REAL
MEETING

"Leadership is time and a simple cup of coffee"

ANETA DARLINGTON – BRIAN DARLINGTON

National Library of Australia Cataloguing-in-Publication entry

Authors: Darlington, Aneta and Darlington, Brian

Title: Real Meeting

ISBN: 978-0-646-70875-1

Subjects: People Aspects of Leadership and Connection with Others.

Dewey Number: 302.12

Contact email

Leadership.embodied@gmail.com

Contact Website

To order this or previous books by Brian Darlington, please visit www.embodied-leadership.eu

Scotoma Press

10 Jens Place

Kambah ACT 2902

Graphic design and layout by Justin Huehn.

Contents

Figures

Foreword 1

As a student, I was assigned to do a practical placement at a busy office in Elizabeth, South Australia. It was then, and I suspect is still, the largest office of the government department of Community Welfare. In the early stages of my study, I was authorised to do nothing but observe. Keen to learn, I arrived at the office early on most days, which was a bit silly, because my supervisor generally arrived late. Most of the professional staff entered their offices via the public front entrance passing through the waiting room; and therefore, it was the logical place for me to wait for my supervisor.

One morning in the waiting room, there was a rather overweight aboriginal woman, her presence dominating the confined space. As social workers entered through the space and into their offices beyond, it seemed clear to me that each one of them noticed the sobbing woman and each one had no desire to be caught up in whatever it was that was bothering her. Many of the social workers glanced at me, I presume trying their utmost to avoid the lady. I interpreted the facial expressions as something like, "I haven't got time to start this engagement. No doubt there is a can of worms to be open and if I stop and listen, I'll lose the best part of the morning". I kept hoping someone would attend to the lady, but I was just a student with no experience. I guess everyone, including me, had a reason to avoid her. "It's not my case. There is someone on duty for this kind of call so let them deal with it".

Most of the social workers employed were relatively young, although there was an elderly man, whom I presumed was not far from retirement. He was an overweight, grey-haired and grey-bearded man. He lamented that the department seemed in recent years to promote young people into senior positions and who were managers by training. This old gentleman had seen many restructures in during the later years of his employment and he took the view that most of the changes were about giving a new name to an old form and earning a promotion in the process. He entered the room and went straight to the sobbing lady. He knelt down, took one of her hands and said, "What's up?" I could not hear the conversation well, but it was clear that the old man saw her, heard her and quickly assured her about who it was she needed to see and that he would try to speed the process up for her.

I stress the word "quickly" in that last sentence. I was amazed at how the dozen social workers, who had walked past her caused her distress to grow. The old social worker took just minutes to transform that room. He brought the lady a cup of tea and assured her again that someone was coming to see her, and then went on with his day. What astonished me at the time was how efficient this process had been.

Like everyone else, I had judged that engaging with the lady would be an expensive time waster, but the old social worker demonstrated that the opposite was true, and his meeting had made a difference to the distressed lady.

At the time, my head was exploding with readings from Sigmund Freud and other psychotherapists, and I loved talking with my supervisor about such things at every opportunity. The old bloke thought that life was too short to fill the air with verbal pollution. I have remained hungry to read and learn throughout all the years since, but I have also come to understand and appreciate the wisdom of that dear man, who knew people need to be seen, heard and appreciated more than they need to be fixed. He knew people will move toward their own health if they have been met, in the process, or perhaps accidentally, solving many of their own problems. Problem solving is a game that both therapists and clients partake in, endlessly.

The authors of this book, Aneta and Brian, know business. They know what is key in leadership. They have described something that unfortunately not many managers know. People will work together for the common good, if they know they are not alone but are part of a bigger picture. All of us are at our best when we are necessary, significant but not central. Thankfully this book is practical, life is too short for anything else.

As good friends with both Aneta and Brian, I have seen how they continuously give of their time to others, they see others, show social care, and engage at every opportunity, and they refrain from acting "quickly". This will become evident as you read this book.

Graham Long

Author and Former CEO of the Wayside Chapel

Foreword 2

I first met Brian and Aneta at a conference in Denmark some years ago where both Brian and I were presenting keynote sessions. The three of us sat and chatted for a while afterwards, and, in that moment, I realised that there was a genuine connection, between us all. Taking the time to converse, to actively listen is not just something that Brian and Aneta talk about, they truly embody this in their everyday actions and values.

In today's fast-paced world, where efficiency and output often overshadow connection and understanding, meetings have become routine exercises in protocol. Leaders at all levels rush through preset agendas, aiming for control and authority, but rarely engage in what we might call a "Real Meeting". The idea of meeting has been reduced to a formality rather than a genuine opportunity for connection. This book challenges that notion.

Drawing inspiration from the profound philosophy of Dr Martin Buber, specifically his concept of "I-Thou" relationships, this book titled "Real Meeting" invites us to rethink, how we interact with others in both personal and professional settings. There are so many personal stories woven throughout the book, taking that insight to heart and offering a roadmap for leaders seeking to bring it to life in their everyday.

As Brian and Aneta reflect on, leadership is not just about holding power or executing tasks. It is about offering your time, your undivided attention, and your presence; whether through a formal meeting or something as simple as sharing a cup of coffee (similar to the sub-title of this book). In these moments, real leadership is born, grounded in empathy, caring, trust, relationships, understanding, and genuine human interaction.

This book will not only inspire you to rethink your approach to leadership, but will also provide practical guidance on how to transform routine meetings into "Real Meetings", where connections thrive and both leaders and their teams become more whole.

Mandy Hickson

Author and Female Fighter Pilot

Dedications

This book is dedicated to a number of special persons who gave us life or entered our lives and have made a huge difference to who we are today.

Brian: Firstly, to the late Raymond and Margaret Darlington, my parents who were always there for us giving us a good education and upbringing and instilling good morals and ethics in life. Dad passing away after a long illness in 2007, and Mom passing away suddenly in 2020, together with my dearest sisters, Wendy and Susan, we miss you dearly and you remain embedded in our hearts.

Aneta: The book is also dedicated to my dearest mother, you have always been there for me, supporting me in my dreams, my years of living in different countries to achieve those dreams, even when I decided to move to and study in the United States of America as an eighteen years old girl, I know as your only child, it must have been difficult. Whilst working for an international airline you were always willing to travel with me to all corners of the world, to experience other cultures, foods, visit endless museums, shrines, temples, and churches, to widen my horizons, my understanding of the world. After all, you encouraged me to write my first book, "Fifty Shades of Red" and you believed in me, even at times when I was wondering if it would be published one day. Although you are a fantastic mother, you are simply my best friend, you are my "Kryszczi". In us we have always entered the hyphen between the "I and the Thou", we have always had Real Meeting, we have always had each other, for which I will be forever grateful, thanks Mom.

Brian and Aneta: and of course, we also dedicate the book to our good friend and mentor, Dr Robert Long (Rob). Although geographically separated, we remain in close contact – be it on a personal or business basis. Over the years, Rob has provided so much guidance and support to both of us, shifted our mindsets, not only in how we see leadership, but also how we see the world. Our worldview has changed tremendously since the initial meeting with Rob in 2018, in Belgium, followed by numerous trips to Australia, many one-on-one coaching sessions when both of us were studying for our Master's in Social Psychology of Risk (SPoR). On a personal side, the cherry on the cake was when Rob sang at our wedding in Auckland, New Zealand, singing the same song that was sung at Rob and Helen's wedding forty-eight years before. Rob you are a dear friend, filled with love and so much care and giving, you are a friend second to none. Without you by our sides over the years, our journey in Social Psychology of Risk, our understanding of the importance of semiotics, listening for metaphors, humanising our approach to others, and much more would not have begun, and this book would not have been possible.

Acknowledgements

Special thanks to Rob, for all your support and guidance provided to us over many months, from the minute we informed you that we were planning to write this book, right until the final full stop in the book prior to going to the printers. Thanks for all the proofreading, editing, responding to emails and for putting up with many hours of discussions and for bouncing off ideas with us.

Thanks to Graham Long and Mandy Hickson for agreeing to write the Forewords. Graham, meeting you in Canberra, Australia in 2023, inspired both of us in writing this book and contributed tremendously to what is written in the chapters that follow. Your efforts to "Meeting humanity" over decades are an inspiration of note. Mandy, the way you meet with people to share your story as a fighter pilot and the importance of teamwork would always feature in our writings.

Finally, Katia Guerreiro, as a performer you inspire us with the passion that you have, not only for your music and lyrics, but in engaging with your audiences, giving them that embodied feeling with each song that you sing; you are an inspiration to us both, muinto, muinto obrigado.

Meaning Behind the Title of the Book "Real Meeting"

Our definition of "Real Meeting" is "how we develop relationships when connecting with others, being with others, allowing deeper understanding of the other, and when we as humans become whole by being influenced by another".

It is common for many leaders to hold meetings, however never meet, sticking to pre-set agendas, maintaining their authority, telling and controlling others, all this without meeting in the true sense of the word. Martin Buber, who was born in Vienna, Austria on February 8, 1878 and died on June 13, 1965, was an Austrian Jew and Israeli philosopher best known for his philosophy of dialogue, a form of existentialism centred on the distinction between the "I–Thou" and "I–It" relationships. He was nominated for the Nobel Prize in Literature ten times, and the Nobel Peace Prize seven times. In his writings, he speaks about the connection between beings, and therefore, inspired us to create the title of this book "Real Meeting".

Influenced by his writings, we decided to change from our original title "Embodied Leadership" to "Real Meeting". As Martin Buber said, "all real living is meeting" or "all real life is an encounter". In Real Meeting we get to know the other, we connect, we listen, and we show interest. Doing so develops good, positive, and trusting relationships, be it in our private lives or as leaders of organisations, operations, departments, and teams. In meeting we get to know "about" something; however, in Real Meeting we get to know the "Who" as well. In Real Meeting, we simply get to know the other. It is all about "meeting to Meet", "engaging to Engage", "listening to Listen", "understanding to Understand", "connecting to Connect" and "knowing to Know". This is a far cry from being stuck in the I-It mode all the time, where we are focused on objects and using or experiencing the other.

As leaders, most meetings are structured and not experiencing Real Meeting in the true sense of the word. The meetings are directed by formal agendas, fixed time slots, taking of minutes, filled with decisions and actions, often looking back at what has happened, identifying trends, focusing on achievements and outcomes. The time slots often dictate how long a certain discussion takes place, how much time is given to a certain topic and when nearing the scheduled end time of each discussion, the chairperson speeds up the conversation, often not completing the discussion in full. No doubt that there is, of course, a need for these meetings in the business world, mostly held in the I-It. However, leaders need to challenge themselves on how many meetings are conducted where there is Real Meeting, engagement and connection taking place. Real Meeting happens where agendas and authority are suspended and aligned with the sub-title of this book, "Leadership is time and a simple cup of coffee". We are inspired by how Sir Richard Branson relates to being with people around the fireplace, telling stories, just another way of giving of one's time to another and in doing so, being in Real Meeting with others.

It makes one think of the Hebrew word "Yada" which, as per formal definition (although many definitions exist), means "to know" or "knowing the other". This Hebrew word appears early in the Bible to convey a special kind of knowing, implies intimacy, and is much more than just cognitive "knowing". For example, when I say I know my children, I mean much more than just head knowing, I have an in depth understanding of them, I know what makes them sad, what makes them happy. Just being with them, I get the feeling of whether they are stressed or not, whether they need a shoulder to lean on or just an ear to listen to, it all boils down to knowing them, "knowing the other". When we know someone through Real Meeting it confers connection, experiential embodied knowing, not just "knowing".

By meeting in Real Meeting is this kind of "Yada" (positive yada). We explain the Yada as a semiotic in Chapter 3. As leaders allow another person or persons to tell their story, they get to know the other, in this case it is about more listening and refraining from just having a telling approach. However, on the opposite side of the coin, "yada, yada, yada" (negative yada) is the same as the phrase "blah, blah, blah" which refers to discussion that is boring, has little meaningful content or value and provides little knowing.

A leader who does not enter the hyphen of the I-Thou, who meets just for the sake of having meetings (due to lack of trust) is often seen by others as a leader who is full of "blah, blah, blah" or "yada, yada, yada". It is up to leaders to decide which one they prefer to be identified with. Is it the positive "yada, yada, yada" or the negative one related to the "blah, blah, blah"?

Meaning Behind the Sub-title of the Book "Leadership is Time (Listening) and a Simple Cup of Coffee"

A couple of years ago, a colleague and myself (Brian) were on a large annual maintenance shut in Finland and observed a contractor coming out of a high smokestack after finishing a week's work and about to travel home. I was concerned about her driving a long-distance trip home, so I invited her for a cup of coffee, I gave up my time, suspended my agenda and had a lovely chat with her. When reflecting some months later on our engagement, I came to realise that I had given her time over a cup of coffee to listen to her story, and this was when I developed the quote, "Leadership is time and a simple cup of coffee", and when planning this book, we both immediately knew that in the light of "Meeting to Meet", this story would fit the book well and also be a great sub-title for the book.

The key word in the quote is "time", the word "coffee" can be replaced with anything like for example, a cup of tea, a Coca-Cola, a cigarette, sharing lunch, a walk in the park, or simply just a chat. It is all about giving someone the time to tell his or her story, it is about us as leaders suspending our own agenda or our authority and giving someone else the opportunity to share what is on their mind, to take an interest in what they are saying and to give undivided attention to others. As social beings, this is important and is all about the I-Thou, showing interest in others. What is meant is not about having a cup of coffee, but rather about listening with intent whilst giving someone your time. Everybody somewhere in the world has a cup of coffee with someone, but it is about what is shared and discussed between the parties whilst having that cup of coffee.

We both have the quote, "Leadership is time and a simple cup of coffee" displayed in our offices as a reminder of the importance of giving time to others.

We will explain this Meeting over a cup of coffee with "the lady in the smokestack" further in Chapter 5 in this book.

Figure 1. shows *The Quote* on the wall of our office and *Figure 2.* shows *Coffee Mug and Coasters* having the quote embossed on them.

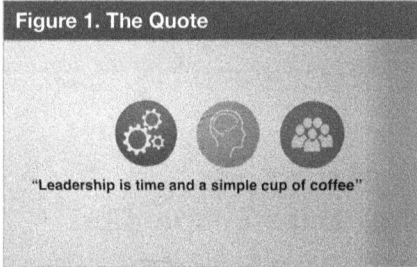

Figure 1. The Quote

"Leadership is time and a simple cup of coffee"

Figure 2. Coffee Mug and Coasters

Explaining the Cover

Aligned to the title of the book "Real Meeting" as well as the sub-title, "Leadership is time and a simple cup of coffee", the two hands holding the cup depicts those of a leader offering another a cup of coffee. In the steam of the coffee are two symbols, one is an hourglass which relates to the time given to others in Real Meeting and the second symbol is the citation symbol which depicts discussion between beings. The cup affords the sharing of a cup of coffee. Although the cup of coffee could be replaced by amongst others, a drink of another nature, a cigarette, or a simple walk in the fresh air. "Time and a simple cup of coffee" relates to the I-Thou by Martin Buber, on which many elements of this book are based.

This book is based on the I-Thou and the importance of moving into the hyphen of the I and Thou. Co-writing a book is always a challenge, there is a need to agree on content thereof, the need to discuss and compromise to allow each of the authors to put their point of view across, tell their stories whilst, at the same time, ensuring there is a flow to the book. Therefore, it was of the utmost importance for both authors to move into the hyphen of the I-Thou, and therefore, we included the hyphen between our two names on the cover "Aneta Darlington – Brian Darlington" rather than "Aneta Darlington and Brian Darlington".

Thanks to Martin Buber (and because of our interest in his writings on the I-Thou), as he prevented many disagreements and allowed for many discussions, debates, compromises between the two of us during the many months of drafting this book, by moving us into the "hyphen" (instead of us having to book an appointment with a divorce lawyer).

Reflections Throughout the Book

This is not a book of abstract academic ideas, nor a book of theories, removed from reality. Throughout the book, we have given some very practical constructive reflections for the reader to apply what is learnt, related to the reader's reality. This opportunity for reflection is highlighted throughout the book by a grey shaded box. Dear Reader, when you see one of these shaded boxes it is time to slow down your reading and move into a reflective mode, to think about what has been discussed from our experience and to consider how to apply it to your own.

Explaining the Inside of the Back Cover

On the inside of the back cover of the book is a photo taken in Canberra, Australia of the two authors in Real Meeting with our dear friend and mentor Rob, as well as Graham Long, sharing a great Australian red wine and with all four of us entering the hyphen in the "I and Thou".

The Use of Capitalisation, Indentation, and Italics

Some of the words such as "Meet", "Real Meeting", "Community", "Human Beings", "Leader", "Engage", "Listen", "Understand", "Connect", "Mind" and "Know", "Dreamtime" are capitalised throughout the text to give those words a wider and more powerful meaning.

We purposely indented certain paragraphs to reflect personal stories and experiences of others. Italics are used in sentences to match the title of the relevant photographs.

The Wolves of Reflection

"The wolf that wins is the one that you feed".

Wise Old Cherokee Man

When designing the structure of this book, we both felt that there should be a chapter on reflection, as self-reflection is an art, and unfortunately, not always practised. We felt there could be benefit to the reader, if we included a short section at the end of each chapter with some prompting comments and self-reflection questions relating to the specific chapter. As mentioned, the reflection sections are highlighted in grey shaded areas and complemented by our reflection icon of the two wolves.

We came up with a couple of ideas for a symbol or icon that we could place on the reflection pages. However, after meeting "Nukumij Wape'k Paqtesm" ("Grandmother White Wolf") in Canada and having a discussion about the meaning of the two wolves' heads for the Indigenous Canadians, we felt this would be a suitable symbol to use. So why did we choose this symbol?

The Indigenous Canadians or also known as the First Nations see alikeness and connection with the Wolves and have huge respect for them. As with persons, wolves are playful, they defend and educate their young, hunt for food and feed their pups. Wolves, like elephants and dolphins, are extremely intelligent animals, they live in family groups and are devoted to the members of their family, taking care of them. Wolves demonstrate a strong sense of responsibility and have tight social bonds with their pack, they nurture their young and have been known to adopt unrelated pups, they love and grieve, they protect what is theirs, are loyal and have respect.

The Old Cherokee Grandfather and Grandson

One day as part of his teachings, a wise old Cherokee man sat down with his grandson and shared a parable about life. The legend went something as follows:

"A fight is going on inside of me," he says to the boy. "It's a terrible fight between two wolves. One is evil – he is full of rage, jealousy, arrogance, greed, sorrow, regret, lies, laziness, and self-pity. The other is good – he is filled with love, joy, peace, generosity, truth, empathy, courage, humility, and faith. This same fight is going on inside the hearts of everyone, including you". The grandson thinks about this for a few minutes, and then asks his grandfather, "Which wolf wins?" His grandfather replies, "The one you feed". The grandson thinks about this for a few minutes, and then asks his grandfather, "Which wolf wins?" to which his grandfather replies, "They both win if you feed them right".

The grandfather continued, "You see, if I starve one wolf, the other will become imbalanced with power. If I choose to feed only the light wolf, the shadow one will become ravenous and resentful. He will hide around every corner and wait for my defences to lower, then attack. He will be filled with hatred and jealousy and will fight the light wolf endlessly. But if I feed both, in the right way, at the right time, they will live side-by-side in harmony. There will be no more inner battle. Instead, there will be inner peace. And when there's peace, there is wisdom. The goal of life, my son, is to respect this balance of life, for when you live in balance, you can serve the Great Spirit within. When you put an end to the battle inside, you are free".

Our Yin-Yang Choice

Because of the story above and discussions with "Nukumij Wape'k Paqtesm" ("Grandmother White Wolf"), as described in Chapter 5, we decided to use the Indigenous People Wolves connected to the Yin-Yang symbol similar to the tattoo of Melanie ("Grandmother White Wolf"), although in our design we added the words "Reflection" to the icon. The Yin-Yang symbol was developed by the Chinese believing that our universe comprises complementing as well as competing forces of nature, such as the darkness and light, happiness and anger, female and male, to name a few. The symbol conveys the meaning of balance and harmony between two opposing forces and depicts that when there are two opposing forces, they appear to have a contradiction to each other and although they are totally independent, they best work together.

Leaders are continuously challenged by the two opposing worlds, two opposing forces, and therefore, reflection is key in understanding one's own biases, actions, stresses, ethics, behaviour, etc. People will always have different opinions, however in compromise, listening to each other and through mutual engagement the two opposing forces could best work together.

The symbol that we have chosen for our reflection pages at the end of each chapter is similar to the traditional Yin-Yang symbol as shown in *Figure 3. Yin-Yang*, however, as seen in *Figure 4. Wolves' Heads*, being our symbol, is aligned to that of the Canadian Indigenous People. What we have added to our design is the words "reflection".

Figure 3. Yin-Yang

Figure 4. Wolves' Heads

CHAPTER 1

Introduction

"Through the Thou a person becomes I".

Dr Martin Buber

Austrian-Israeli Philosopher

As we believe that leaders need to tell their stories and by doing so, support understanding and learning, therefore, as with our three previous books written separately by us, this book is filled with personal stories, both from us, as well as a number of personal narratives of others, who we know and have been privileged to have met over the years. They have not only inspired us, but who have been kind enough to allow us to retell their stories in some of the chapters of this book. These people range from personal mentors, coaches, a female fighter pilot, lecturer, Indigenous People from Australia and Canada and friends that we have engaged with during our travels.

Semiotics and Semiosis (the making, meaning and purpose) influence humans on a daily basis, in everything that we do. Therefore, the signs, symbols, images, icons, slogans, banners and messages that we have on our office walls, communication boards, TV monitors and in the factories, as well as gestures, myths and metaphors are all of significance in life in general, but also in leadership. Semiotics are also of benefit when telling stories, and therefore, we have included many photographs and some diagrams in all the chapters to reflect in a semiotic way, aspects of the relevant stories and focus areas.

As humans we need to "step into the hyphen" in connecting or building relationships with others, in what is known as personhood. Whilst doing so, building trust, bringing things out into the open, whilst less things remain hidden, where there are fewer so-called secrets, where people get to know each other, and where there is continuous learning, etc. Entering the hyphen with others, assists us as humans in stepping out or letting go of our own worldview for a moment in time and seeing the world through the eyes and stories of others.

During our travels to cities around the world, we have often approached persons and asked them if they would be willing to give us some of their time to explain something of significance to us and in doing so telling us their story. When doing this one's worldview changes constantly and at times rather significantly, be it through their stories, feeling their culture, understanding their traditions, their beliefs, their rituals, and their myths. We have used some of their stories in articles and books that we have written over the years and have selected some of the inspiring stories which are included in the chapters of this book, stories of Real Meeting with others.

As you will read throughout the chapters of this book, there are some "Golden Threads" to many of the stories and throughout the chapters. These golden threads are all related to the title of the book, Real Meeting, and include being in the I-Thou, the importance of community, personhood, meeting others in the true sense of the word, leaders telling their stories, being ethical, showing care, giving of one's time to another and many more. Through this we enrich ourselves and there is continuous learning for us as well as the persons with whom we interact through Real Meeting.

The quote from Martin Buber that fits well with the structure of this book is, "I knew nothing of books when I came forth from the womb of my mother, and I shall die without books, with another human hand in my own. I do, indeed, close my door at times and surrender myself to a book, but only because I can open the door again and see a human being looking at me".

Relating our lives as leaders to this quote by Martin Buber, there are times that we are focused on things that keep the business running, things that take up our time of the day, events that we need to close our door and focus on, nothing wrong with this, however, it is important that, at times, we open that door and engage in Real Meeting with others. We need to find the balance, we need to find the Yin-Yang, we need to feed both of our inner wolves.

Aneta and I are both avid readers and have our preferred interests, such as semiotics, Indigenous cultures of Australia and Canada, social psychology, military history, the Australian Bushwhackers, such as Ned Kelly, the Clarke Brothers and writings of Carl Jung and Martin Buber. Although continuous reading ensures continuous learning and understanding, reading the books is nothing compared to the experiences through Real Meetings with others. We have been fortunate to have had Real Meetings with people, friends and total strangers of different backgrounds and ethnic groups in many countries around the world, listening to their stories, their experiences, their cultures and worldviews.

Many of these interactions have been inspirational, be it standing at a first nations ceremonial grounds in beautiful Canada, in numerous churches in Europe, the Blue Mosque in Turkey, various temples in Malaysia on two occasions (five years apart), around an Indigenous Person's smouldering fire in the capital city of Australia, interviewing a dear friend Graham Long on a park bench in Braidwood, New South Wales, Australia, learning about a "Talking Stick" on a cattle ranch close to the Rocky Mountains, over a cup of coffee in a meeting room in Austria, having a cup of tea with an Indigenous Elder during a dinner in Alberta, Canada, or the two of us sharing a good bottle of Pinotage red wine on a wooden deck overlooking the African bush, hearing lions' roar, and the gecker of a vervet monkey in the distance at a Safari Park in South Africa.

In reading this book, we trust that you reflect as a leader in whether you take time out, and give enough of your precious time to others, be it in your professional lives as a colleague, or in your private life with friends, your family and even at times with strangers. May this book also trigger your thoughts and reflections on whether you meet with others by listening with intent, whether you spend time in Kairos Time rather than only in Chronos Time, and most importantly in doing so, being with others in Real Meeting and in the I-Thou.

If at the end of reading this book and on reflection you feel that you fit the mould, we then encourage you to pass this book on to some other leaders in your organisation, family or a friend, who might benefit from its contents. Be it by the sharpening of their leadership style, through understanding the importance of engaging and caring for others, acknowledging the need of not always having to control the discussions, or fill the space with noise and the importance of allowing others to tell their stories. And of course, the power of self-reflection and meeting in Real Meeting.

CHAPTER 2

From Golf to Real Meeting to Love

"All journeys have hidden destinations of which the traveller is unaware".

Dr Martin Buber

Austrian-Israeli Philosopher

Aneta's Story

Immediately after graduating high school, I moved to the United States to complete my degree in journalism. After a couple of years, of writing for a number of newspapers, I decided to move into a more exciting chapter of my life; moving to Dubai and working for a large international airline, flying to many destinations around the world, meeting interesting people, learning different cultures, changing my worldview, and experiencing life was one of the best decisions I have ever made.

As Martin Buber said, "all journeys have hidden destinations of which the traveller is unaware". In September of 2016, I decided during my off days to travel home from Dubai, to surprise my father on his birthday and spend twenty-four hours with him and my mother. To use the words of Martin Buber, this trip would take me to many hidden destinations of which, at the time, I had no clue about, as the destiny was clearly out of my hands. After a fantastic and happy twenty-four hours at home, my father was driving me to the bus station so that I could catch my transport to the Warsaw international airport and finally board the flight back to Dubai. Unfortunately, my destination changed within a blink of an eye, as about thirty kilometres from home, we were involved in a head-on collision with a car that swerved out into our lane as the driver attempted to overtake a truck. With little reaction time of both drivers, the two cars slammed into each other, killing the passenger of the other car, and injuring my father and myself. Later, I heard that I had broken my back in multiple places as well as other bones in my body. My destination had unfortunately changed from Dubai to the operating theatre of a local hospital, followed by many months on my back, recovering at home.

Some months after experiencing this horrific car accident, I decided to close this chapter of my life, as although I loved flying and the lifestyle, I concluded that flying was no longer something I wanted to do forever. During my time off recovering from my back injuries, I had completed a Master's Degree in economics and studies in marketing and communications. The time had come for me to change careers and enter the educational field. As a result, I moved to the island of Malta to take up a teaching position.

One day whilst enjoying the sun, relaxing beside a pool in Malta, I received a call from my mother, telling me the story that she had heard from a friend of hers, of a man that had lost his wife in a freak accident after she had fallen at home and sadly passed away. I recall the feeling of sadness that overcame me on hearing the story and I said to my mother, "I wish I could simply give the man a hug of support". During the following weeks, I often thought about this man, when lost in my thoughts, whilst walking back and forth to work or lying next to the pool at my apartment in Malta.

Then in 2020, I was spending New Years Eve with my mother in Warsaw, Poland, saying farewell to the old year and welcoming the new one under the moonlight, watching the fireworks and as with many millions around the world in celebration and sending well wishes, when my mother said, "I just have a feeling that this year something super amazing is going to happen". In March of 2020, I would often joke that with that sentence, she had probably foreseen the COVID-19 epidemic, but soon enough, I figured that she meant my life was finally falling into its place.

At this point, I had moved to Warsaw and became a university lecturer; however, not being totally inspired by the university where I was employed, I was keen to move back to the United States and get a lecturer's position in the university where I used to study.

I was still looking at various possibilities and options in the United States when one Saturday morning I decided to join my mother for a round of golf on a course in Torun in Poland, close to the old walled city that was built and occupied by the Teutonic Knights in the thirteenth century. Well, what more can I say, this game of golf and drinks at the "Coffee and Whiskey House" some months later would change my destiny forever; the idea of moving to the United States faded off in the distance; living and teaching in Warsaw would come to an end almost three years later; and I met someone who made me happier than I have ever been.

Strangely enough, my journey had brought me to the man I envisaged wanting to hug in compassion when I was talking to my mother, at the time, of hearing of the passing of his wife back in January of 2019. What a strange coincidence, from a round of golf and to Real Meeting to eventually love. What a journey, what a change to my destiny … and the rest of the story is explained by Brian below.

Brian's Story

In January of 2019, I lost my wife, Bela, through an accident and at that time my world fell apart, I tried to be strong for my children with the loss of their beloved mother, whilst unknowingly withdrawing myself from society to some extent. My dreams had come to an abrupt ending, my purpose and destiny in life had suddenly changed. Spending Christmas in Auckland, New Zealand, with my children Clayton, Jolene and Nastasha, their spouses Angie and Jonathan and at that time three grandchildren, Jena, Blaire, and Ellie, was the first time we would be together as a family since the passing of my wife, their mother. My whole world had changed, my focus was now on them and for two weeks nothing else mattered, but my family. I felt the closeness that they shared with me, the care and support that we gave each other, although mixed emotions of happiness being together, but also sadness as Bela was missing from the table, the chats in the lounge at night, or relaxing at the beach. It seemed to me that our emotions were on a roller coaster ride.

After a wonderful two weeks in New Zealand, Nastasha and I left with a heavy heart as we said goodbye to the family and walked through the doors into the airport's departure hall, boarding our flight and started the long journey back to Austria, I went back to work, and she returned to student life at the art university in Linz. I sold up our family home and moved to Vienna. My life became totally focused on work and playing golf and not long did the world come to an abrupt ending with the arrival of the COVID-19 pandemic.

Like most of the world, Austria went into complete lockdown and as social beings we were forced into becoming anti-social. Life had changed from almost one day to another. People were prohibited from leaving their houses, no meeting others, less interaction, and engagement. Dreams of holidays, spending time with others, being at work amongst peers, visiting families and friends and just being social with other humans had become a thing of the past and was no longer an option. Life had changed for billions of people in all corners of the globe.

Many people could not even visit the elderly, the sick and the lonely. Sadly in 2020, my mother, living in Pretoria, South Africa, fell, breaking her hip and passed away in hospital a couple of days later. I could not travel to South Africa, as no airlines were operating out of Vienna, my sister living in KwaZulu-Natal in South Africa could not travel the six hundred kilometres to attend the funeral, due to lockdown. There was a maximum of ten persons allowed to attend the funeral, with my sister Wendy attending on our behalf. Susan and I, as well as all other family and friends had to join via a Zoom call. Closure of losing a mother and grandmother was not that easy, and once again as social beings, we could not even mourn her death together.

How my life had changed within just over one year and was one that was unrecognisable to the life I had prior to January 2019, reminding me that as humans we are fallible, and life will throw challenges at each and every one of us, throughout our lives.

Some two years later things started opening again and although I had throughout the pandemic maintained my focus on my work, I started playing golf again, sometimes alone, and other times with other people whom I did not know. I preferred to play on my own, as that meant I did not have to engage with other people and even when I played a round of golf with others, I tended to keep to myself, not really wanting to engage.

Once borders had opened up again and over time life returned back to normal, Jan, a retired colleague and good friend of mine, living in Poland invited me to play golf with him over a weekend, to which although uncertain at first, I agreed and decided to travel to Poland and spend the weekend playing golf, enjoying good wine and food at French and Polish restaurants. I thoroughly enjoyed the companionship, the banter on the golf course and catching up on the past, memories of working together for a period of around eleven years.

This trip was followed by two more, and it was on the third trip that we were joined by two ladies, Krystyna and her daughter Aneta, for a round of golf. We were about to tee-off when they approached the tee box and asked us if they could join, as what is commonly known in the game of golf as a four-ball. We played the eighteen holes without much mingling, the ladies were playing their game, walking together, chatting, as did my friend and I, amongst ourselves. We at times between holes chatted a bit with Krystyna and Aneta, however not of anything significant and most of it just small talk.

One evening, some three months later, Jan and I walked into the "Coffee and Whiskey House", for an after-dinner drink, and surprisingly and coincidently we noticed Krystyna and Aneta, who we had not seen or heard from since our game of golf having a drink and chatting. We joined them in the corner close to the bar, relaxing on sets of cigar lounge couches and once again involved in small talk, telling jokes and just having some fun. This was just a casual meeting, enjoying the warm summer evening.

Well, when leaving at the end of the evening, we all agreed to stay in contact and arrange another round of golf. This happened some weeks later and over time the four of us became rather good friends. Each time we met, the meetings became Real Meetings, where we took more interest in the discussions and experiences shared. Without realising it at first, we became much closer, ending up with Aneta and I having dinner and drinks a couple of times in Warsaw and Gdansk, Poland, as well as Vienna, Austria.

We started seeing each other more frequently as time moved on, and my destiny that I thought had faded away and was to some extent non-existent, seemed to resurface and soon thereafter we started dating. My life had developed the semi-colon (;) with having been so sad and withdrawn after losing Bela, my story could have ended there, but it continued with Aneta entering my life. The belief in the semicolon by the Canadian Indigenous People is explained in Chapter 5. We, then some years later travelled to Athens for New Years Eve celebrations and then to Rhodes in the Greek Islands where we spoke about our relationship and looking at the future. A few months later, we were on a flight to Australia to our dear friend Rob Long, and as Aneta had flown for a Dubai-based airline for almost ten years, and loved the Airbus A380, I arranged to propose to her in the plane's bar shortly before landing in Australia. The pilot together with the air-crew members who had set up the bar area with flowers made from balloons, good champagne and a breakfast joined us in celebration as I asked Aneta to marry me. *Figure 5.* shows the two authors playing a *Round of Golf* together and *Figure 6.* shows *The Celebrations* on the flight to Australia.

Figure 5. Round of Golf

Figure 6. The Celebrations

During the months to follow, we found more common interests which would strengthen "the hyphen" between the two of us in our relationship. Prior to going on honeymoon, Aneta attended training in scuba diving and within a couple of weeks, we found ourselves on a boat in the Maldives preparing for her first dive. I had stopped diving in 2013, after completing more than one hundred and thirty dives, as that passion too had disappeared some years back, but when planning the trip to the Maldives, and when seeing Aneta training in a diving centre in Vienna, I was once again inspired to service my scuba gear and return to the reefs of Maldives, Saipan and Greece. *Figure 7.* shows Aneta S*cuba Diving in Saipan* and *Figure 8.* shows Aneta *Diving in Crete, Greece.*

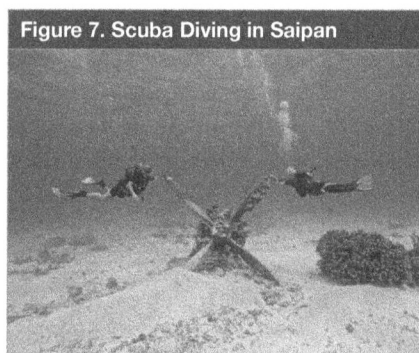

Figure 7. Scuba Diving in Saipan

Figure 8. Diving in Crete, Greece

As Buber said, you cannot rely on dreams, but must have a destiny. Well both of our dreams had changed, our destinies had altered and we both came to realise a year later when reading the works of Martin Buber, our life's journey had a secret destination, one that we had not planned for, one that we both were totally unaware of, one that happened because moving from only playing golf to building a friendship that was based on many Real Meetings over time.

We had found the I-Thou in our friendship, we had connected through understanding, common interests, and experiences together as Beings, not individual inner feelings but connection between us, the hyphen between the "I and the Thou". Initially we were just meeting, to play golf, have small chat, however, over time these meetings became Real Meetings. There was genuine interest in each other's stories and true connection, as social beings we gave time to each other in sharing. Aneta is a great follower of Martin Buber, and inspired by many of his quotes, however, one of her favourites is the quote that relates to this chapter where he said, "Our relationships live in the space between us which is sacred", meaning the hyphen between the I and the Thou.

CHAPTER 3

Entering the Hyphen in the I-Thou

"The meeting of two personalities is like the contact of two chemical substances: if there is any reaction, both are transformed".

Dr Carl Gustav Jung

Swiss Psychiatrist and Psychotherapist

Graham Long and Martin Buber - an Inspiration

I (Aneta) have an interest in the writings of Carl Jung and Sigmund Freud and have written some academic papers based on their worldly views. During two of my trips to Canberra, Australia, I have been fortunate and honoured to meet Graham Long and through Real Meeting, we have become fond friends. Anyone who knows Graham understands that he has read the book "I and Thou" probably more than any other person and who has a wealth of knowledge, and interesting personal interpretations of the writings on Martin Buber. Through listening to Graham in a training venue, during on-line sessions and during interviewing him on a park bench in Braiden, New South Wales, Australia, I have found Buber to be an enormous inspiration to me as well as Brian, so much so that we have based several of the chapters in this book on his writings.

Buber's I-Thou

When it comes to connecting with others, not many (in our opinion) described it better than Dr Martin Buber, one of the most influential philosophers of the 19th and 20th centuries (and today). Buber was born in Vienna, Austria, in 1878, and died in Jerusalem in 1965. The online sources describe him as a "prolific author, scholar, literary translator, and political activist whose writings - mostly in German and Hebrew - ranged from Jewish mysticism to social philosophy, biblical studies, religious phenomenology, philosophical anthropology, education, politics, and art. Most famous among his philosophical writings is a short but powerful book 'I and

Thou' (1923) where our relation to others is considered as twofold". For decades, historians also appreciated him for a translation of a Bible from German to Hebrew, which took him an astonishing amount of time, almost thirty-seven years.

Since, in many of his writings, Buber would often say that his whole life was, "a journey toward 'I and Thou' and what he described as genuine meeting", portraying some parts of his biography seemed to be essential to explaining his work on communication.

Buber was born to an Orthodox Jewish family and was a direct descendant of the 16th century rabbi Meir Katzenellenbogen, known as the Maharam, as well as Karl Marx. The philosopher's bibliography mentioned a strong influence on his scholarly development (as until the age of ten, Martin was homeschooled) created predominantly by his grandfather – Solomon Buber, who was a scholar of Midrash and Rabbinic Literature, and his grandmother (who thought that), "language-centred humanism was the royal road to education". From a very early age, Buber had an unusually high maturity level, which allowed him trying, at the age of sixteen, to translate Nietzsche's "Thus Spoke Zarathustra" into Polish. Unfortunately, that plan failed after finding out that a prominent Polish poet had already signed a contract to translate it, obliging the young Buber to give up on the project, but even the attempt at translating a piece of literature as difficult as any of Nietzsche's writings was very impressive for a teenager, even a very intelligent one.

Buber spent most of his childhood days with his grandparents Adele and Salomon Buber, with whom he lived after his mother left his father for a Russian army general. In his notes, Buber recalled the moment in which he felt abandonment, it was when he was watching his mother leaving the family home. As he was observing her through a window and hoping that while leaving, she would turn around and look at her child one more time, but she never did, which (according to Buber) was one of the most painful memories which deeply affected his adulthood. The worst of all was the fact that it was not his family who introduced the "new reality" to him and, as a matter of fact, Buber was constantly hoping that his mother will come back. Until one moment, when he was already living with his grandparents, while playing in the backyard with one of the neighbour's children, Buber recalled (in many of his writings), "we both leaned on the railing. I cannot remember that I spoke of my mother to my older comrade. But I hear still how the big girl said to me: 'no, she will never come back'. I know that I reminded silent, but also that I cherished no doubt of the truth of the spoken words". In many of his writings, Buber mentions, "whatever, I have learnt in the course of my life about the meaning of meeting and dialogue between people springs from that moment when I was four".

As a matter of fact, the "big girl" was correct, but only to some degree, after about twenty years Buber saw his mother again, as she, "came from a distance to visit (him) and his children". Unfortunately, the meeting was not as, "meaningful as Buber hoped, as it is strange to make meeting between two familiarly unfamiliar strangers".

Throughout his adult life, he was always very critical of his family, even by the end of his life, at the age of eighty-five, two years before his death, he said, "Freud says that angst stems from terrible childhood experiences. I do not believe so. I do not have *angst* and I had a terrible childhood".

That childhood, later in his early adult years, resulted in Buber having trouble meeting people and creating meaningful friendships. However, the university was not only a place where Buber got his degree and a doctorate in the History of Art, but it was also a place where he met Paula, the girl who was to become his wife, with whom he had two daughters (who both, at some point of their adult life, were just like their father – university lecturers). Paula was also a writer, who used a pen name Georg Munk, as women back then had trouble getting published. Throughout his life, Buber taught at many different universities, but he never described himself as a lecturer; instead, all he would say about his own teaching style was, I just, "open a window, take people to it, and say: 'look out'".

One of the most remarkable friendships in his life was the one with Franz Rosenzweig (1886–1929), who still ranks as one of the most original Jewish thinkers of the modern period. Rosenzweig founded Freies Jüdisches Lehrhaus, the school of Jewish adult education in Frankfurt in August 1920, where Buber started to polish his lecturing skills. That establishment was a place where Buber would commence eight lectures on "Religion as Presence" which, "would attest to Buber's turn in from a Romantic Erlebnis – mysticism to a philosophy of dialogue that affirms the transcendent Otherness of God. The stenographer's transcriptions of the lectures would, as Buber told Rosenzweig, serve as 'the prolegomenon to the work' he had been engaged in for the next several years. The lectures were, in effect, a draft of 'Ich und Du' ('I and Thou')".

During writing of "I and Thou" Rosenzweig, who often would edit parts of Buber's writings, was diagnosed with amyotrophic lateral sclerosis (ALS, now particularly known as Lou Gehrig's disease). On the beginning, he "would offer critical comments to Buber either orally (when it was still possible) or in writing (with the assistance from his wife) (...) Buber would gratefully respond to Rosenzweig's critiques and duly attend to the clarifications and revisions his friend suggested". During his six years of sickness Rosenzweig had suicidal thoughts and according to his mother only the friendship with Buber, "made her (…) life possible, just as it joined in sustaining Franz's". Rosenzweig passed away on December 12th, 1929. "At his request, no eulogies were delivered at the funeral (…) It was also his wish that Buber read Psalm 73, which contains the verse that Rosenzweig had selected for his gravestone: 'I am continually with thee'".

The "I and Thou" was meant to be Buber's call to engage the world – our life with others – in dialogue; he also recognised the painful truth of how difficult it is to achieve, how often life's journey is filled with mismeetings and the failure of I-Thou encounters to take place. Buber also spoke about the fragility of human relationships, of the ideological and psychological "armor" we as humans invariably wear to protect ourselves from such mismeetings. As mentioned above, this masterpiece was also heavily impacted by the friendship with Rosenzweig, whose incurable, life-eating disease spread powerfully through Buber's thoughts on life, connecting with people, one's religiousness, and overall ideas on communities and the necessity to belong.

The belonging was significantly described by Buber in introducing the phrase, "I see you", "if now I say, 'I see you', or, 'I see the thee', perhaps the seeing is not real in the same way in both, but the I in both is real in the same way". Here, "I see you" refers to seeing the "real you", by seeing the purity of all perfections as well as imperfections of another person. An Urban Dictionary explains the term as, "often used to express when (one is) impressed by someone whether it be what they wear or something they do". Back in the day, this sentence was attached (mainly by literature) to primitive nations, as it was described in the triple Oscar-winning movie "Avatar" from 2009, written, directed, co-produced and co-edited by James Cameron, where the main characters using the term, "hello" would be referred to as "I see you", which signified that the characters were accepted despite their physical differences.

Even though, nowadays, the phrase is closely used more in the slang version of communication, the sentence can be very positively charged (since it recognises someone's efforts), which is why, especially lately, it has been widely used in rehabilitation centres around the world. On the way to recovery, "I see you" is always used only in situations where it can be positively charged; it has the power of recognizing someone's efforts and praising them for trying to accomplish a goal which they put in front of themselves.

Over the years, Buber did not want to revise the publication, as he mentioned that the readers should read his initial thoughts on the matter. Additionally, as mentioned before, the first edition was "proofread" by his best friend Rosenzweig, who died later, so perhaps that was one of the ways in which Buber wanted to honour the friendship by not changing anything in the first version of "their masterpiece". In the beginning, the book was supposed to be just the first chapter of a much larger piece of writing; however, the process of writing led Buber to the conclusion that he should leave the piece as it was – just a little over a hundred pages long, which today is referred by many as more of a poetic than a literary piece of writing; others describe it as rather, "a frustrating read", where seemingly simple words are used in new and alien contexts.

The truth of the matter is that the book might be described as a rather difficult lecture, as "'I and Thou' is full of aphoristic formulations and evocative figures of speech and has an almost musical cadence. Indeed, the work is configured in a quasi-musical form of three parts, akin to the movements of a sonata, each with a distinctive internal rhythm, punctuated with thematic motifs. It is written in sixty-two short sections that grow along the way with an ever fuller conceptual resonance. 'I and Thou' thus been characterised as a philosophical poem". In the translator's introduction of "I and Thou", written by Ronald Gregor Smith, the linguist wrote, "we might call 'I and Thou' a 'philosophical-religious poem', it belongs essentially to no single specialised class of learnt work. It has a direct appeal to all those who are interested in living religious experience, rather than in theological debates and the rise and fall of philosophical schools. It has first and foremost to be judged on its intrinsic merits – by the impact, that is to say, which it makes on our actual, responsible life, as persons and as groups, in the modern world".

"I and Thou" (also often written as "I-Thou") translates into seeing another person as a Thou. It happens in meeting, where the other person is treated as an unknown person. As Buber explained, "in the I-Thou relationship, one does not experience, but meets the Other". Each person then is treated as an "end" in themselves. In other words, just a meeting with a person and engaging with them should be enough. Together with trying to suspend one's bias, personal agenda and the need for knowing, the other should be a sustained notion of being – considering that the other person is unknown and equally sufficient to be enough of an answer to any relation.

"Philosopher Martin Buber detailed the qualities that characterise a real 'encounter,' or I-Thou meeting, between two people. (...) According to Buber, an interpersonal encounter contains wonderful potential that far exceeds two separate people in conversation. This potential becomes apparent when two people actively and authentically engage each other in the here and now and truly 'show up' to one another. In this encounter, a new relational dimension that Buber termed 'the between' becomes manifest. When this between dimension exists, the relationship becomes greater than the individual contributions of those involved. This type of meeting is what Buber described as an I-Thou relationship".

On numerous occasions Buber mentioned the importance of "intimacy" in the idea of knowing. As according to him in the state of true "intimacy", we know "no thing" about each other, we "surrender" everything we know about the being so far and we, "quest a conversation as a new adventure". For example, the philosopher mentions that the, "universe addresses us as Thou", which could be understood as the universe always wants, "to get to know us" and in order to do that it always "suspends" its agenda and bias. According to Buber, relation occurs in three main areas:

- the relation to nature;

- the relation to each other ("I-It" between people and objects and "I-Thou" between people);

- spiritual life – the I-Thou according to Buber does not "just happen," it occurs as per God's grace – God's unmerited favour to humans, as we need to submerge our purest version of ourselves in the conversation or relation.

That last point was reached when one morning the mindful teacher was visited by an unknown young man – who had some questions regarding life. Years later, Buber described the meeting in the following matter, "I conversed attentively and openly with him – only omitted to guess the questions which he did not put. Later, not long after, I learnt from one of his friends – he himself was no longer alive – the essential content of these questions; I learnt that he had come to me not casually, but borne by destiny, not for a chat but for a decision". The literary reviewers believed that also this experience had a tremendous impact on Buber's understanding of the importance of a dialogue and the potential in a Real Meeting. As per God's grace, Buber had a chance to save the life of someone who wanted to commit suicide; by human mismeeting, he did not respond to that grace in the most intimate approach.

In today's Vienna, there is a place named after the philosopher, which is a university dormitory located at Fritz Hahn-Gasse 1. In *Figure 9.* is *The Dormitory* and in *Figure 10. The Dormitory's Entrance.*

Figure 9. The Dormitory

Figure 10. The Dormitory's Entrance

MARTIN BUBER
1878-1965

Der in Wien geborene Sozial- und
Religionsphilosoph gilt bis heute als einer
der einflussreichsten Denker, Politiker und
Schriftsteller der deutschsprachigen
jüdischen Kultur- und Geisteswelt.
Als Mitbegründer des „Freien Jüdischen
Lehrhauses" in Frankfurt a.M. und
bedeutender Übersetzer der hebräischen
Bibel ins Deutsche erwarb er großes Ansehen.
Der interkulturelle Dialog war ihm stets
ein Anliegen, ganz nach seinem Motto:
„Alles wirkliche Leben ist Begegnung".

At the entrance to the dormitory, there is a placard, explaining in German who Martin Buber was (*Figure 10*), where the translation of the sign states:

"Martin Buber, the social and religious philosopher, born in Vienna, is still considered one of the most influential thinkers, politicians and writers in the German-speaking and Jewish cultural and intellectual world. Most known as a co-founder of the 'Free Jewish Teaching House' in Frankfurt and an important translator of the Hebrew Bible into German. Intercultural dialogue was always important to him, true to his motto:'All real life is an encounter'".

Although Buber was a very accomplished scholar, he could be described as one of the most "award-unappreciated" philosopher of all times: he was nominated for the Nobel Prize in Literature seventeen times, and the Nobel Prize in the Peace category once, but unfortunately did not receive any of them. However, in our eyes his creativity deserves all those prestigious awards.

The Length of the Hyphen in the I-Thou and I-It

In his writings, Martin Buber explains the hyphen between the I and Thou (I-Thou), and with our biases most people see it as the short hyphen which is positioned on the bottom right of most computer keyboards. However, as reflected in the semiotics of the next section, the metaphor of the hyphen could be of different lengths, from short to extremely long, and at times, alternating in length, depending on the situation and relationship.

To explain the above, let us use the example of falling in love, getting married and living together for decades. When meeting someone for the first time, the length of the hyphen is short as we know very little of the person. As one develops the relationship and understanding of another then the hyphen lengthens. For example, one person might know his wife for thirty years and then one day along comes the first grandchild, all of a sudden, the grandfather sees a totally different side to his wife, as she becomes a grandmother. This results in more understanding and appreciation of her being, and therefore, the length of the hyphen, lengthens even more. When being married for say forty years, the hyphen is longer than when a couple met, however clearly as things change in life one still is getting to know the other, be it with the birth of a grandchild, in stressful situations, in sickness and also in death, and in doing so still giving of oneself to another, still listening, showing care, compromising and being human together.

Understanding the I-Thou and I-IT Semiotically

We believe that Martin Buber missed the semiotics of the I-Thou principal, and therefore, we decided to explain some of the I-Thou semiotically. The hyphen used is not simply just a hyphen between two words, but rather seen as a true word in itself; it is seen as the embodiment of joining persons or the embodiment of meeting others.

In *Figure 11.* the hyphen in the I-Thou is a *Short Hyphen,* where there is only a limited relationship or understanding between two persons. In *Figure 12.* we see the *Hyphen Being a Longer One*, thereby indicating that there is more understanding between the two persons. We have also here, brought in our icons indicating an individual speaking with another, which could also be more than one person in some situations.

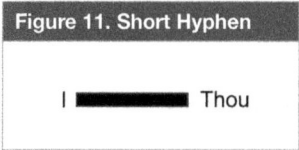

Figure 11. Short Hyphen

I ████████ Thou

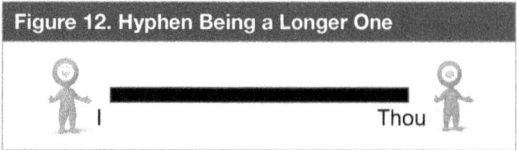

Figure 12. Hyphen Being a Longer One

I ███████████████████ Thou

In *Figure 13.* we show the *Hyphen Being an Extremely Long One* where there is much in common, understanding or in relationship between the two persons. Here too we have brought in the icons to demonstrate relationships.

Figure 13. Hyphen Being an Extremely Long One

In *Figure 14.* we reflect the *Differences in the Length of the Hyphen* that people enter. As mentioned, when meeting someone for the first time, the length of the hyphen is short, as indicated by the position arrow on the left side. As one develops a relationship and understanding of another, the hyphen lengthens. For example, when starting a relationship, one is on the far left of the hyphen, however as time moves on, the further we move on the hyphen.

This is indicated by the position arrow on the left. This position arrow obviously moves as time progresses and can move in both directions, depending on how we treat the other, how we listen, how we care, how much we allow others to get to know us, how we build on relations and of course how people meet to Meet, even in a family environment.

Figure 14. Differences in the Length of the Hyphen

Although using a personal-based example above, it is no different in professional life, the more leaders spend time with their teams in Real Meeting, the better they get to know them, the more they are able to enter into the hyphen and make a difference, and as time develops so does the semiotic hyphen extend in length. How can leaders enter into the hyphen? Well, it is getting out on the "shop floor" to have open discussions with employees, listening to them and showing interest with intent. Often the approach of leaders misses the elements of listening, learning, helping, caring, and even ethics at times, as well as personhood.

When meeting someone, instead of delving directly into work-related topics, at times, try to have a discussion about things of interest to them. Obviously, the better one gets to know the other, the easier it is to enter that hyphen. For example, if the leader knows someone is interested in a certain sport, sports team, pastime, or hobby, it becomes easier to start the discussion. I visit operations around the world on a regular basis, and when walking on the shop floor, I do my best to Meet with individuals and sometimes small teams. Although, not knowing everyone, due to the size of the company where I am employed, it is obviously difficult to know what everyone's interests are, never mind even knowing their names. Therefore, I observe the semiotics around them to give me an indication of what interests them. It could be a photo of a loved one, a poster on the wall, their keyring, sticker on their helmet, a baseball cap (when in the USA) or artifacts on the shelf or desk. Asking them to tell their story about any of these not, only breaks the ice, but unconsciously sends a message to them that the leader is showing interest and care in them.

In today's era, so many people have tattoos, and therefore, one way of engaging is to ask them if they are willing to explain the significance of their tattoo. One would be amazed how quickly the conversation opens up, and in most cases the individual is more than willing to explain the meaning of the tattoo, and in many cases, they show other tattoos that they have. By doing so, the leader has immediately entered the hyphen in the I and Thou. This approach of showing interest, listening with intent, and suspending one's own agenda contributes to developing the culture in an organisation.

Then on the opposite side of the coin, we have the I-It where the focus is on object rather than relationships. In *Figure 15.* we show the hyphen in the *I-It* principle and in *Figure 16.* we have included *Two Icons* reflecting person focusing on objects. I have seen leaders approach persons on site and focus the discussions solely on the work issues, the controls, systems, and the procedures, with very little or any focus on the personhood. We are by no means saying that focusing on the work issues is incorrect, as this could be no further away from the truth. The work issues are important; however, it is key that leaders find the balance in their approach. At times, the focus is, of course, solely on the work issues, but other times it could be a balance between the work issues and the personhood. And then, at times, it is also important only to focus on the personhood. Our preference is to start with the personhood issues and then the work issues. No approach is wrong, but it is of utmost importance to find a suitable balance. To be stuck only in the I-It is definitely not a productive way and can only be a step to disaster for any leader in their efforts to gain respect, appreciation, and building a team based on trust.

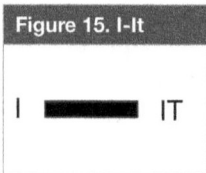

Figure 15. I-It

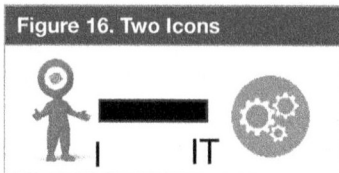

Figure 16. Two Icons

In the beginning of the book, we explained the meaning of Real Meeting and getting to know each other by "meeting to Meet", "engaging to Engage", "listening to Listen", "understanding to Understand", by "connecting to Connect" and "knowing to Know". This is what is meant as the Yada in Meeting. In *Figure 17.* we show the *Yada* in the hyphen between the I and the Thou. In *Figure 18.* we have replaced the word Yada with words that we feel make up the Yada.

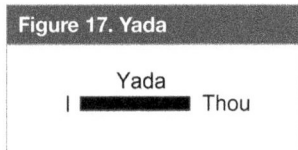

Figure 17. Yada

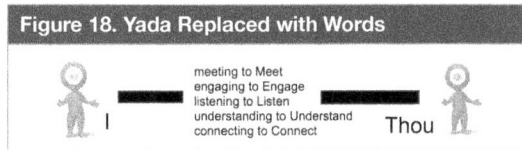

Figure 18. Yada Replaced with Words

Seeing the Meaning of the Hyphen in a Different Light

During a business trip to Chicago, I had been talking to some leaders about the writings of Martin Buber and had explained the meaning of the hyphen in the I-Thou. During the tea break, one of the participants, Shelly, came up to me and in discussion she made the comment that when one looks at the dates written on gravestones or headstones, there is a hyphen between the two dates, for example 23.12.1934 – 29.06.2020. Shelly mentioned that for her this hyphen could depict the life that one has lived. I found this comment interesting, and it definitely shone a different light onto the understanding of the meaning and the semiotic of a hyphen between two dates.

That evening, during reflecting on the day's events, the comments made by Shelley came to mind, and in thinking of what she had said, my thoughts drifted off to my late mother, Margaret, who had for many years dedicated much of her life being there for others, which included years of voluntary work, and raising money for the Hospice association in South Africa (an association that supports terminal cancer patients). The hyphen between the dates of my mother's life from birth to her passing made sense and inspired a new meaning for me; she had meant so much to so many people, cared for people, her hyphen was long and filled with so much of the positive Yada, so much time spent in the Kairos Time.

I am sure that Martin Buber never regarded this aspect of the hyphen in his I-Thou, relating to the hyphen between dates on a gravestone, headstone or on a remembrance card. However, for us, there was this new meaning, a deeper understanding of the hyphen.

Community – A Much-Desired Social Need

Gemeinschaft and Gesellschaft

Without going into too much detail, the German sociologist Ferdinand Tönnies (1855 – 1963), used the words Gemeinschaft and Gesellschaft. He referred to the word Gemeinschaft (Community) in defining an "ideal model" of society, in which there are bonds and networks between people, where relationships are social, personal, and direct and where there are strongly shared values and beliefs and there is a sense of togetherness. Gemeinschaft also refers to a relationship where there are personal interactions which are based on sentiment, where people feel a sense of belonging. In this type of Community there is little need for any external control or arbitration.

On the other hand, the word Gesellschaft (society) is different, as it refers to more complex and impersonal societies and a form of social integration based on impersonal ties, focused on one's own interests, competition with others and negotiations. Gesellschaft is also considered as being more an association than what is meant by Community when referring to the word Gemeinschaft. In Gesellschaft or society, there are contractual-type agreements, the individuals' rights and obligations are spelled out and often governed by legislation and rules, and in turn people are controlled by authorities, bodies, and institutions. Gesellschaft could also refer to a contractual relationship between two entities.

There are various definitions for the word Community, however some of the common words that come up include care, relationships, empathy, collaboration, consultation, and communication. All of these words fit into the word Gemeinschaft and in turn into the elements of Real Meeting as well as entering the I-Thou. When researching various interviews with Graham Long, he commented on Community, which highlights its importance, be it at the workplace or in private lives. Without a sense of Community or a sense of belonging there is division, stress, sadness and discrimination. This is no different to the workplace, the stronger the sense of Community, the happier people will be, and in turn, this feeling of togetherness as a team, contributes to a desired company culture.

Graham Long in Real Meeting

In Graham's years heading up the Wayside Chapel, he and his teams opened their arms to all those who were at the margins, whether because of poverty, sickness, mental illness, homelessness, or addiction. By doing so they have returned many people into the loving embrace of Community, where all humans belong.

Developing the sense of Community in the true sense of the word, can only be developed through Real Meeting and by entering the I and Thou. During a cold winter's night walk through one of the famous Christmas Markets, close to the "Rauthaus" (City Hall) in Vienna, we walked past the City Hall. Projected on the walls were the words, "All Humans are equal", so fitting to this chapter of the book, and when seeing the words Aneta murmured, "Graham would have been so impressed". Although the photo seen in *Figure 19. Rauthaus,* does not capture the full sentence, one sees the words "All Humans" projected on the walls.

Figure 19. Rauthaus

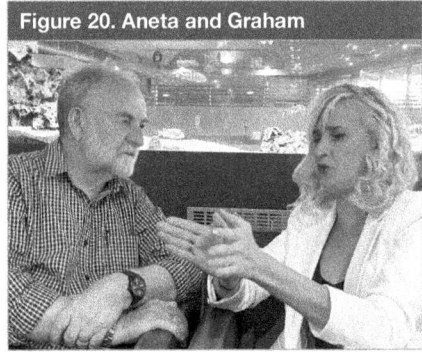

Figure 20. Aneta and Graham

Sadly though, as life has become more hectic, we humans tend to pass one another with little Meeting, little acknowledgement of co-being, no time for one another as we move through this "rat race" that we find ourselves in. This problem has become an even bigger one since the world went into lockdown due to COVID-19; during this period, as social beings we were forced to become anti-social. When walking the streets in Vienna, it was as if humans had become scared of each other. I recall shortly after countries had opened up again towards the end of the pandemic, I was walking in the centre of Vienna on the way to the office when I noticed an elderly lady battling to place her bag into the rear of a taxi, whilst the young taxi driver simply watched her. I immediately walked up to her and assisted her in placing the bag in the taxi's luggage compartment. When I had done so, the taxi driver told me that I was stupid, because I did not know whether the lady had COVID or not. I felt saddened by the comment, and seeing how the lady was battling to lift her bag before I had assisted her, I realised how unsocial we had become. (On entering the office, I guess that you know what I did, though, I immediately washed and disinfected my hands.)

In an interview, Graham Long expressed his desire to meet people and create a Community that looks like a community centre that welcomes all comers. I have no doubt that what Graham meant when saying his desire was to meet people was the capitalised version of the word "Meet". *Figure 20.* shows *Aneta and Graham* in Australia in 2024.

In Chapter 5, we share our discussions with numerous Indigenous People from totally different corners of the globe, including Kevin and the "Medicine Lady with Knowledge" in Australia as well as Melanie, Lisa, and the Elder Joe in Canada. All of them expressed the importance of Community in their cultures, be it around a fireplace in Canberra, Australia or social events in Hinton, Canada. Both these cultures although thousands of years old had no knowledge of one another, but their need for Community, their need for engaging, their need for Meeting was the same. When researching these two cultures, we are reminded of the powers of the "Collective Unconscious". They had never met, however very similar in their traditions, connection to nature, dances, body painting and much more. What stands out most for us is their desire to Meet, to meet in Real Meeting.

The Sense of Community – We are not Individuals

While we were writing this book, one weekend we were watching a reality show based on survival in a remote part of Mongolia, and the interest we both had in following the challenges of isolation meant many late nights or early mornings, watching the stories unfold. What was clear was that no matter how strong an individual was, hunting for food, eating items that probably most of us have never eaten before such as mice, tree bark, leeches, to name only a few, what did get to many of the team members was the isolation, being apart from Community.

One of the participants, named Randy, needed to give up the challenge, even though, it meant that he would be giving up the prize money of half a million dollars. Why? Because, he said, he was impacted by the lack of Community and then by being out in the wilderness; there was a huge part of his world that was missing. Although as winter had crept in, he was no longer successful in hunting and fishing for food and was hungry, he mentioned that there was a whole different aspect that was affecting him: the lack of social interaction, lack of people, lack of Community. He also mentioned that he was hoping that the environment would fill that gap, however realised that it was a temporary fix. The contestant made the comment, "it's like putting a band-aid on a bullet hole".

We are definitely not only individuals, as humans we are continuously connected, one of the participants in the reality survival programme even became emotional when hearing the echo of his own voice, "wow" that was an eye opener for me, although he had been alone for over a month and not seeing any persons, his own voice made him emotional.

Larry, one of the other contestants on the same reality show, said that at times it is nice to be alone, however he mentioned that he misses what he calls, "the sweet in life" and when one has the sweet in life, the sour is not that bad. After the respective episode, we discussed this metaphor used by Larry and we agreed that it was a nice metaphor to chase when in discussion with somebody. He mentioned that one needs to cherish the sweetness of being with one's family, close friends and even pets. These all fit into the I-Thou. The sour he mentioned was the bad day at work, the daily commute, people that frustrate others in the traffic, all of these linked to the I-It. He also mentioned that although at times it is great to be alone, other times one feels good having others to depend on oneself, feel needed and wanted, appreciated and to be loved. The need is great to love one's family and to love one's friends, so important in life, so in touch with the I-Thou of Martin Buber.

Key comments made by the contestants related to the I-Thou and sociality were: "I miss my family", "I need someone to talk to", "I need my family in order to survive", "I miss my family's companionship", "I think of my family constantly", "I miss interaction" and one contestant made the comment that, "it is extremely lonely to share experiences just with one's self".

One contestant made the call to the show organisers telling them that he was, "officially tapping out" and thereby making the request for them to return and fetch him. He mentioned that when he entered the challenge, he thought it would be about outlasting the hunger and the cold, if he wanted to win, however even though he was warm, dry and comfortable and he had more than a week's stock of food, he "tapped out". He mentioned the sitting around waiting for time to pass. Knowing that his children were going about their daily lives was in his words, "driving him nuts" and all of it was not worth the prize money. He was missing being happy, being a dad, missing his kids' life and his joy in life was being a husband and dad and that is what he lives for, and what makes life worthwhile.

To some degree, I understand this comment made by the contestants of the reality show "Survivor", as in my professional life I travel a lot all over the world for business. However, very rarely do I visit the cities on my own, as I always have the feeling that it is too lonely having nobody by my side to experience all those things with. To experience, amongst others, the sounds, the smells, the views, the beauty of nature, or the cities, the sunsets and sunrises, the semiotics of the semiosis that we find ourselves in.

At first when reading the comments by Martin Buber that we are not individuals did not make sense to me, as it was clear that everyone is different and that we are in fact individuals. However, when watching the reality show about survival, it all became clearer and made more sense to me. Yes, to some degree we are individuals, however we are always connected to others, and therefore, the comment that there is no such thing as individuality. We are humans and as humans always connected to another, be it in reality, or simply in our thoughts, we are always socially connected. Even though, the ten participants never met anyone else during the days in solitary living, they were always connected in their thoughts to their families, friends and pets back home.

The same applies to prisoners in solitary confinement, although they have been removed from society, but also from their fellow prisoners, they remain connected to other human beings, not only for the few times a prison guard delivers the food with each mealtime, but more importantly being connected with others in their thoughts. This proves Buber's point that we are members of a Community, we are constantly connected with others, we are together Human Beings.

Entering I-Thou, Shifts Focus from Fixing, to Focusing on Persons

In an interview with Graham Long, he made the comment; "We definitely live in a culture where we treat one another as problems to be fixed, rather than people to be met". Graham also mentioned that he had mostly overcome that approach, and he knows that he cannot fix the problem, but he is happy to meet the person. This resonated with me, as in my field of work, people often believe that they need to fix all the problems that people face out there, and I do not think that this is uncommon for leaders in general. In the I-It, people feel it is their duty or responsibility to fix all the problems, despite the fact that there are probably team members or others, who are more qualified or suitable and have a better understanding of the problem, if only given the trust and the chance to do so. I think (even worse) managers' belief that they can fix people are entrenched in the I-It. In the I-Thou leaders focus on the person and in doing so, they are not treated as objects to be fixed.

I think, it was in another interview, during which Graham Long made some key comments that I felt would support the thinking of Community. Graham mentioned that, "ever since we stopped hanging over the fence talking to our neighbours, our list of mental illnesses has mushroomed and because we're hardwired as social, to live your life in a bubble is to be unwell. You can only distract yourself or entertain yourself". Definitely, nothing social about this.

Graham also mentioned that when one person experiences another, it is not a good thing, if one uses another, the person is being used by the other for their benefit. Therefore, experiencing or using another person is nothing like Real Meeting, in fact it is totally the opposite. It is clear that not many persons like to be used. This is probably a controversial comment, but people consider sex workers as being used, I have my doubts whether many of them like the fact that they are used. For them there is no I-Thou, they are treated in the I-It and for sure there is no Real Meeting taking place. However, I do confess that I am generalising, but this is my impression.

Consider this in a working environment, if after having a discussion with your boss, you leave his or her office afterwards knowing that there had been a Real Meeting, this would be a much more positive experience than feeling that you had been used.

When considering the I-Thou principle, there could be a fine line of how deep you drive a discussion. When allowing persons to tell their stories, there is always the chance that it gets personal and at times even emotional. Unless the leader is qualified to address a problem, he or she should refrain from attempting to be a counsellor, rather refer the person to professional support, for assistance and addressing the situation. Much better to show sympathy and to determine, if suitable help could be arranged to address the issue.

Coincidentally, when writing this chapter, I happened to hear a snippet of an interview on one of the broadcasting channels with a lady who lost a baby due to a miscarriage, and how, at times, she felt that she was to blame. She mentioned that losing a baby, no matter how many weeks old, is extremely emotional. Although I missed the entire interview, she mentioned that many people make the mistake of trying to fix the situation. This is often done with words like "you are still young", or "you have time" and "you can try again". I am sure that people making these comments are only trying to do good and trying to give support; however, are not aware that the comments that they think are suitable for the situation are more likely causing emotional distress. We all know what it is like when we attend a funeral, for example, most of us do not know what to say to the parent who has lost a child, or someone who has lost their partner. As Graham says, we do not have to fix the situation, we probably cannot say anything that would help, nor do we really know how the person affected is feeling. All that we need to do is show sympathy, through body language by giving them a hug of support in Real Meeting.

My mother passed away during the COVID -19 lockdown and I could not travel from Austria to South Africa to say farewell and attend her funeral. Neither could my younger sister Sue, travel within South Africa to attend and nor could my children get there from New Zealand or Austria. We all had to dial in remotely into the service, with my other sister Wendy and only a handful of persons attending. When seeing the sadness on the faces of my siblings and the grandchildren during the service, I just wanted to give them a hug of support, a shoulder to cry on, but this was not possible. I received many messages of support from friends and colleagues, however what I missed was the simple hug from my family and a shoulder to lean on. No words could take away the sadness that we all felt, the sense of loneliness in the loss of our beloved mother, as we all joined from many thousands of kilometres apart. We were not experiencing the Real Meeting on the day, and nobody could fix the situation and take away the sadness experienced.

For months after our mother had passed away, I would get into my car and dial her number, wanting to have our weekly chat. My unconscious mind was controlling my thoughts, but then the reality hit home that she was no longer there to talk to. My sister Sue said the same, she would at times want to pick up the phone and make the call back home, before also remembering that it was no longer possible, there would be no answer on the end of the line or in today's world at the end of the signal. I am convinced that as we were not there in Real Meeting with Wendy and the children to say our farewells, we probably have not had complete closure, especially in the months immediately after mom's passing. By contrast, in 2007, I said the eulogy at my father in-law's funeral and at my father's memorial service, I had closure, I said my goodbyes ... but not this time. This time I was alone, no community, no meeting, and definitely no Real Meeting with family and friends.

Listening Brought Tears and Friendship

So much of what we are sharing in this book comes through discovery and experience and "switching on" to placing persons at the centre of what we do. One such occasion occurred when out for dinner one night with Rob Long in a restaurant in Canberra, prior to the COVID-19 global lockdown.

After finding a table and taking our seats, our waitress arrived, introduced herself to us and we responded by introducing ourselves to her. We asked her if she would like to share "her story" with us, interested in how she ended up in Canberra and working in the restaurant. She smiled and started to tell us a part of her story, and then took our drinks order, before leaving and attending to a table adjacent to ours. Even though, the restaurant was busy, every time she returned to our table, enjoying the interaction, she continued telling us details of her past, why she was waitressing and her interests. This resulted in the three of us discussing various issues with her, and even included some card tricks, to which she once again appreciated the interaction.

We noticed that she was enjoying the continuous interaction, so we suspended our own agenda, took the focus off ourselves and even what we wanted to order, and instead opened up the opportunity for her to talk to us. At some stage during the discussion, she began to cry, and tears rolled down her cheeks. She was embarrassed and apologised, but we made her feel at ease. She stated that no one had wanted to hear her story before and that no one knew of her struggles in life and the pressures she was under.

At the end of the meal, we simply asked if we could have a selfie with her, and she was delighted to have her picture taken with these two old guys, old enough to be her grandfathers. Prior to leaving the restaurant, we gave her a nice tip and said our farewells, knowing that we would probably never see her again. She said "thanks" and gave both of us a huge hug, which led us to realise that we had left an impression on her – and she on us.

On returning to my hotel, I reflected on the dinner and the conversations we had that night. It all involved key aspects in social psychology, starting with intent listening, suspending our agenda, and showing interest in what our waitress was saying. It was about caring and building a relationship, even if it was a short-term one.

Knowing that we would never see her again, I often thought about her over the years that followed, wondering what had happened to her, whether she was doing well and if she had achieved at least some of her dreams. Fast forward around five years, Aneta and I were visiting Canberra and decided to have dinner at one of the many restaurants near our hotel. We entered the restaurant and were waiting to be seated when out of the corner of my eye, I noticed someone running towards me, then throwing her arms around me and greeting me at the same time. Well, surprisingly, it was the same waitress who had served us years before. Even though, between my visits to the restaurant, she must have served thousands of hungry customers, she remembered me. This is proof that if one suspends one's own agenda and gives time to someone else to tell their story, they create significant impact and lasting memories.

Had Rob and I, five years prior, only focused on ourselves and had no personal contact with the waitress, she would never have remembered me many years later. We had, through her stories on the initial day, entered into the hyphen of I-Thou, and by doing so showed interest and care and built trust, which in turn made a difference to one person's life, but also created a friendship between the three of us. *Figure 21. Engaging with Rob and I* and in *Figure 22. Meeting Five Years Later.*

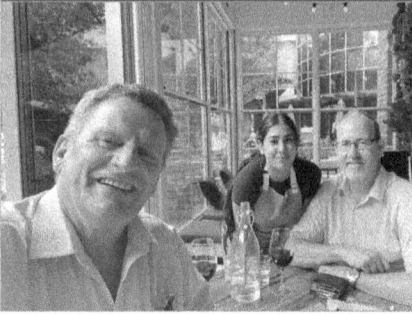
Figure 21. Engaging with Rob and I

Figure 22. Meeting Five Years Later

Relate this story to leadership in general; at times, we as leaders underestimate the importance of finding the issues of the other persons' significance, and giving of ourselves to them, allowing them the time to tell their story. Throughout some of the chapters of this book, we share some insights into events where others have been given the opportunity to share what is important to them, to share their narrative. By allowing others to tell their story, ensures learning as leaders, and in many cases learning about important aspects that in no means can be measured.

SELF-REFLECTION

Chapter 3 - Entering the Hyphen in the I-Thou

Our selection of elements for self-reflection from the chapter are as follows:

- How often do I shift from focusing on the I-It and move towards entering the hyphen in the I-Thou, thereby engaging with employees and others?

- As a leader or part of a community, I refrain from experiencing or using another for my benefit.

- When meeting someone, do I, dive directly into the workplace related issues, or do I at times, start a discussion with issues that are of interest and of significance to hem?

- Is it my style to pass others in the office, along the passage, in the car park or on the shop floor without any Real Meeting, little or no acknowledgement of co-being, showing no time for others?

- How often do I try my best to refrain from "fixing others", and rather place my focus on the person?

CHAPTER 4

Meeting with "No Meeting"

"We expect more from technology and less from each other. We create technology to provide the illusion of companionship without the demands of friendship".

Dr Sherry Turkle

American Sociologist

The word Meeting (capitalised) is characterised by mutuality, listening, suspending one's own agenda, suspending or relinquishing one's power, being in relationship with another and being present, all of these being in the I-Thou. Using the word meeting (non-capitalised) is often in the I-It mode, and focused on objects, control, utility structure, efficiency, as well as based mainly on inputs and outputs. When being in the I-It, the word "communication" is interpreted as "telling", and not as listening as when being in the I-Thou. In our private lives, there are several examples where we meet others, but actually where there is no Real Meeting taking place. These examples include amongst others, Facebook, Instagram, WhatsApp and LinkedIn.

Two Young Ladies in Colombia

I recall sitting in a restaurant in Colombia quietly having dinner on my own and reading a book. The setup of the restaurant was similar to a typical American-style diner with nobody else but myself and two young ladies in their early twenties who were sitting directly behind me. Whilst watching the waitress fill up my glass with a good Argentinian Malbec red wine that she had recommended and waiting for my Argentinian Angus steak to arrive, I could not help overhearing the conversation between the two ladies, as they were talking rather loudly.

At one stage they were sharing information about their friends, when one of them said to the other that she has over one thousand friends on Facebook from all over the world, friends from her school days, work life, friends of friends as well as people that she had never met in person. I got the impression that the second lady was rather impressed, as she used the words "oh my gosh, that is unbelievable", after which she mentioned that her group of friends was around half of the number mentioned by the other lady. They then agreed to open their Facebook accounts, I guess using the app on their phones to check the numbers.

After eavesdropping for a while and feeling a bit guilty for doing so, I purposely lost track of their conversation, and I went into reflection about what I had just overheard from their discussion. It dawned on me that in today's world with all the social media options, people naively believe that those connected to them on various apps and platforms are actually part of their friendship groups. The reality is that, apart from sharing their photos and comments on Facebook or any other social media, they do not actually know the person or persons, and even more striking is that there is never any Real Meeting taking place. It is so misleading that people believe that they are friends, or even have the foggiest idea or understand of what the other person is all about, without ever meeting them in person and apart from messaging and commenting, actually never even talking to them.

The discussion between the two ladies led me to reflecting on my own LinkedIn account, in which I have over the years regularly had requests for people to follow them, as they are following me. If I recall correctly, the words that popped up on my computer screen included, "you have four new invitations", "you appeared in thirty searches", "see who searched your profile". The worst of them all, for me, was the message that often appeared on the computer screen was "congratulate so and so, for working for a certain company for a certain number of years", and then what people do is click on the button to congratulate the person, without any need to type a single word. How false can one get, definitely a case of meeting without any Real Meeting.

By no means am I saying that social media is a bad thing; however, what I am saying is that there is a false sense of belief on how many friends one has, or active followers, similar to what the two young ladies in the diner were in discussion and in awe about. I regularly upload my articles in LinkedIn, to share them with the wider community, rather than only those who read the magazine in which I have a column. I also belong to some closed groups on Facebook, some professional, others military and sports, however, do not open it up to the traditional friendship groups. Aneta, on the other hand, does not participate in any social media, whatsoever, as she feels that if people look at the photographs uploaded and then interpret them as they feel fitting, believing that they have a good understanding of what is happening in their so-called friend's lives without actually knowing the full context of the picture or information posted. Sadly, Aneta is right, so many assumptions made about the lives of others without any Real Meeting at all.

As we were writing this book, there was a heated debate among Polish politicians (where one party wanted to follow an already implemented law in France) about banning smart phones in schools, especially primary educational establishments. Apparently, many kids who were asked in a survey what they thought about the idea for the new law, stated that they are "mortified" as it would mean that without the phones, they would have to talk to their classmates during the recess. Personally, we cannot think of many things that would be more "mortifying" than those answers provided in the survey.

Meeting at the Workplace

Unfortunately, at the workplace, it is common that when people "meet" on an individual basis or in groups there is little engagement in the true sense of the word. This means there is far more telling than listening, little suspending of one's own agenda and power, controlling discussions and all this resulting in meeting with no Real Meeting. Without encouraging and having two-way open discussion, and engagement in the meetings, there is at times dialogue, but not necessarily any "Real Meeting" between the parties.

I am not only referring to formal meetings, but also meeting others in general. Putting it in a business or industrial context, these meetings include meeting for induction training sessions, on-line training sessions, general safety training, toolbox talks, shift handovers, pre-shut and pre-start meetings, productivity, and operational meetings, to name only a few. Meetings of these kinds are based on getting the documentation in order, getting the task "done and dusted", a "tick and flick" approach – or as I recently learnt in Canada – a "pencil whip" approach, and signing off on the paperwork and formalities. Yes, as leaders, these types of meetings have a role to play and are critical in the need to manage any organisation, operation, department, or smaller teams. However, at times, we as leaders need to move out of the I-It and into the I-Thou, where people are placed at the centre of our discussions. Being in the I-Thou does not naturally occur all the time, leaders must be aware of being in the I-It, and then consciously focus on moving into the I-Thou, being with others in Real Meeting.

A typical example of meeting without "Meeting" is the infamous induction training, as mentioned before; this is in many instances a meeting without "Meeting". In our view, induction training sessions of this nature should rather be called

"Indoctrination Sessions". At the end of the session, everyone signs an attendance register, in case there is a need to prove there was a meeting, even if, in fact, there has been no "Meeting" whatsoever. Then leaders wonder why the employees or contractors working on the site do not follow the rules and requirements. Well, it is simple, the persons were put through what I call "Death by PowerPoint" or shown a five minute video, and then it is expected that firstly they understand what is required and secondly that they even listened to what was being said, probably as the metaphor that my late father would at times use, "in one ear and out the other". The Australians have a nice metaphor explaining the approach which is referred to as "tick and flick", depicting that it is an exercise done, only because it is required by legislation or corporate requirements, even if it adds little or no value.

As mentioned, Real Meeting" is about time together, suspending one's own agenda, engaging, connecting with people, allowing others to tell their story, and promoting two-way, open discussion. We as leaders need to reflect on how much of our efforts is just meetings and how much engagement is in Real Meeting. Do we find a suitable balance between the two? We cannot be stuck in only one of them, however, there needs to be a certain balance. As Martin Buber said, Real Meeting requires unconditional trust, and therefore, it is also key that leaders are ethical and genuine when being in the I-Thou.

Over time, both of us have attended business Meetings, me at the workplace or in various organisations that I have belonged to, and Aneta at the universities at which she has worked and lectured. Many of these were formal meetings, often with fixed agenda and timeslots, but at the end of many of the meetings there was no outcome and there was absolutely no Real Meeting. I recall someone once making the comment, "this meeting was about taking minutes, but losing hours", I thought the comment was rather comical, however sadly true in some instances. Leaders should understand that people become disengaged and distance themselves from others as soon as meaning, purpose and the motivation to connect is lost.

On the other hand, in many social meetings where there are no fixed agenda topics, but rather where there is open discussion, there is Real Meeting taking place. These meetings are mostly informal, consist of a simple social contract, and yet add value. Some examples are given throughout the chapters on Real Meeting and how we as humans enter the hyphen of the I-Thou.

It is key to point out that not all meetings are going to be Real Meetings where deeper discussions are held. We all know that in management at various levels of an organisation and in a typical working day at the office, there is the need to run and manage the business, to be focused on the I-It elements of running an organisation, for example, only to mention a few, issues like being focused on specific tasks, responsibilities, following up on actions, providing instructions, developing processes, sorting out technical issues, problem solving sessions, strategic plan and many more. However, during all these activities there is still the possibility and the need to treat people with dignity and respect, to listen with intent, to be respectful in dealing with them, handling their comments and suggestions and thereby, even though, focused on the objective we can still treat them in the I-Thou domain. Managers, at times, need to take tough decisions, navigate difficult situations, like restructuring or dismissing a person, however once again, this can be handled with as much compassion as possible and treating the receiving persons with care and respect. How this is perceived depends on how we as leaders are being with others, how we conduct ourselves when in meeting with others.

Two Types of Time in Greek

In the Greek language there are two types of time: one is known as "Chronos Time" and the other referred to as "Kairos Time". Chronos Time is measured by clocks and watches and by the evolutionary phases of earth's moon. For the Greeks the second word for time is "Kairos Time", which is known by fewer people, however despite this, it is what philosophers refer to as the "deep time".

In Chronos Time one measures time, it is quantitative and exact. Chronos Time is based on the second hand of a watch or the ticking of a clock, the sound of an alarm waking someone up, a tower bell ringing, or the amount of time for an appointment or meeting. On the other hand, in Kairos Time one finds opportunities to engage with others, be it family, friends or work colleagues, it is seen as opportune time.

Holding a meeting, conducting a meeting, organising a meeting, the outcomes of a meeting – these have nothing to do with Real Meeting. In leadership, we have mythology about time, however in management we have time management, and both the mythology of how leaders use time and all courses with time management relate to Chronos Time, where time becomes a monetary value. It becomes an economic thing, theretofore relates to the I-It and not much of the I-Thou. Dot points (bullet points) are a quick tool for managers, however leaders understand that stories take time, dot points are about Chronos Time, where stories are related to Kairos Time as reflected below. The I-It and Chronos Time focuses on the outcome, where the I-Thou and Kairos Time focus on the Meeting.

Chronos Time

Most leaders, in fact most humans, run and manage their lives in Chronos Time. Life as we know it today has become a "rat race", so busy, we hear metaphors being used so often like, "time is of the essence", "time is money", "my time is precious", "she was wasting my time", "time is running out", "time waits for no one" and many more. These expressions are often taken literally in everyday language; however, they stem from a metaphorical concept of time, as time is neither money, nor a fluid thing. In fact, we speak metaphorically in the unconscious mind, in most instances we do not think consciously of which and when to use a metaphor, the words are spoken without any thought.

One of the metaphors mentioned above, "time is money", is a metaphor that compares time and money, and it does not literally mean that the amount of time you have equals the money that you have. Instead, it means that time is a valuable resource, and it should be used effectively to be productive and earn money. This is all seen as Chronos Time.

Have you ever wondered why so many of us do not give ourselves the time to take a breath at times, to relax and even reflect? Why are we always on the run, doing things quickly to move to the next activity? We rush our morning coffee, almost downing it in a couple of gulps, so that we can get to the office. Then when driving or walking to the office, again this is at full speed. Lo and behold, we get caught up in traffic, resulting in words not commonly used by us (or at least not in front of our children), blood pressure rises, frustration creeps in, all because we are thinking at full speed.

Think about a normal day in the life of a leader, we manage our diaries, as if controlled by our calendars, our watches on our wrists, the clocks on the wall, or the time shown on the bottom right-hand side of our computer screen. Leaders run from meeting to meeting, cut discussions short when the "time is up", however in these circumstances often there has been meeting, however with no Real Meeting. We say this, as in these meetings there is often no connection between people in the true sense of the word. In Chronos Time we monitor our day, control our activities, measure our days and our lives in general in a quantitative manner. In Chronos Time we as humans are unconsciously controlled, demanding on ourselves as well as others and in fact probably allow life to fly past, without smelling the roses at times. In Chronos Time, one can meet with someone for a whole day and in that have no Meeting at all.

Kairos Time

Kairos Time is totally the opposite from Chronos Time. In Chronos Time it is all about control, demands, restrictions, etc., it is all about the measure of quantitative time or exact time, whereas with Kairos Time it is all about the right time or the time of opportunity. Kairos Time can be seen as the "timeless" duration of a discussion; it appeals to emotions of the time or event one finds oneself in at the moment. It is the time where things seem to stop, where we connect with others, with nature and even during reflection. Other examples of Kairos Time could be a walk along the beach, meditation, yoga, a chat around the fireplace, sketching, in other words doing things that allow us as humans to enter the moment and not be controlled by time. In my view, people who I have known suffering from burnout were living their lives in Chronos Time and not enough in Kairos Time.

Even though, we live in different continents to many of our family members, both Aneta and I make time for our grandchildren to enjoy time together via video link, sometimes for only a couple of minutes or other times over an hour. We suspend our agenda, our power and hand it over to the children. We allow them to direct the discussions, we spend the time in Kairos rather that Chronos Time. There is no looking at the watch, speeding things up, importance of time stops, it is all in the moment and they decide how long the moment will be. It is all based on Real Meeting and giving of one's time without an appointment. If the girls decide that they are not too keen to chat, because something else is happing in their lives, that is fine with us. We find another day or time when they will want to have the call.

As mentioned in Chapter 3, Ferdinand Tönnies used the word Gemeinschaft, and what he meant is what takes place when in Kairos Time, where "community and society" are central, where bonds are formed, networks and relationships between people created and a strong sense of togetherness.

I recall in the early 1999, we had decided to participate in the annual one hundred and nine kilometre Cape Argus Cycle Race in Cape Town, South Africa. We were inspired by a good friend of ours, Bob who had just completed the previous race and had mentioned how challenging it was. We purchased some racing bicycles, spent every Wednesday night training on spin-bikes in a gym at the local cycling shop, Thursday evenings cycling around the old Kyalami Formula One Racing track and on Saturdays out on the road. It was all about getting fit to finish the race in a given time, a time that we had set ourselves. This was obviously all in Chronos Time. However, on the day of the long race in Cape Town, we decided not to be concerned about the finish time at all, we decided to enjoy the event, to relish the moment. We had moved from Chronos Time to Kairos Time, and by doing so, we had enjoyed the race, and because of that, returned for the next four years (and with our time, each year, actually getting slower).

I read and enjoyed the book "Silence" written by a Buddhist monk, the late Thich Nhat Hanh, where he mentioned something that connects my thoughts to Chronos and Kairos Time. The words are, "Don't worry about the future, because the future is not yet here. There is only one moment for you to be alive, and that is the present moment. Come back to the present moment and live this moment deeply, and you will be free".

These words resonated with me, and a couple of months later we met an Indigenous Aboriginal lady around a fire in Canberra and she used words that were similar to that of the Buddhist Monk. Her words were "there is no rupture, no heaven, just here", and we have included her story in Chapter 5.

Visiting "Doctor Listen-Little"

Whilst in the process of writing this chapter, I had to visit an ear specialist as I was battling with a slight tinnitus as well as a blocked ear, or in other words equalise the right ear, very similar to what one does when flying in an aeroplane or descending whilst scuba diving. We had been diving in Saipan a couple of weeks before, and ever since then, I had battled with the ear as it always seemed blocked.

My appointment was at 10 a.m., I had filled in the necessary paperwork, waited fifteen minutes, and was then called by the nurse to undergo some acoustic tests in the sound booth. When finished, I was directed back to the waiting room and asked to wait to be called by the doctor. I waited about forty minutes to be called into the consulting room by the ear, nose, and throat specialist. I greeted him, and without greeting me back, he immediately asked me what the issue was, and before I had completed my first sentence, the doctor interrupted me and said, "let's take a look". I continued trying to explain the situation and he once again said, "let's take a look" without giving me the time to explain my story.

I was somewhat surprised and thought, here is a doctor who treats patients with hearing loss and ear problems, however he had absolutely no manners, people skills and even worse absolutely no listening skills (ironic since he treated people for hearing issues). At no stage was he truly interested to hear my full story or my concern, and he was not listening with any intent. He was dealing with the tinnitus only and not the problem with the blocked ear. He was dealing with me in Chronos Time, all he wanted to do was get me looked at as soon as possible with little discussion, prescribe something (that he said might help treating the tinnitus) and then get me out of his consulting room as quickly as possible. I thought to myself that he should invest in a production line where patients enter his consulting room through a rubber trap door on a conveyor belt and he questions them, "takes a look at them", hands them a prescription and then off they go through the exit rubber lined trap door, and then the next patient arrives through the entrance trap door, delivered just in time for the same treatment. I imagined the process as something like a production line in a Coca-Cola bottling plant.

The doctor commented on the tinnitus, and prescribed something for it, however ignored my questions about the blocked ear, and only after repeating my concern three times, he prescribed something which I thought was a bit strange; a nose spray. I knew he was an ear, nose and throat specialist, but my ear was blocked, not my nose, however after all, I am not a doctor, so what would I know, but two weeks later my ear was still blocked and my nose as clear as a newly purchased musical flute. My time at the doctor's consulting room is a typical example of being treated as an object, "something" sitting in his room, but at no time did he enter the I-Thou and connect or listen to my story. At the end, he gave me a prescription and said, if the medication helps for the tinnitus, I should come back within a month. Well, guess what, I never went back to him, and searched for an ear, nose and throat specialist who understands the meaning of care in her patient and listens with intent, suspends her power, rather than talking and controlling the discussion. In total, I spent ten minutes in the sound booth, forty minutes in the waiting room and a whole eight minutes with the doctor. The appointment at the doctor had in fact just occupied my time, I would rather visit a Buddhist monk who has taken the vow of silence than return to "Doctor Listen-Little".

This encounter fitted well into the notion of meeting with no meeting, or mismeeting, as described by Martin Buber. There was no connection between the doctor and me, there was a lack of communication and absolutely no listening on the side of the doctor. When I walked out of his consultation room, I had the feeling of mismeeting, probably wasted my time and as a result developed mistrust in him. When leaving, I told the story to Aneta and when doing so I gave the doctor the nickname, similar to the movie "Dr Dolittle", except for the doctor I gave him the nickname "Dr Listen-Little". We will send him a copy of this book and ask him to read this chapter, and hopefully the penny might drop. He might learn something about treating others with dignity and empathy.

The Dance

I recall visiting an operation in Italy, focusing on a large rebuild project and to take a break, we decided to spend two days in the coastal city of Trieste, finding some relaxing time and visiting various historical sites, including royal castles, a Basilica and some Roman ruins, as well as visiting one of my friends, Claudio, at his wine farm (OBIZ), close to Aquileia, which is an ancient Roman City founded as a colony by the Romans in 180 BC. Together with Claudio, we shared good Italian wine, cheese and salami whilst talking about everything from Italian culture and the history of the area to the art of wine making.

Driving back home, we crossed over the border between Italy and Slovenia and visited the Skocjan Caves. Having visited various caves in South Africa and Austria, this visit was exceptional, and second to none. What an amazing experience as we entered the first chamber, noiseless and filled with an abundance of stalagmites and stalactites created over millions of years. Then as we were approaching the second part of the cave, which is named the Murmuring Cave, one could hear water gushing and when entering, one gets this awesome feeling when seeing the river flowing. This part of the cave is between ten to sixty metres wide, over three-kilometres long and one-hundred metres high. The cave is the home to one of the largest underground river canyons in the world, and is filled with so much beauty that leaves one in awe and speechless. The caves are a unique natural phenomenon, which over time have been carved into form by the Reka River.

We sat on benches, at times, staring at the water gushing past below us, we stood on a bridge forty metres above the canyon and flowing river below us, walking along pathways lit up with lights and carved into the walls, taking in the experience, living the moment, at times in discussion and then at times in our own world, in our own thoughts, in our reflections and in connection with nature. The biosemiotics giving us an amazing, embodied feeling that was exceptional. After an hour and a half, the tour through the cave ended and we were given three options, which were to climb back up to the surface a short way, a medium route, and the long way. The medium and the longer options took visitors past waterfalls and smaller caves. We decided on the medium route, as we still had around five hours' drive back to Vienna. However, the medium length route continued giving us an embodied feeling with nature and the connection to something that had been created over millions of years, something not man made, but rather by nature itself.

Our visit to the caves was solely focused on Kairos Time, we were living in the moment, not worried about anything, not managed by the time on our watches. Sitting on the benches, standing on the raised bridge, reflecting on what we were experiencing was all in Kairos Time. After finishing the tour of the caves and returning to the surface, we decided to have lunch and then continue our journey by car back home. This is when we moved back into Chronos Time, where time once again became the essence, where our watches on our arms and the speedometer in the dashboard came back into play and influenced a trip back home. Although the time in the car was like a dance between Chronos and Kairos time, wanting to get home, but still enjoying the moments together.

A couple of days after returning to Austria from Slovenia and visiting the caves, I travelled to Poland to support our team on a large paper machine rebuild project. Aneta had engagements with a company that she was consulting for as well as at the university at which she was lecturing. Like the project in Italy, I moved back into Chronos Time and before I realised it, I had returned to the daily routine of being in project environments, running from meeting to meeting, supporting in the drive to meet the start-up date, attending discussions, addressing issues on the site and fitting in as much as possible during the limited three days that I was on site. There is nothing wrong with this approach, as this is how we run our daily lives as leaders. It is part of business, in fact, how we spend a large portion of our personal lives as well. What is important though, is that we need to try find some sort of balance, attempting to find the possibilities to move back into Kairos Time and engage with others, live the moment, and not be managed by the watches on our arms, or clock on our phones. In today's world it can be a challenge, however it is possible.

For most persons, no matter whether at work or in private lives, life is like a dance moving between Chronos and Kairos Time, the challenge is to force ourselves to enter Kairos Time and not to be forever trapped in Chronos Time. Being with others, living in the moment is what makes a difference and moves leaders to engaging with others without worrying about time. Leaders who are stuck in Chronos Time, miss some of the important things in life. By being trapped in Chronos Time, life passes us by, and in doing so we miss important aspects of life, things that cannot be measured, for example relationships, self-reflections, finding the joys of life, being with others, and quite plainly, smelling the roses. All humans need to find the opportunities in moving into Kairos Time, simply it just makes sense. Finding the balance is the key, very much like me having been in mainly Chronos Time in Italy, then moving in Kairos Time whilst walking through the caves in Slovenia and then back to mainly Chronos Time on the rebuild project in Poland. It is taking part in that constant dance between the two Greek categories of time, it is up to us as leaders to decide how much of the dance is in Kairos Time. One thing for sure is that if we get stuck in Chronos Time, we will miss out on so much of the joys of life.

SELF-REFLECTION

Chapter 4 – Meeting with "No Meeting"

Our selection of elements for self-reflection from the chapter are as follows:

- As a leader, I often suspend my own agenda, my own power and focus on being present with others in the I-Thou, listening to them tell their story.

- How often do I reflect on whether I had Real Meeting when talking and engaging with my team members?

- I focus on shifting out of being controlled by Chronos Time and in turn moving into Kairos Time, when being with others, being in the moment.

- Do I treat all meetings like appointments, therefore totally in Chronos Time and in the I-It mode, or are there times that my meetings are balanced between Chronos and Kairos?

- I encourage informal social meetings without any fixed agenda, allowing the discussions to take their path in Real Meeting.

- Does my behaviour probably give me a nickname amongst my team members like "Dr Listen-Little", or do I give them the time in Real Meeting, listening to them and reflecting care?

CHAPTER 5

Meeting in Real Meeting

"A human being becomes whole not in virtue of a relation to himself [only] but rather in virtue of an authentic relation to another human being(s)".

Dr Martin Buber

Austrian-Israeli Philosopher

Martin Buber's Take on Real Meeting

Martin Buber wrote about Real Meeting. What he focused on was, in his words, "all real living is in meeting" and in Real Meeting we ensure what he called "inclusion" where all parties in the conversation and / or relationship are significant and valued at the same time. Buber's approach is that Real Meeting takes place in the present (Kairos Time) and is in Meeting with humans, nature, and animals. Buber's thinking and writings, at the time, was very important to the way human beings have relationships with others, how people connect, give time to the other and by doing this, share stories and in turn ensure learning.

We have, therefore, covered several personal stories in this chapter to explain the importance of practising Real Meeting. One of the best examples of being in the present with humans and nature are the Indigenous People also known as the First Nations and Aboriginal Persons of Australia and Canada. This chapter takes you into conversations and our experiences, be it through rituals, listing to traditions and myths, all whilst listening to the stories of the inspiring First Nations people, who we have been honoured to meet during the writing of this as well as other books.

Each one of the stories, we have heard in person, variously in a conference room in Switzerland, on a construction site in Finland, around coffee tables in Canada and Australia, standing at an Aboriginal sacred site in Canada and twice sitting around a fireplace in Australia. During all of these it was Real Meeting, keeping quiet, being immersed in dialogue, suspending our agenda, letting someone else tell their story, and explain what is of significance to them.

The Lady in the Smokestack

"At times, leadership is time and a simple cup of coffee".

Brian Darlington

Whilst writing my second book "Humanising Leadership in Risk", I was on an annual maintenance shut at a paper mill and as I was walking on the site with a colleague of mine, we noticed that there was a crane with its slings and hook lowered inside a high smokestack (industrial chimney). We approached someone, who was conducting some work in close proximity to the smokestack, introduced ourselves and enquired about what tasks were being conducted inside the smokestack. He informed us that he was not part of that team, however he had noticed that there was a person inside the stack conducting some activities, but he was not sure what it was. We "hung around" (excuse the pun), until the person was lifted out of the stack in a person cage and was subsequently lowered to the ground. The engineer exited the cage and after giving her some time to put down her equipment and sort things out, we approached her. We introduced ourselves, asked if she had a couple of minutes for us and informed her of the purpose of our visit. I then asked her, if she would mind telling us her story and explaining what she was doing inside the smokestack. She described what her task was, that she had been performing some tests and in turn explained what some of the challenges were in conducting her activities. During the discussion, she then mentioned that it had been a long and energy-draining, busy day and that she was going to pack up her tools and equipment, complete some reports, after which she was looking forward to returning home to her family, as she had been on the site for several days. Whilst giving her the time to tell her story, she mentioned the area of Finland that she lived in, and if I recall correctly, it was about three hundred-odd kilometres from the site.

Listening to her language and unconscious meanings (things she automatically told us without being asked) she used language, metaphors and gifted words such as "energy-draining", "busy day", "family", and "distance home". It was clear she had a physical and challenging task and was pleased to have finished it. However, considering her language and meaning, I was a bit concerned that after a challenging day, she was planning to embark on a long drive back home. As she had mentioned that it was an energy-draining day, I was concerned that she was probably tired and perhaps fatigued. Therefore, I asked her an open question about how she was feeling, and whether she would be fine driving back home. She said that she was a bit tired, but assured me that she would be fine for the drive back home to her family and stated that she would make a stop halfway through the journey for some dinner. She also mentioned that if she felt tired along the way, she would take some additional breaks to get some fresh air and to stretch her legs.

Obviously, I remained concerned, but knew that I had no influence on her drive back home and was unable to convince her to stay overnight at the hotel and travel back the following day. I, therefore, asked her if she would like a cup of coffee before leaving. She accepted the offer, and I invited her to join me for the coffee, in the main administration building once she had finished packing up her equipment. After an hour or so she joined me, and we spent around twenty minutes having coffee together, talking about her family and life in Finland – time spent in Real Meeting. As she prepared to leave the office, I offered her a second cup of coffee to take with her on her journey back home, as South Africans would say, "one for the road", or as a good friend of mine, Arthur, would say in Afrikaans "Loop Dop", however in this case it was coffee and not a glass of wine.

This was a "simple cup of coffee" of little financial value, but with enormous personal value, as a gesture of care from someone that she did not know.

In hindsight, such gestures are much more than "a simple cup of coffee", more like a "caring cup of coffee". A cup of coffee with significance, a cup reflecting the humanising part of leadership. What accompanied that cup was the gift of time, focused listening, a spirit of care and helping with no "telling" and no "control". It was a moment of unconditional acceptance in trusting another person in influencing her life through a moment of reflection and care.

This moment is no different to the time we as leaders spend with friends, family, children or grandchildren, be it in person or virtually, both just a case of giving time to another in engagement and reflecting genuine care. The lady making her coffee for the road can be seen in *Figure 23. "Simple Cup of Coffee"*.

Unfortunately, many leaders believe that their sole role is to manage others, focusing on telling, instructing and policing others. Most often these are an expression of absolving connection, saving time and not listening. So often, leaders focus on what to control rather than on the adult person, who is conducting the work. It is all about telling to explain and not much about listening to understand. Yet, in the small relational moments much more can be achieved through engaging in Real Meeting.

Had I focused the discussion simply on the task and missed those key words like: "busy day", "family" and the "long trip home", I would have slipped into management control rather than practise leadership in listening. When we focus on Workspace elements (and not also Headspace and Groupspace issues) we tend to fixate on controls not leading others with vision and learning through relationships engendered in trust. Although I could not change the means of transport back home or shorten the distance for her, what I could do was show some care and help, in making it a bit more comfortable with that "simple cup of coffee" and all that came unconsciously with it.

Yes, I guess you knew it was coming, that I would relate to one of the quotes by Martin Buber where he said, "The world is not comprehensible, but it is embraceable: through the embracing of one of its beings". That I believe occurred when I invited the lady for a cup of coffee, showing care, giving up my time to Meet.

Whilst writing one of the chapters of this book, I was once again on the exact same site in Finland for a period of five weeks involved in a large project. Much of my time was spent supporting an Italian team rebuilding a large part of the paper machine. I often spoke to members of the team and entered into the hyphen of the I-Thou and whenever I saw fatigue creeping in, I would give the team a chocolate each. Although we maintained the professional relationship and there were often times that we moved into solely the I-It mode in managing the work being conducted, we always found time to move into the I-Thou. Eventually the Italian team realised that even though, we worked for different companies, with different priorities, cultures and sub-cultures, we needed to work together in order to complete the project successfully, on time and on budget with as few injuries as possible.

Within a couple of days of being on site, although we still had our challenges and differences, they soon began to realise that we were to be a team, a team that cared for each other, a team that aligned our objectives, a team that were interested in getting to know each other and providing the desired support for each other. It was not long before they would invite me to have a strong Italian espresso on the site, next to the machines being installed. They had given me their, "Time and a simple cup of coffee", even though at times it was difficult to communicate due to language barriers, however it was all in the gesture, the smile, and the connection. *Figure 24. Cup of Italian Coffee* with the Italians.

Figure 23. Simple Cup of Coffee

Figure 24. Cup of Italian Coffee

Hostage Negotiator (Scissors Event)

I met George Kohlrieser during my studies in Switzerland on an International Management Development (IMD) programme. This is when I heard the story of one of George's experiences as a young hostage negotiator. I later read it in his book titled, "Hostage at the Table" and was privileged to have George agree to write a Foreword in my book titled, "Humanising Leadership in Risk". The story intrigued me of the importance of showing care and how caring is very much person centred. Having a background in clinical psychology and hostage negotiations, George understands the importance of meeting to meet, engaging, bonding, dialogue, ethics, respect, helping, caring and winning trust, in other words engaging in "Real Meeting", and therefore, when planning the structure of this book, both Aneta and I agreed that we needed to reflect on George's story and how the testing events of that specific day are so much aligned to the "I and Thou" of Martin Buber.

The words, engaging, bonding, dialogue, ethics, respect, helping, caring and winning trust, unfortunately are often not considered important, or are often overlooked by leaders, however all of these fit into the I-Thou principle related to leadership and not in the I-It of management.

George's story concerns hostage negotiators and how the words above are extremely important to them in their line of work. However, these are all characteristics of truly high-performing leaders in any line of business, profession, or category of industry. Without considering these aspects, it is impossible for leaders to fulfil their best potential.

Indeed, hostage negotiators achieve a 95% success rate (as measured by Interpol and the FBI) by empathetically connecting, listening, understanding the pain that motivates the hostage taking, and making effective concessions. This process builds the trust needed to influence the hostage taker to release the hostages. The golden thread of it all is a "caring attitude" to build trust. No different to leadership in general, be it in the boardrooms or at site level of organisations. Only focusing on controlling and managing, with no Real Meeting, is the journey to failure, all based on the I-It and little on the I-Thou.

Because I was inspired during the week that I had spent with George in Switzerland and had learnt from his experience in leadership, we are honoured that George has agreed to share one of his key learning and life-changing experiences in this book. The story goes as follows:

George's Story - a Hostage Situation

The first time I witnessed the importance of these dynamics was in the 1970s. While riding with a lieutenant named Dan, we got a call that there was a possible hostage situation at a local hospital. We rushed to the emergency room, where we learnt that a patient with a stab wound was holding a nurse hostage. He was in a psychotic state, screaming and shouting, he wanted to kill everyone.

After assessing the situation, the lieutenant decided that we can't use gas as we were in a hospital emergency room; we can't kick the door down and rush in as he might impulsively kill the nurse. And so, he made the decision that someone needed to enter the room and calmly try to talk him down.

Dan slowly looked around the room into the faces of the doctors, nurses, and police officers there. I was standing behind him. And then he turned around and asked, "George, would you be willing to do this?" Talk about social pressure! I trusted him and being a risk taker, I said, "Sure, I'll give it my best".

I entered the room. The scene I faced was the patient, a man named Sam, screaming and shouting in a psychotic state, and holding a pair of scissors to the throat of the nurse, Sheila. He was stabbed near his heart and was bleeding, shouting and screaming that he wanted to kill as many people as possible.

He did not respond to any of my questions or transactions. Then after about three minutes of screaming and yelling, he cut the side of Sheila's throat with the scissors, so that she started to bleed on her white nurse's uniform.

He then took the scissors from Sheila's throat and stepped back from her. Instead of deescalating, he now flew across the room with the scissors. I had a nanosecond to choose – do I call in the officers who were just outside the door, do I throw myself at his feet, or do I continue to talk? *I chose to* talk, *and he put the scissors to my throat, screaming, "I'm going to kill you and everyone I can!"*

Keeping calm, I put my hands onto his arms, looked into his eyes, and continued to ask questions. I asked question after question with no response. From a short briefing I'd had before I entered the room, I knew that his ex-wife had stabbed him during an argument over the visitation of their children. So, I asked him, "What about your children, Sam? How do you want them to remember you?"

He pushed the scissors into my skin and screamed, "Don't talk about my children! Bring them here and I'll kill them too!"

This was an important moment. While this wasn't the answer I wanted, it was a positive step in the negotiation as he had, for the first time, answered one of my questions. I chose to continue. I said, "Sam, we need to talk about your kids. I know you love your kids". I then asked him how he wanted his kids to remember him. As a murderer? He again responded, "I will kill everybody I can and kill myself". Again, a direct answer, but not what I wanted. Daring myself, I came back again and said, "you want them to remember you not only as a murderer, but also as someone who commits suicide? Come on Sam, I know you love your kids".

Within three or four minutes, he backed off from me. And within another ten minutes, he had calmed down enough so that we could negotiate for Sheila's release. "She is a mother; you are a father. I am a father. She's bleeding. Will you let Sheila go?" So, he agreed.

After she had left the room, we carried on talking. So, then the scissors became a barrier. Always with a question, we moved forward. I asked, "Do you need the scissors? Do you want to throw them on the floor or hand them to me?" In a shocking reaction, he hesitated and then gave me the scissors – the very weapon he had been using to defend himself. You see, I had become a secure base for him; he had begun to trust me. I am sure, it was the caring attitude he saw in me.

His wound was life threatening, and it was urgent to get him to another secure unit of the hospital. To do that, he had to be in police custody as he was considered a dangerous felon. He had to be handcuffed. These can be the most dangerous moments in a hostage negotiation as the hostage taker is entering a new space.

Always asking questions, I asked, "Would you like me to handcuff you, or shall I ask a police officer to do it?" "I want you to do it George". We are now on first name terms! I then asked, "Do you want to be handcuffed in the front or in the back?" He asked to be handcuffed in the front, and we then walked out of the room and made the handoff to the waiting lieutenant and officers.

As he was being led away by the police, Sam stopped and asked the lieutenant, "Can I go back and say something to George?" The lieutenant said, "sure". So, he came back with a police escort, looked me in the eye and said, "George, you're all right. I'm glad I didn't kill you". I replied, "Me too, Sam". He then thanked me. I asked, "What are you thanking me for Sam?" He said, "For reminding me how important my children are to me".

This story is just one of many examples of how important it is to sincerely care for others, to achieve the best results. Imagine if George only cared for himself, refused to empathise with Sam, or tried to force him to follow his orders - the outcome could have been totally different and even fatal!

Marie O'Hara was my coach during a High-Performance Leadership Programme in Lausanne, Switzerland, and played an important role in me dealing with the loss of my wife. Marie together with George had challenged me, encouraged me to tell my story to a large audience and in doing so taught me the importance of telling one's story, as part of the healing process or dealing with difficult situations or periods in a person's life. Most of the support was provided over cups of coffee, encouraging and supporting me on the journey dealing with loss, to what Marie often referred to as, "Finding the Joys of Life". Marie had asked me to set some personal challenges in finding the joy of life, which I did and which including writing a book, a dream that I had, but never believed that it would materialise. There were a number of other challenges that I agreed to and shared with those in the training. Thanks to the approach of Marie, within a couple of years all of the challenges had been met, including the writing of the first book, followed by two more and a couple in the making. I will forever be grateful to both Marie as well as George for their direction in my journey of, "Finding the Joys of Life".

Figure 25. With George and Marie

George showed the care for the hostage taker and Marie demonstrated true care to me, listening to my story and encouraging me in, "Finding the Joy of Life". Both George and Marie, in two totally different situations, entered into the hyphen between the I and Thou and making a difference in the lives of two individuals. See *Figure 25.* together *With George and Marie* in Switzerland.

No matter what profession, whether in law enforcement, business, medicine, education, or any other profession or line of work, it is so important for leaders to show integrity and genuine care for others. Yet, despite these sacred ingredients for success, it is so often ignored by so many. Some may falsely perceive this as exhibiting weakness; maybe others are uncomfortable to show a more human, personal side in the workplace. Whatever the reason, this is a leadership characteristic that must be developed, especially in our new, post-pandemic world. This is the approach of the Wayside Chapel in Sydney that has been providing unconditional care and support for people on and around the streets since 1964, and under successful leadership of Graham Long, who has kindly written the Foreword for this book.

Leadership at the Coalface – Entering the Hyphen of the I-Thou

We recall listening to Rob Long tell the story of the Beaconsfield disaster and then followed up in Rob's latest book reading about the event. Rob has kindly given us permission to retell his story in this book, a story which goes as follows:

Beaconsfield - The Everyday in the Catastrophic.

In 2006, Rob was working for an EAP (Employee Assistance Program) company called "WorkWise" and this involved: education and training development, leadership coaching and learning, organisational and cultural development, and counselling. One of the companies Rob was working with was Beaconsfield Mine, a Joint Venture (BMJV) which had come out of receivership and was rebuilding the business. BMJV was a gold mine that got started in 1877 and is 41 km north of Launceston Tasmania. Beaconsfield was situated on a rich Quartz reef, but overtime the problem emerged of pumping out water the deeper the mine went. The mine closed in 1914, and like all gold mines, depended on the gold price and the cost of extracting the ore.

Beaconsfield was reopened in 1998, and at times struggled to make a profit given the costs of extracting water and ore. In 2006, when Rob was at the mine helping as a consultant, educator, trainer and counsellor, there was a collapse. This event proved to be the most exceptional mining accident in Australian history, projecting Beaconsfield across the world stage.

The rockfall occurred on Anzac Day 2006, and Rob was in Canberra that morning swimming laps in the Tuggeranong Pool. During his break, Rob looked at his phone and there was a message from the Mine Manager. Rob returned the call, got the picture of what had occurred, and was on a plane the same morning.

When Rob arrived at the mine, his first job that the Mine Manager gave him was to go to the pub and talk with the workers who had just come off shift and were overwhelmed by their experience. Rob's next job was to engage with Jackie Knight, who was anxiously waiting with her family in the Beaconsfield's Community Hall for any news about Larry (one of the team members trapped underground). Rob then engaged with the spouses of Todd Russell and Brant Webb (other two men trapped in the mine) in a support and counselling role. And as described by Rob, "so it all started".

The next fourteen days was a roller coaster ride that no-one could imagine. Beaconsfield was to become the biggest media event in Australian history. The little town of a few hundred was to quickly swell up to thousands of media from all over the world.

For a few days, most people were convinced that Todd, Brant and Larry were dead and on the morning of the 27th, such was the case for Larry. Rob had known all three men previously through much of the training that he had undertaken in the mine on risk, safety, and teamwork. Rob had known Todd's wife - Carolyn because she worked in administration at the mine, but Rob had not known Jackie or Rachel (Brant's wife). On the 30th of April it was discovered that Todd and Brant were alive and what was a recovery mission quickly turned into a rescue.

Rob's role at Beaconsfield was to work behind the scenes and avoid all the media hype as this allowed him to move freely to support the three families, the Executive team, and miners. After the rescue was completed the Mine Manager made Rob the Manager of Community Recovery. Rob's involvement at the mine became full time and extended for nine months.

As part of the rescue, Rob was on the Emergency Coordination Operations Group (ECOG), formed to oversee the rescue and his role was to support the Mine Manager to manage the socio-psychological dynamics that played out in the group and in the rescue group 950 m underground. The ECOG numbered about thirty people (mostly engineers, miners, geo-tech specialists etc.), who met four times each day and night, going through everything imaginable. As

Rob describes in his book, "Everyday Social Resilience", there was not enough space in his book to describe all that went on.

Rob's role was to support and have input on those dynamics. Underground there were also another fifty or so persons with another hundred providing all kinds of logistics and support. The purpose of telling this story is to demonstrate, how the "Everyday meets the Unusual and how each informs the other". The whole operation developed its own unique culture as did many of the related sub-cultures that intersected with it, for example, the community, school, media, shopping centre, experts flown in, social supports especially, politicians, recalcitrant unions, media personalities, clergy and counselling support.

As mentioned by Rob, "So let's start at the Everyday".

Rob was lucky to be able to be accommodated with long-time friends (who he had known since Theological College) who lived outside of Launceston. This helped to keep Rob grounded and, at times, distant from the powerful "e-motions" (as he calls it) that flowed through the mine on daily basis. Sometimes a dark cloud would come over the whole mine if there was a setback. On other occasions everyone was elated by good news. In Rob's role, he just hovered about, attended as many meetings as he could touching base with the Mine Manager and other Executives to offer his reflections and observations on a regular basis. The Mine Manager was interested in Rob's perceptions about culture, social dynamics, and the social ecology of the above ground situation. Not surprisingly, knowing Rob, he kept a journal throughout and even mapped a chart of how the e-motions and culture of the mine changed in stages.

The media pressure was particularly intense and affected everyone. It was a frenzy of moving hungry beasts eager for whatever sound bite they could grab. As you can imagine, the world was watching. Nobody could get in or out of the mine without bustling through the hundreds of cameras and video teams. Some handled this pressure well, others did not. Not surprisingly, such a situation "tests" everyone.

"When your ordinary Everyday of coming to work changes from routine to mayhem, how do you respond? It is extraordinary that the media hype creates this silly world of heroes and the superhuman. There were no heroes or superhuman at Beaconsfield, just ordinary everyday people working together to save two men trapped one thousand metres underground. The tasks that were performed every-day by everyone, combined in such diversity and complexity, developed a life of its own. People just did things, allostasis and homeostasis just cut in and people did things without explanation, good and bad. Every day of the rescue started by people arriving, clocking in and assembling for a handover from night shift. In that moment, everyone was together coming or going. It was an opportune moment for extended communication, observation and evaluating how all were psychologically going".

To help this process, Rob and the mine team strategically limited the entry ways into the mine. Normally access to the mine could be made through four gates, but they closed these all off and deliberately "funnelled" everyone though the central admin area. In the central admin area, they set up chairs, benches, BBQs, drinks and conversation space, so that those coming in and out of the courtyard could be seen and engaged. The BBQs went all day for breakfast, lunch and dinner as the team knew that food was vital in binding people together, to create sharing and empathy. In a way they helped create a social ecology, a living moving place where every word, gossip and gesture could be observed and tackled. This was a sign of Real Meeting, and in doing so focusing on the I-Thou.

All of the fencing early on in the rescue, had to be covered up to limit access to media viewing. In a similar way, communication across the site and underground had not been conducted by landline phone as the media, from the start, used listening devices to access radio communications. For those in the ECOG, including Rob, managing the media was of primary importance. Inside the fence, they were consumed by the rescue, outside the fence was a media frenzy eager for any sound bite. This was fulfilled by the National Secretary of the Australian Workers' Union (AWU). What the TV audience saw everyday were updates by the National Secretary, who received second-hand information from miners and then relayed to the media. The National Secretary was not on the ECOG.

Unfortunately, every time the National Secretary provided incomplete information, Rob was delegated to visit the families of Larry, Brant, and Todd, to consult, counsel and communicate with them directly. Whenever there is a catastrophe, and the media are involved, TV audiences struggle to work out the difference between reality and performance. This was no different at Beaconsfield. Later, when the movie was made and other media was presented it was loaded with misinformation and distortion, most of which those on the inside of the fence knew was unhelpful and inaccurate.

Todd and Brant were trapped under tonnes of rock, 1 km underground in a tele-handler box (wire cage) and any disturbance of the rock above them was too dangerous. Whilst the media above stirred looking for any story, the ECOG and rescue team took ages in planning, innovating, and testing the rescue plan and implementation. Speculation and misinformation spread above the ground like a virus. The best way to describe what was happening above ground outside the fence was "a circus". Indeed, during the media circus outside the fence, someone set up donkey rides and a jumping castle.

"Early on a 90 mm pipe was able to be drilled into the location of Todd and Brant, but to develop an extraction hole 650 mm in diameter was going to take much longer. This time pressure was where the resilience of everyone was tested. For those in the rescue the every-day was filled with the Everyday, they worked from moment to moment, event to event and risk assessed every move with the ECOG four times a day. The world looking on, the last thing needed was a blunder. A camera, food, antibiotics (Todd was injured), water and communication were enabled by this 90 mm pipe". Those involved, including Rob, could see, talk and manage things using camera vision and audio. The whole team (over two hundred people) involved in the rescue had a role and every role was critical, even if it was turning bacon and eggs on the barbecue.

Rob's job was to work at a meta-level with Mine Manager and the Executive team and the ECOG to monitor and work with the dynamics at work in the social ecology created by this unique event. Even though, everything about Beaconsfield was unique, they still came to work each day and worked normally, as if they all shared in a project like any other. "There was nothing special or heroic about any of it, but they all knew that they were in the Every-day not the every-day. Then after nine days straight, with the bore in place, miners flown in from other sites, working 24/7 and managing all that was thrown at them, the team got some positive news late in the night that the probe had gone through, and they could see Todd and Brant".

Todd and Brant eventually "tagged out", were taken to ambulances, supported by paramedics and then off to Launceston Hospital to be checked out. Larry's funeral was the next day. "On that day, there were even more emotional experiences, from the surprise appearance of injured Todd, the bikie cavalcade and Todd's prayer over the casket. Then there was the torrential rain for two hundred faithful standing by the graveside for the burial".

The rollercoaster of emotions over the fourteen days was at a heightened level. Larry's funeral was delayed and rescheduled, because the team thought the extraction would be slower. The final probe was actually a surprise and demonstrated that the technicians had overestimated the drilling up distance to Todd and Brant. "The balancing of Internal Integration, External Adaption, Organic Processes and Mechanistic Processes" were just some of Rob's primary roles. On many occasions, Rob was in meetings with technical people, engineers, geotechnics, seismologists etc. and he had no idea what they were talking about, but then again none of them was self-aware of their own emotions, personalities or socially conscious.

The Mine Manager often turned to Rob and asked him what he was thinking. Rob was very conscious of the social ecology of the rescue culture, understood and analysed all its dynamic activity, very often spoke about excitement of some, the arrogance of others, emotional blindness, over-confidence or any other socio-psychological factor. Interestingly, the team flew in psychologists, who together with the Employee Assistance Programme (EAP) were available to everyone, however, they were not used. People found their support in trusted family members, friends and local clergy.

Listening to Rob tell the story and after reading the chapter in his book on resilience, it is clear that at all times he was in Real Meeting, he was entering the I-Thou with those that he was engaging with and in all of this, supported by counsellors and psychologists. The team were at the coalface providing guidance and support, the team were placing persons at the centre of their focus, and by doing so, were showing true leadership, one where there is care for others. They had moved from the I-It to the I-Thou.

"Dreamtime"

After meeting an Indigenous Elder known as "Uncle Kev" in Canberra, Australia in 2019, I (Brian) have over time become interested in reading and learning about Indigenous cultures of Australia and more recently Canada, with many of them aligned with waiting, listening and intuiting. The Indigenous People are connected to nature, symbols, and rituals. "Dreamtime" for the Australian Indigenous People represents the period when their Ancestral Spirits proceeded over the land, created life, as well as significant formations and sites. "Dreamtime" is also related to the interrelation of all persons, all things, and the legends live on, and are passed down from generation to generation through storytelling, songs, art, rituals and ceremony.

I was lucky enough to experience all of this during my almost one-hour Meeting with "Uncle Kev" around a campfire at the "Tent Embassy" in Canberra. The storytellers are chosen by the Elders, who in turn have a duty to pass the stories on and through generations, thereby ensuring that the younger members of the Indigenous People retain the sense of who they are and in turn pass the stories, rituals and traditions on to the next generation.

"Dreamtime" or dreaming stories are told through various mediums including, amongst others, song and dance, symbolic drawings, body paint as well as drawings in the sand for ceremonies. The art is a visual expression of their beliefs, history and of course their amazing and interesting culture, dating back for around fifty-thousand years. No wonder the Indigenous People of Australia were not happy with the words in the Australian National Anthem, "we are young and free", but fortunately these words have since been removed from the National Anthem. Sadly, though, whilst I was writing this book the Indigenous People of Australia were not given a voice in parliament during the "Yes or No" vote on the matter in 2023. A typical example of people not wanting to enter the hyphen in the I-Thou nor engage in Real Meeting. I can only imagine how sad and disappointed "Uncle Kev" must have been when hearing the outcome of the vote that was once again a "no".

You may ask, why we are sharing this story as part of a leadership book, however for us it is clear, the Indigenous People of Australia and similar to other Indigenous People in other countries around the world including Canada, Namibia, South Africa and New Zealand, celebrate in rituals and ceremonies that are all aligned with Real Meeting and Martin Buber's principle of the I-Thou. See *Figure 26*. New Zealand Indigenous Person's *Body Art and Dance* and *Figure 27. Zulu Dance* being performed on a beach in South Africa.

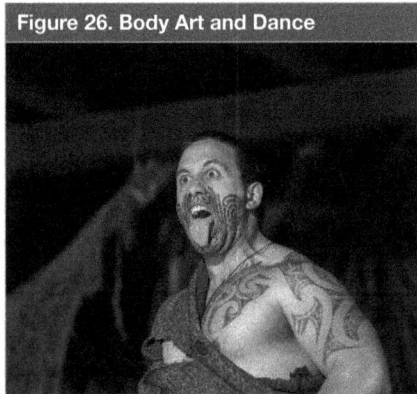

Figure 26. Body Art and Dance

Figure 27. Zulu Dance

A good friend of both Aneta and mine, Robert Long, attended a conference in Canada, which was opened by the First Peoples of the Songhees region, of the Salish People. During the opening an elder gave the "welcome to country" and was wearing traditional garments having significance and spiritual importance. The vest was worn to protect the heart, and the headband, made of woven maple bark and worn to protect the use of wrong language. These rituals are aligned to body, mind, and spirit and the Three Ways of Knowing as shown in a model explained in Chapter 11.

I was fortunate to engage with "Uncle Kev" (Kevin) in Australia, "Grandmother White Wolf" (Melanie), The Elder, "White Headed Eagle Man" (Joe) in Canada and both Aneta and I were fortunate to engage with Lisa Higgerty and then the "Medicine Lady with Knowledge" in Australia. Each time, to listen to their stories, the stories of their cultures, rituals, beliefs and myths, the stories handed down from generation to generation over centuries by their respective elders. These stories are shared below.

Kevin at the Tent Embassy

Some years ago, I was visiting Canberra, Australia on a business trip and as part of some training in Social Psychology of Risk that I was undertaking. I had some time off, during the weekend prior to flying back to Europe, and therefore, decided to spend the Saturday morning visiting some of the museums and galleries around the city.

This was my second trip that I had done to Canberra, and being a city full of fantastic places, filled with an abundance of semiotics, supporting so much learning and understanding of the Australian culture, I took every opportunity to discover more. I had started the day off at the Australian War Museum, and although I had visited it once before, I decided to visit it again to spend some time in certain sections of the museum, including the area that focused on the Boer War that took place in South Africa around the turn of the twentieth century.

After visiting the War Museum, I took a walk down the Anzac Parade, which is a long road leading from the Museum towards the lake in front of Parliament House, a beautiful stretch with military statues of various wars, some of them nestled amongst gum trees along both sides of the road. After walking around the edge of the lake, I approached the Old Parliament Building and noticed the "Tent Embassy" on the grass area in front of the building. I immediately knew that I had found the place that I had interesting discussions with Rob in the past. The "Tent

Embassy" was started on 26 January 1972, by four First Nation people (Aboriginal) protesting against the Australian Government and in support of Indigenous land rights and reconciliation. Now, over fifty years later, this protest continues.

I walked slowly over the grass section, not seeing anyone around, not knowing what to expect, I continued walking through the area, seeing a couple of tents, a caravan, and smaller temporary type buildings, however stayed away from them, not wanting to disturb or be of any nuisance to anyone. I then from the corner of my eye noticed some smoke rising from a smouldering fire, in the centre of the camp, and then realised that there was an elderly gentleman sitting on a chair in front of the fire. When he noticed me wandering around, he stood up, called me, and invited me to join him at the fire, shaking my hand, he introduced himself as Kevin. Whilst shaking his hand I immediately felt a sense of kindness and friendliness, he had this sense of calmness in his eyes.

Kevin added some couple of pieces of wood to the smouldering fire, pulled up an old chair for me and with hand gestures invited me to take my place next to him, close to the fire. As we sat down next to each other it felt like we had been friends for a long time, he gave me a huge smile and then asked me about my family, where I came from and what I was doing in Australia. For me my story was not important, I wanted to hear about Kevin and his story, the story of the Aboriginal people.

We then spent most of the time in discussion about Australia and the struggles of the Aboriginal people over the centuries, since the Europeans settlers had arrived and set foot on the country's shores on the western side of Cape York Peninsula back in 1606, (first documented landing).

I found the conversation fascinating, as Kevin explained how they began the protest all those years ago and have kept it going ever since. He enlightened me on aspects of Australian Aboriginal culture, including their belief that man, animals, nature, and ancestral dreaming are all inextricably linked and share the same fate. He explained that their culture regards the earth as eternal, and how through their various rituals, the beings that created the earth remain accessible to them. In reflection of the time spent with Kevin, I recall he touched on the term "Dreamtime", which was fascinating to listen to. In Kevin's culture they believe that the "Dreamtime" occurred around sixty-five thousand years ago, when the Spirits created the land and people. They believe that the Spirits created everything connected with the land and then gave them the tools for hunting.

Kevin told me about some of their ceremonies, which have been part of the Aboriginal culture for thousands of years. These rituals include dancing, symbols, and body decoration, and they are passed down from generation to generation. All these rituals are part of "Meeting" with others.

While we were chatting, two other Indigenous people approached, took off their shoes and seated themselves close to us, as if almost sitting in a circle. They stared intensely into the fire without saying a word. They did, however, seem like they were listening with interest to what Kevin was telling me. At the end of our chat, Kevin invited me to participate in an Aboriginal ritual by placing a branch on the fire and saying a prayer for peace and healing.

When it was time for me to leave, I shook Kevin's hand and thanked him for the time that we had spent together, in "Real Meeting". I valued the fact that he had given me the chance to listen to his story and that of his people – a story of perseverance and hope as well as the meaning of "Dreamtime". Listening with intent to what he said, helped me understand his world, a world filled with traditions, signs, and symbols, signifying a connection to the earth and nature. Somehow, we felt connected, we had engaged for around forty-five minutes, we had felt like good friends in "Real Meeting". "Wow", he made an impression on me, this fella born in Africa.

He had inspired me, he has left an impression on me, one of care, one of giving up one's time for another, one having the impact a person gets from meeting in "Real Meeting". After leaving, I sat on a bench close to the Old Parliament House in a rose garden and reflected on what had just happened, I realised that sitting there in Real Meeting with Kevin around the fire, ending up with me smelling of smoke (not sure what the taxi driver must have thought) made me realise the importance of suspending one's own agenda and letting the other person tell their story. If leaders in organisations can practise the art of listening with intent, suspending their own agenda, power and authority at times, they would be surprised what they can get out of a simple chat with their team members.

In this case, Kevin gave me his time and intriguing experience around the fire. We had both entered into that hyphen in the I-Thou, immersed in Kairos Time. I had returned to the Tent Embassy now on two occasions, hoping to see my friend Kevin again, maybe introduce him to Aneta, but no luck, I somehow knew that I would probably never "Meet" him again, however the Real Meeting that we had back in 2020, and the discussion will remain in my memories for ever.

During a recent visit to Canberra, Aneta and I decided to, once again, visit the "Tent Embassy" hoping to learn more about "Dreamtime" and were fortunate to engage in discussion with an elderly lady. During our discussions, I informed her that I had, during one of my visits some years ago to the "Tent Embassy", met an elder named

Kevin and always hoped I would meet him again. The lady's face lit up with a gentle smile and she told us that she knew him and that "Uncle Kev" as she referred to him was in his "own country", however his health was deteriorating. She gave me "Uncle Kev's" telephone number, but sadly I was not able to get hold of him. When we got into a taxi, Aneta then "Googled" his name and we were astounded to read that he was actually a well-known icon and had featured in numerous documentaries, articles and attended many events. This inspired me even more as "Uncle Kev" had never mentioned anything about himself, his fame, or achievements, during our Meeting some years back. It was all about his culture, his country, and his people. I thought to myself, if only leaders could follow such a humble example, by not always placing themselves in the centre of things, suspending their power, authority and agenda, at times, and letting others tell their story and whilst doing so, listening with intent. I have mentioned "Uncle Kev" in my previous books, as he is a true role model and inspiration for me. I felt that the more I share his story, hopefully the more people will be inspired. However, I must admit that telling the story does nothing to explain the feeling that I had sitting around the fire just listening to him and feeling his presence.

In my view (Brian), moving 180 degrees from "Uncle Kev", let us use the 45th President of the United States of America (and at the time of writing, the 47th President-elect), Donald Trump, as an example of the leadership style of the billionaire, someone who always places himself at the centre of his own worldview. Without any doubt, for me, totally the opposite to inspirational leaders such as Mandela, and my friend "Uncle Kev". He has absolutely no regard for the dignity of others, whether it be persons who he knows or does not know, whether female or male, or any other gender, and even whether allies or enemies. When being challenged about his comments and behaviour, he often refuses to apologise. Some examples of his insults are the names he came up with: "Crazy Kamala", "Crooked Hillary", "Sleepy Joe", or the Late Senator John McCain, whom he called a "Loser" and not a war hero. Trump also labelled the press as being the most dishonest persons ever created. Trump is a leader, who sees only his way of thinking, is under the impression that he is always right, and believes other person's comments are of no or little significance. He has a simple style, when challenged by anyone, he gets rid of them, as evident when considering how many people he fired during his first term as President of the United States of America.

Donald Trump has written a number of books, however many of them focused on the object rather than persons. In his book titled "Think Big", he mentions the words, "do not trust anyone". He also wrote, "when people wrong you, go after them, because it is a good feeling and because other people will see you doing it". Trump also said that he always gets even. I wonder how many meetings with Trump could be considered as Real Meetings, probably very few indeed, if any, would be my guess.

Sadly though, like Trump there are many leaders who too think they are the most important person in the company, department, or shift. When challenged by others they silence them by making derogatory remarks, applying bullying tactics, demoting them and shifting people sideways, making them feel part of the outgroup or even worse dismissing them from the company. Trump as well as leaders like this, hardly ever enter the hyphen of the I-Thou, and do not suspend their own bias, agenda, power and authority. In my time in the military and years of employment, I have personally witnessed some leaders, who have a total disregard for others, believe they are "God's gift" to an organisation, and are totally self-centred. On one large construction project that I was involved with, I had a discussion with a leader, who barred certain persons from attending meetings as they would put the "smelly fish" on the table and raise issues of concern. This type of management style develops a sense of mistrust, hiding of issues and ends up in failure. Sadly though, in many instances the good team members are the ones, who leave an organisation when managed in such a manner.

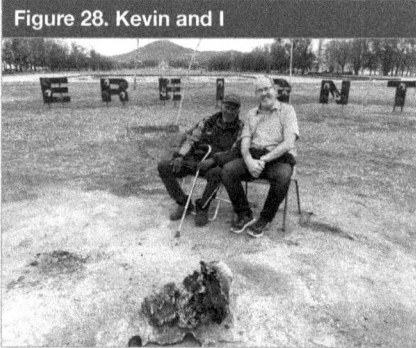

Figure 28. Kevin and I

Figure 29. Aneta at the Tent Embassy

"Uncle Kev", on the other hand, at no time showed any signs of self-focus at all, had no attitude, and was not at all self-centred during our conversation and time spent around the campfire. For "Uncle Kev", it was all about the other persons, the land, and the culture of his people. A totally different approach to that of President Donald Trump and many leaders across the globe. I would much rather spend ten minutes with Kevin than any amount of time talking to President Trump, as well as some other world leaders of today. See *Figure 28. Kevin and I* sitting together at the fire, engaging in the stories, beliefs, and traditions. In *Figure 29. Aneta at the Tent Embassy* two years after I had met Kevin.

Learning from the Canadian and Australian Indigenous Cultures

The company for which I work acquired a pulp mill in Hinton, Alberta in Canada and on our first trip to the site I was introduced to a colleague named Glenn, and in discussion over dinner, we spoke about the Indigenous People of Canada, during which he mentioned that he had married into an Indigenous family. Well, with my interest in Indigenous cultures in many countries across the globe, he certainly got my interest and the discussion going. I suspended my agenda and let Glenn tell his inspiring story, with full concentration from me taking in all that he was saying. When we had finished our discussion, I asked him if he would be willing to arrange that I could Meet with an Indigenous Elder to hear their story. Well, the next day, I was delighted when Glenn informed me that his niece, Lisa, was willing to meet with me. This meeting would take place some months later, however not in person, but through virtual means.

Significance of Melanie's ("Grandmother White Wolf") Tattoos

Some months after meeting Glenn for the first time, I was visiting our operation in Hinton, Canada again and was conducting training in Social Psychology of Risk, during which we were discussing the importance of connecting with others. To demonstrate how we can connect with people (entering the I-Thou) and how we can chase discussions depending on comments made by the person that, as a leader, we are talking to, I asked whether anyone had a tattoo, to which two ladies put their hands up. One of the ladies, Melanie, showed us that she had two wolf heads on her left arm. On being asked the significance of the tattoo, Melanie explained that it had significant meaning for the Indigenous People of Canada. I asked if she would mind telling us more about the significance of the tattoo. Melanie gladly elaborated and explained that in the Canadian Indigenous culture, the Native Wolf Symbol represents strong family ties, good communication, understanding, loyalty and intelligence. It is believed that the wolf has strong supernatural powers. The Indigenous People of Canada believe that inside each of us are two opposing wolves, with one being the evil one and the other the good one. Depending on the one that a person feeds is the wolf that wins. Melanie mentioned that when she is experiencing emotions such as anger, sorrow or frustration she looks at the tattoo or a larger symbol of the wolves in her house, which then reminds her to shift her emotions to positive ones such as joy, hope, kindness and faith, thereby feeding the good wolf.

Whilst Melanie was explaining the meaning of her wolf tattoo, I happened to see that she had a second tattoo, this time on her right wrist. The tattoo was unique as it was a small semicolon. Again, I proceeded to ask her what the meaning was, to which she explained that the semicolon in grammatical terms represents a place in a sentence where the sentence could end, however carries on. Melanie then went further to explain that the true meaning has been adopted for suicide awareness and prevention, as a symbol for people battling through difficult times having suicidal thoughts, actions or behaviour, as well as persons, who have been touched by suicide in their lives, in one way or another.

The semicolon tattoo gives hope not only to the wearer, but it also serves as a symbol of encouragement and solidarity to others, who may be trying to overcome tough times and impossible struggles. To some degree, when someone that is experiencing mental well-being issues, sees another person having the semicolon tattoo, interprets the person as caring, and in fact, is feeling the hyphen in the I-Thou without any words being exchanged. I later found out that some people wear a lapel pin depicting a semicolon. The pin is meant to spread awareness of mental well-being issues.

Throughout the short discussion with Melanie, I had engaged with her regarding two symbols on her wrists that had huge significance to her, being the wolf and the semicolon tattoos. She had a smile on her face explaining the meaning of the wolf tattoo, however when talking about the semicolon one, I could see in her body language and tone of her voice that the discussion was becoming personal. I, therefore, refrained from delving any deeper into the topic and thanked Melanie for sharing her story with me and the other twenty-three persons in the room. I had entered the hyphen in the I-Thou through her tattoos, I had shown interest in her story. I would, however, later get the chance to engage with Melanie, during which she shared so many interesting stories and explained some of the rituals, myths and symbols that have been passed down from her ancestors, through the generations.

It was two days after our initial discussion in the group about her tattoos that Melanie and I grabbed two chairs and sat together privately in a room at the Indigenous People Friendship Centre, giving each other the time to talk and share our stories. My aim was to suspend my own agenda and listen to her story, however Melanie being the caring person that she is, was also keen to listen to my story and that of my life. And "wow"! We must have sat for almost an hour and a half chatting and partaking in Real Meeting. During this time, I was overcome by a sense of calmness, filled with emotions of happiness as well as sadness as we shared and listened to each other's stories. How sad that the Catholic Church in the 1500s and the colonial immigrants who followed over the centuries, did their best to dominate and supress the culture of the Canadian Indigenous People, through many means including criminalising many aspects of Indigenous life from spiritual to self-governance as well as the residential school systems, where the children were taken away from their families. Melanie explained to me how her grandfather would tell the stories of their ancestors, but by gesture of his forefinger on his lips told them not to tell others. This story was backed up in a discussion I had one evening with an Elder, Joe Cardinal. Whilst occasionally sipping from his cup of tea, he explained the difficult times that he and other children had experienced in residential schools. They had experienced atrocious physical, mental, and sexual abuse by the members of the clergy, both priests and nuns. Joe explained how he had ended up involved in alcohol and drug abuse as a result of his past. However, thankfully he overcame all his issues and has left the past behind him and is now very spiritual. Some years ago, he moved closer to the mountains in order to be connected to his ancestors and the spiritual world. We had a wonderful chat, with lots of shared learnings, however that is a story for another day, maybe another book.

Melanie, whose Indigenous name is "Nukumij Wape'k Paqtesm" ("Grandmother White Wolf"), started the discussion by giving me a gift, and whilst doing so, explained that in her culture it is important to hand a gift over to another, as they believe that they should not be anchored to physical objects. Melanie gifted me with her stories, but I was honoured to receive her personal travel "Smudging Kit" as a gift. The ritual of smudging is a cultural ceremony practised by many Indigenous People in Canada and other parts of the world. Smudging is the practise of burning various medicinal plants as a cleansing ritual and to connect themselves with their spirit as well as with the Creator. The smudging gift consists of a feather protected in a sleeve, packets of tobacco, sage, cedar and sweet grass, a seashell in which to burn the three items, a small wooden carved stand on which the seashell can be placed.

Melanie explained that smudging is also used when one is worried, not feeling well or overwhelmed and is also used to cleanse, purify, and bless the part of our Mother Earth. For example, they smudge around the sweat lodge or powwow (Indigenous gathering with dance) and their houses to purify or bless special objects like ceremonial objects or totems, such as jewellery, rattles, or clothing. Melanie mentioned that when smudging a home, they start from the left side of the walls, windows, doorways, and corners of the room and open the windows and doors to let negative energies out.

Smudging ceremonies must be entered into or begun with good intent, during which smoke rises, and prayers rise to the Spirit world of their grandfathers, grandmothers, and the Creator. During our discussion Melanie used her eagle feather to demonstrate how the feather is used during the ceremony to disperse the smoke towards the eyes, ears, and mouth, as well as heart and soul and then ending by wiping the feather on my back. The smudging ceremony helps participants centre or ground themselves. Negative energy, feelings, and emotions are lifted away, and the ritual is used for healing of mind, body, and spirit, as well as balancing energies.

During our time together in Real Meeting, Melanie explained so many of their rituals to me, which amongst others, included the "Talking Stick", the dance rituals, the blessing of the drums and how the sweat lodges are used to encourage the sweating out of toxins and negative energy that create disorder and imbalance in life. In this way, the sweat lodge ceremony cleanses the body, mind, and soul. What I found most intriguing is that sweat lodges are sacred and are likened to Mother Earth's womb. One therefore, understands why the sweat ritual is deeply spiritual and cultural to those, who partake in the ritual.

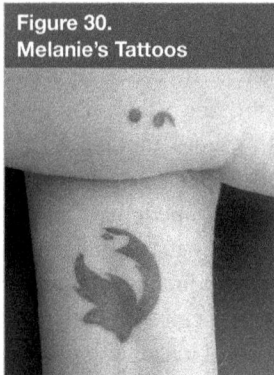
Figure 30.
Melanie's Tattoos

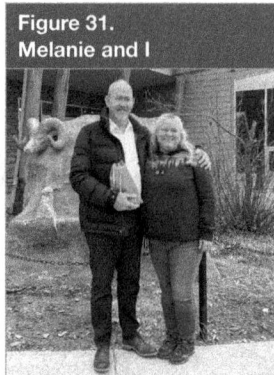
Figure 31.
Melanie and I

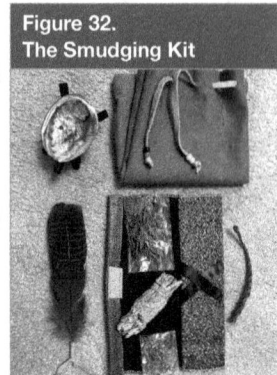
Figure 32.
The Smudging Kit

She also gave insight into the "Highway of Tears" where over the years many Indigenous women and girls have disappeared without any trace. Melanie mentioned that during a certain time of the year, red dresses are placed at strategic places along the highway and in the Hinton town as a semiotic display, and as a reminder that these persons are still missing without any trace.

The time spent together with Melanie was inspirational, we had connected with both of us giving each other the time to tell our stories, and in doing so, we connected and entered the hyphen in the I-Thou, both of us suspending our agendas and letting the discussion flow in any direction it would go. This is not always the case with leaders as there is a tendency to fill the air with noise and enter the discussions chasing their own predefined agenda. Just like I was inspired and honoured to have engaged in Real Meeting with "Uncle Kev" around the fire in Canberra, I once again felt inspired and honoured in Real Meeting with Melanie. See *Figure 30. Melanie's Tattoos* of the two wolves' heads and the semicolon, followed by *Figure 31. Melanie and I* after Melanie gave me the Smudging Kit. In *Figure 32.* one sees *The Smudging Kit.*

Glenn and the Cultural Sites

Having met Glenn for a second time during the training in Hinton and upon him hearing my discussion with Melanie, related to her two tattoos, Glenn offered to take me to the Ceremonial Grounds of the Nakcowinewak Nation of Canada to share some of the Indigenous culture with me. Obviously with my interest in various Indigenous cultures, I grabbed the opportunity to visit the site with Glenn. As we drove towards the site which close to the Jasper National Park on the slopes of the Rockies, it was quite surreal, as the mountain range lay ahead of us with the iconic silhouette of the mountain depicting an Indigenous chief's face and headgear facing the sky. It was as if the mountain range is reminding everyone who are the ancestors of the land. See *Figure 33. The Chief's Head* shape of the mountain.

Some kilometres down the road, we passed an Indigenous gravesite (see *Figure 34. The Indigenous Gravesite*) and shortly after that turned sharply left off the national road, tackling the snow-covered gravel road up towards one of the mountains where we ended up at the Ceremonial Grounds. This is where we observed the tipis, fireplaces and the structures of the indigenous sweat lodges, which are used during ceremonial events, and when standing in the area, one gets this sense of calmness. On our way out of the ceremonial site, Glenn and I walked through the natura forests, climbing over branches and manoeuvring around trees, until we came across an area where many trees were wrapped with different coloured cloths, including red ones, exactly what Melanie had explained to me. These were decorated as a memory of the more than forty women and girls, who have gone missing or were murdered along the "Highway of Tears". When being surrounded by these decorated trees, I could not help feeling emotional and an embodied sense flowing across me.

See *Figure 35. The Tipis* at the ceremonial site and in *Figure 36.* one sees the *Sign at the Entrance* to the Ceremonial Grounds that we visited with Glenn.

Figure 33. The Chief's Head

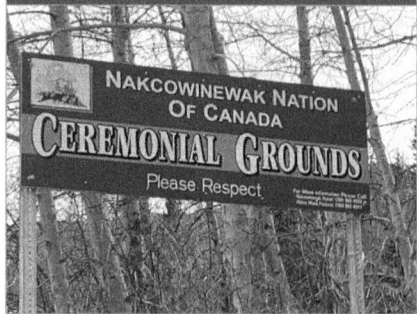
Figure 34. The Indigenous Gravesite

Figure 35. The Tipis

Figure 36. Sign at the Entrance

NAKCOWINEWAK NATION
OF CANADA
CEREMONIAL GROUNDS
Please Respect

We could go on forever sharing details of stories told to us by Kevin, Lisa, Melanie, Elder Joe and Glenn, however, the chapters above indicate the power of Real Meeting, entering the hyphen of the I-Thou, suspending one's own agenda and listening with intent. In all four cases, those telling the stories were eager to do so as we are sure that they all realised our interest and curiosity in what was significant and dear to them, their history, their rituals, myths, beliefs, culture and importantly their people.

If only, leaders would do the same, by giving of their time to others, allowing their teams, their people, the opportunity to tell their stories, whilst in turn listening with intent, and not filling the air with noise. By doing so, trust is developed, which leads to open and honest communication, reflection of care, and in turn contributes to a healthy culture at work. A culture where people feel important, engaged, respected, and listened to, contributes to a positive working environment where there are authentic relations between human beings, between leaders and employees.

Meeting Lisa Higgerty

Meeting Lisa was a truly inspiring experience for both Aneta and me. I know Aneta enjoyed it, as it took her back in time to when she was a journalist working in the United States. At the time of the interview, Lisa was the Assistant Deputy Minister Indigenous Health for the Government of Alberta, Canada. Her career has spanned over twenty years and the bulk of it has been providing holistic healing programs to survivors of residential schools and their families. On top of Lisa's years of contribution to the Indigenous People in Canada, her mom is an Elder in the community of Hinton, Alberta.

As mentioned, our first meeting was remote which is not always ideal, however it went well, and was a stimulating discussion for both Aneta and me. We are hoping to eventually meet up with Lisa during a future trip when passing through Edmonton on the way to Hinton on the foothills of the Canadian Rockies and share some time with her in Real Meeting.

The meeting with Lisa was a long time in the making, not due to any reason from Lisa, but rather from our side in trying to find a suitable date and time to fit us all. As mentioned, meeting Lisa was truly inspiring, with her coming across as a humble person, throughout the discussions showing a warm smile and giving reflection from her heart. When meeting Lisa, we were in different time zones, in Canada it was around 3 p.m. and we were in Greece where it was around midnight, however time meant nothing to us, we were solely in Kairos Time, in the moment, listening to Lisa tell her story.

As I did with Kevin in Australia some years back, we had some pre-planned questions to ask Lisa during the discussion, however, we soon realised that there was no need to fill the room with noise or control the discussion. We listened with intent, and at times following through on key words that Lisa had mentioned. Very similar to the stories told by "Uncle Kev" in Canberra and Melanie in Hinton. Lisa explained the significance of giving back to Mother Earth. She explained that when requesting a session with an Elder, one would offer cloth and tobacco. The cloth could be of different colours and is tied to trees, eventually over time disintegrating and returning to Mother Earth. These cloths tied to the trees are similar to the ones I had seen with Glenn at one of the Ceremonial Sites as well as reiterated during my discussion with Melanie. See *Figure 37.* the *Decorated Trees* in memory of the missing women and girls.

Lisa often related to the importance of meeting in various forms with others, in ceremonial traditions, and when doing so always sitting in a circle, or smudging that is used for various things like cleansing space or conversation, which is often used before going into a meeting. It is about opening up people to themselves for the conversation. In a nutshell, it is preparing for Real Meeting. Lisa also spoke about the significance of the "sweat" and how sacred it is and how it forms part of the cleansing ceremony and this ritual too being done with persons sitting in a circle.

Figure 37. Decorated Trees

Figure 38. Missing Lady

SHELLY ANNE BACSU
MISSING SINCE 1983

"My dearest daughter, you are so loved and we will desperately search for answers until we find you"
Love Mom

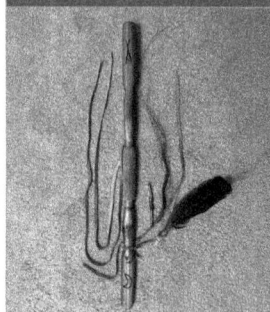
Figure 39. The Talking Stick

Throughout the conversation, we just listened to Lisa tell her story, and it went from the Indigenous culture, the missing Indigenous ladies (*Figure 38. Missing Lady* posted on a billboard on the site of the "Highway of Tears"), to her grandmother being buried in an Indigenous cemetery that I had driven past with her uncle Glenn, during two of my trips to Canada. Lisa mentioned that there are numerous different First Nation Reserves around Canada and then told us that she was from the Mohawk tribe. All of this information was shared with us by initially only asking Lia to tell her story, and during the interview, Aneta followed through on some of the metaphors and gifts that Lisa had gifted us in her words.

One of the intriguing elements of the discussion was the "Talking Stick", which is used in Canadian Indigenous cultures and is a powerful "communication tool" that ensures a code of conduct of respect during meetings. The person holding the stick, and only that person, is designated as having the right to speak and all others must listen quietly and respectfully. Lisa explained that when sitting in a circle, those having the stick are the only ones permitted to talk during the meeting. When she mentioned the "Talking Stick", I immediately thought to myself that this could be of good use in meetings and training sessions. Lisa also mentioned how those given an Indigenous name, like Melanie ("Grandmother White Wolf"), have the responsibility to care for and live up to the name that was given to them. On a later trip to Canada, I was able to obtain a "Talking Stick" that we now use as part of the training that we provide. See *Figure 39. The Talking Stick*.

Throughout the interview, it was clear that Lisa was so passionate about her culture and everything Indigenous that makes up the Indigenous world. However, towards the end of the conversation, we spoke about the two inner wolves within us as humans. This is when Aneta asked Lisa about a picture on the wall behind her which was about wolves that lived in the area of Alberta. Immediately Lisa's face lightened up as she realised that Aneta had observed the semiotics and what was of significance to Lisa. Our interview then continued with Lisa showing us various artifacts around her office and with each one of them she explained the story and their significance.

During the interview, we used the power of silence, after Lisa had mentioned something, we just kept silent for a couple of seconds, and then Lisa would continue with the conversation. As mentioned later in this book, as leaders we do not have to fill the room with noise. Lisa mentioned that in business, people think with their heads and not enough with their hearts.

Some months after interviewing Lisa, I was involved in investigating a serious incident. As these types of investigations are always stressful, emotional, challenging and difficult, we decided that instead of inviting persons, who had been impacted by the incident to the meeting room for interviews, we would do something different. Taking away from our discussion with Lisa, we set up some comfortable chairs in a quiet coffee corner of the office block with the chairs positioned in a circle. There were none of the traditional investigation charts, timelines, and whiteboards in the area (they were left in the meeting room), which if you have ever been in an incident investigation, you would know what I am referring to. Instead, there was one flipchart at the coffee corner, in case anyone needed to explain a diagram or sketch, a coffee machine, water, biscuits and freshly baked muffins. We had a counsellor joining us for all the sessions, taking care of the mental wellbeing of those with which we were engaging. The investigation was based on showing the necessary care and support to all involved and whilst doing so understanding the events that led up to the incident.

Just like the Aboriginal culture in Australia and Canada, we had sat in a circle, making everyone feel a part of the discussion and feeling that their views were being appreciated. Totally different to the traditional leadership style of meeting in the dedicated investigation room, where not everyone feels comfortable and included. A true reminder for me and my colleagues of how much we can learn from each other and how much we can take away when listening to others tell their stories about their traditions and rituals, similar to those of the age-old cultures of the Aboriginal people. Importantly too, is selecting the right space and place for the meeting to take place, thereby having a positive influence on the discussions.

Sitting Around the Fire with "Medicine Lady with Knowledge"

Two days after Brian had returned from the investigation into the serious incident as mentioned above, we both travelled to Canberra, Australia. After four flights, travelling halfway around the world, we arrived in Canberra on Saturday afternoon, drove straight to the hotel and caught up on some much-needed sleep. The following day, we had regained our energy, shaken off most of the jetlag and by mid-morning we were joined by Rob Long, who escorted us to visit some significant locations in Australia's Capital City. As always, we visited a number of museums, an art gallery and an exhibition at the Australian National Archives, whilst catching up with Rob, and taking in all the significance of the semiotics around us.

We were planning to travel back to the hotel to meet someone and prepare for the week ahead when we happened to drive past the "Tent Embassy" where we noticed an Aboriginal lady dressed in a traditional coat and stoking a fire, the same fireplace that I had met "Uncle Kev" during a previous visit to Canberra some six years before. Unanimously, we decided to stop and have a chat to the lady at the fire. We were keen to ask how "Uncle Kev" was doing, as during our previous visit, we had heard that his health was not that good.

As we have an interest in various Aboriginal cultures, the visit turned out to be the highlight of our day. We experienced, once again, a unique moment of synchronicity (Jung). Our signal to stop, park and approach was the sight of a woman stoking the fire alone. On approaching the lady at the fire, we introduced ourselves and she immediately invited us to sit down, after which she started to tell her story. Amazingly, she trusted us and opened up about why she was there, where she had been and who she was. She gave Brian some feathers tied together and spoke about what they symbolised for her. She gave me a knotted and twisted dried vine wrapped in red cloth and told us this was the rainbow serpent. She then handed Rob a knotted stick nestled into another curved piece of wood. This was a Palm Island egg she said. See *Figure 40*. Brian and I *Sitting at the Fire*.

So, we sat and listened as she talked about these three symbols and how each told a story for her. Nearby was a tin container that she said contained the ashes of her child, who died nine months before. There was a brief period of silence. The fire crackled and a young fresh eucalyptus branch burning in the fire began to slowly excrete water from where it had been cut. "They are the tears of my mother" she said. Her language was rhythmic like a song. Her rich poetic symbolic speech was indeed - so captivating.

We did not learn her name at first, but she said we had been sent to hear her story. There was a dead cockatoo by the fire. It looked like it had died recently. She told us how important the cockatoo was for the "Dreamtime". Everything she spoke was lyrical and poetic. Every sentence was punctuated by rich symbols and myths. She danced about the fire and told us she had medicine for us, and then off she walked. She walked some way away from us towards some trees and we could see her stripping branches of assorted eucalypts and wattles. See *Figure 41. Rituals at the Fire.*

Figure 40. Sitting at the Fire

Figure 41. Rituals at the Fire

We waited for some time, and as she seemed to have gone into a trance singing and standing under the trees, so we stood up not knowing whether to wait or leave. When she saw us leaving, as we started walking towards the car, she called for us to stay. She said, "that's right leave, you're always too busy for time" and more, "that's how it always is for you and your law, but I don't care about your law, I have my lore". It reminded us how she was in Kairos Time, fully in the moment, and therefore, the time of day did not bother her at all. As we knew that we were planning to meet someone a while later, our minds were slowly drifting from Kairos Time back into Chronos Time.

So, we sat back down (back into Kairos Time), and she explained to us about how the fresh branches would smoke and that we should bath in it. We watched "Medicine Lady with Knowledge", as she pushed the branches into the fire, between the larger burning logs and we were quickly engulfed in smoke. She invited us to stand up and follow the smoke as the gentle breeze moved it away from us. As we did this, moving slowly around the fire, she said, "there is no living in your law, but life in my lore". See *Figure 42. Taking in the Smoke.*

She then stood in a dancing pose with these three strange white people, confronted by our preoccupation with time, schedules and watches. She said, "life is time, don't you know that?" "You fellas have never listened" she said, "you are so full of things, in a hurry, chasing things and no time to sit and listen".

She spoke poetically, semiotically and mythically about her years in the Northern Territory and about her tribe, people she missed and places she had travelled. She spoke about some of her suffering and about her greatest risk, interference, dispossession and white law. She told us about how her father and mother had been locked up for stealing bread, only because they had just wanted food to feed their family. Through her story, we realised that She herself had been abused and harmed many times. Unless you can think mythically, semiotically and poetically you would have struggled to understand what she was saying about her story and the "Dreamtime".

By this time, we had lost all track of time (deeply in Kairos Time), but she told us that we had received the message, we came looking for. She stood in a different pose to the one before, as if to say we had her permission to leave. So, Rob asked if he could take a selfie of us all together with her and thankfully, she said yes. See *Figure 43. Selfie Together.*

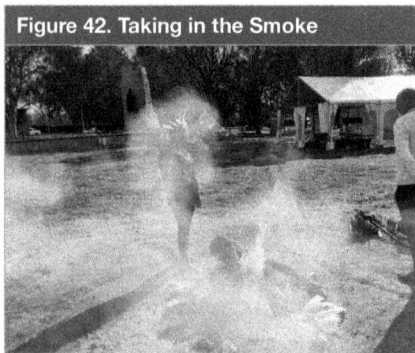
Figure 42. Taking in the Smoke

Figure 43. Selfie Together

She used the term "there is no rupture, no heaven, just here", she was living her life in Kairos Time. At the end of the visit, the lady asked us to gift her with a name. Rob mentioned "Knowledge" and Brian named her "Medicine Lady", so her name became "Medicine Lady with Knowledge". She smiled for the first time and then she thanked us for her new name, and then we left her and her fireplace. As we walked to the car, she waved and wished us well.

Such a remarkable experience on a Sunday afternoon in Canberra. I have experienced nothing like this before. We all felt enlivened and to some degree troubled by her words and message. We knew that people looking like us, the white fellas, were her greatest existential risk, but she welcomed us to sit around her people's fireplace, and shared with us her every anxiety, her every fear.

Despite many similarities, this meeting was different to the ones we had experienced with others, including "Uncle Kev", Lisa, Glenn, and "Grandmother White Wolf". At times, we did not understand the meaning of some of the rituals of the "Medicine Lady with Knowledge", but it once again highlighted the importance of listening to others, keeping quiet, letting them tell their story. This time though it also reminded us of the importance of being in Kairos Time, being in the moment, suspending agendas and power, just simply being with others.

You might ask, why we have included all these stories that have been told to us by the various Indigenous People. For us they are significant, and we believe that they are so relevant regarding embodied leadership and understanding of different cultures through Real Meeting. This is no different to the workplace where multinational companies employ people of different nationalities, cultures, sub-cultures and backgrounds, some working side by side, day in and day out.

The "Medicine Lady with Knowledge" in telling us her stories about the three objects that she gave us to hold was her myth, objects that she carried with her day in and day out on her travels. Her dances, her various poses all of significance to her and in which she believes. No different to the person that goes into a church, lights a candle, makes a sign of the cross and believes that their prayers will be answered. These rituals as well as those of the "Medicine Lady with Knowledge" are all acts of faith, passed down from generation to generation. I am by no means disagreeing with any of these rituals but trying to point out that we need to understand that rituals and myths are significant in all cultures as well as sub-cultures. By letting people tell their stories, we might not always agree with their beliefs, traditions, rituals or myths, but at least we can understand where they are coming from and why we need to respect them.

When we let go of our view of the world, we can learn to understand the culture of others. When we get rid of all the propositional things that seek to control culture by definition, we can learn just how much myth, ritual, symbol and belief are embodied in all cultures. Take a minute to reflect on the various cultures and sub-cultures within a company and we are sure that many come to mind, including: organisational, hierarchical, managerial, as well as sub-cultures of various departments, shifts and working teams to name only a few. These subcultures are developed over time, as groups of employees have different worldviews and values which are in the dialectic with the desired company culture. All these sub-cultures, have an influence on the overall company culture. Although culture cannot be measured, it is important that leaders get a feel of what these sub-cultures are, if they wish to have any influence and in turn make a difference. Mmetaphorically speaking, leaders need to sit around that "fireplace" and speak to people, let them tell their stories, and in doing so get to feel the culture. That "fireplace" could be the canteen, the coffee corner, smoking area or simply being out on the shop floor.

With new eyes, we can strip away the façade of spin in these cultures, deconstruct their dominant faith and see the way each creates myths, rituals and beliefs that are empowered through semiotics, poetics and discourse. All cultures embody belief in semiotics.

With all this in mind by engaging, listening with intent, we can better understand others, their respective culture, leadership and embodied being in order to demythologise beliefs and strip away issues that inhibit effective relationships, social connection and ethical practise. This is what Real Meeting is all about, be it at the workplace or in our private lives.

SELF-REFLECTION

Chapter 5 – Meeting in Real Meeting

Our selection of elements for self-reflection from the chapter are as follows:

- I treat people with dignity and respect, irrespective whether from my department, other departments, other companies, or visitors.

- Does my language reflect me as a leader having good ethics, showing care, encouraging belonging, and thereby developing trust?

- I often invite someone for a cup of coffee and an informal chat about things of significance to them.

- Do I refrain from being a counsellor, but rather bring in the specialists to counsel persons in need?

- In my style of leadership, I provide sufficient and genuine support for others that have been traumatised by events or are under stress, because of their current situation.

- Am I humble, do I, similar to "Uncle Kev", refrain from trying to be in the spotlight, the centre of attention, but rather focusing on others and issues of significance?

- I find my "fireplace" to get to feel the culture and sub-cultures.

- I am aware of my two inner wolves, and do I find the balance in feeding them both?

CHAPTER 6

Leadership in Being with Others

"The world is not comprehensible, but it is embraceable: through the embracing of one of its beings".

Dr Martin Buber

Austrian-Israeli Philosopher

Female Fighter Pilot (Mandy and Support from Other Cadettes)

Mandy Hickson is a former Royal Airforce fighter pilot, who was only the second woman to fly the Tornado GR4, including flights in operational areas at speeds of "420 knots" or just over "777 kilometres" per hour. Mandy throughout her career experienced success, but also failure during her time as a cadette, throughout her time striving to achieve her wings, the coveted silver wings in, at the time, a male dominated profession. Because of her drive, support and leadership of other team members, Mandy went on to complete three tours of duty and fly over fifty missions over Iraq.

Brian and I were both attending a conference in Denmark for the oil and gas industry, as Brian was invited to be one of four speakers at the event to share some elements of Social Psychology of Risk and parts from his book titled "Humanising Leadership". Sharing a table with the other speakers, we got to know Mandy, and during one of the breaks, Mandy and I shared a cup of coffee, chatting about her experiences. After one of the breaks, Brian presented his talk which ended off with inspiration from the late President Mandela. Mandy then stepped up onto the stage and presented her talk based on her book "An Officer, Not a Gentleman".

A talk that mirrored the sub-title of her book, "The inspirational journey of a pioneering female fighter pilot". As she spoke, I thought "wow", and I was experiencing one of the most inspirational talks that I have heard. And trust me when I tell you, I am the kind of person who listens to "TED Talks" religiously. I recall Brian saying after her presentation that he was extremely relieved that he had spoken before Mandy, as she would be a difficult act to follow.

After the conference, Brian and Mandy swapped books and I started reading hers on the plane back to Austria, definitely one of those books that one battles to put down. Amongst several inspiring stories shared during her presentation at the conference as well as in her book, there were several events that stood out for both Brian and me. Events that relate so much to I-Thou, meeting to Meet, team spirit and leadership in general. With approval from Mandy, we share some elements of her the story.

The story of events that I have selected to share is one that comes out of a chapter in her book titled, "The Team Works" and I chose this as not only is it an inspiring story, but it also resonates with me, as in most successful teams, what works is the trust amongst the team members which often comes from the knowing of another. This is the case for sports teams, work teams, the arts, dancing, singing to name a few. The story also relates to the quote by Martin Buber, "the world is not comprehensible, but it is embraceable: through the embracing of one of its beings". The story goes as follows:

A Good Team That Made a Significant Difference

Mandy was entering the final stages of her training programme and was weeks away from earning the coveted silver wings on her chest, however there were still some hurdles that kept popping up. Mandy could feel the pressure mounting, she was battling to sleep, and her gut feel was taking her all over the place. Mandy was spending endless hours studying, practicing her maneuvers and procedures and had flown in excess of sixty hours in the magnificent Hawk fighter plane. The weight on her shoulders and the pressure increased as the days passed and as she got closer to the end of her training, still not confident if she would pass the final tests and become the pilot that she had always dreamed of becoming, she knew that her career and her dreams were all on the line. In her book, Mandy used several metaphors to explain her emotions in those final days. Mandy mentioned that it felt like she was on a downward spiral, and a feeling as if she was being sucked under water (how any psychologist would have worked on these words) and as she was tired, she could not get her head around some of the aspects of flying and every test flight was adding to the pressure and becoming a huge challenge for Mandy.

After landing once she had completed her third last trip, she was informed during the debrief that her manoeuvres had not gone well and that she had failed the test. One can only imagine the sinking feeling of hearing the news, the added pressure it must have placed on Mandy's young shoulders. In her book Mandy uses another metaphor to explain her feeling, she mentions that it felt like she had been "booted in the stomach". She was informed that she would have to have one more test flight and had some additional flights scheduled to practise her maneuvers. At this stage, Mandy felt like she was not going to be part of the team that would be receiving the coveted wings at the end of the training.

That evening after dinner and returning from the mess to her room, Mandy immediately started practising and going through her manoeuvres, when someone knocked on her door. When she reluctantly opened the door, she was faced by three of her fellow team members, who invited her out, to which Mandy thought it was an invitation for a drink at the local pub. After eventually convincing Mandy to join them, they took her to the bicycle sheds, collected their bikes and cycled to the parade ground. This is where they met other team members and to Mandy's surprise they started going through the manoeuvres and they insisted that they would keep her there until she mastered the battle turns. Eventually once convinced that she had managed it, Mandy returned to her room for the well-earned night's rest.

The following morning Mandy was up in the air going through the motions and when landing, her instructor was in awe at what he had just experienced. Mandy went on to tell him what had happened the night before, how her team members had supported her, and wanted her to pass, even though, they were all competing for the open positions. The team members showed the true spirit of being with others, showing leadership in a caring manner, one where they all pulled together for the sake of another, where each one of them acted selflessly, even though, it could have been to their detriment.

This is sadly frequently not the case in business, where people often will do others in just to get a foot ahead, become the favorite for promotion, be seen in a better light than another, win over the attention of others. I have worked with wonderful teams where they have each other's back, however, I have also experienced situations where people do things and act in a way that is detrimental to others and only for personal gain.

Some leaders could learn a thing or two from the team of pilots that were awarded their wings together with Mandy. Taking time to support others, not seeing juniors or subordinates as a threat to their own positions, wanting to see others excel in the jobs and their careers. This is the same in my line of business, as a university lecturer giving that extra time needed to some of our university students to support them in a better understanding of the topic being discussed and in turn see them achieve better marks for the assignments, as well as exams at the end of the semester. In having this approach, similar to those fellow pilots who assisted Mandy in getting the hang of her manoeuvres, develops a sense of trust in the leaders and in turn, leaders as well as lecturers gain huge appreciation and respect from their respective team members and / or students.

Figure 44. is *Mandy and Brian* meeting up one evening in Austria and *Figure 45.* shows *Brian Speaking* just before Mandy and *Figure 46.* is *Me Listening* with intent and awe to Mandy's talk.

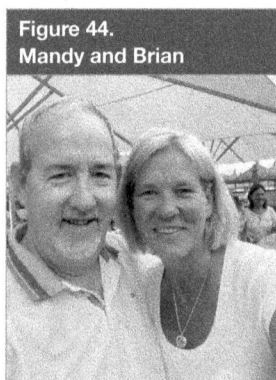
Figure 44. Mandy and Brian

Figure 45. Brian Speaking

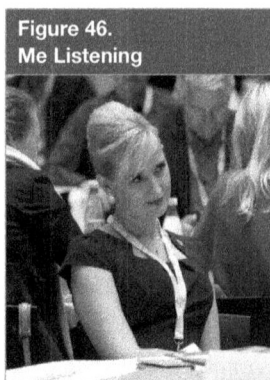
Figure 46. Me Listening

Suspending One's Agenda and Power

There is the need for leaders to suspend their own agenda as well as power when being in Real Meeting with others, be it at work or on a personal basis. Many leaders, however, find it difficult to do so, to move out of the I-It and into the I-Thou mode. When entering into an engagement with another, it is important to suspend one's own agenda, stop thinking of what to say next and be aware of one's own biases. Active listening means listening to the person's comments, allowing them to tell their story, and whilst doing so refrain from thinking what is the next question that should be asked. This is called active listening. Never go into an engagement with a hidden agenda, as doing so kills any Real Meeting.

The only way to really Meet another is to suspend one's own agenda, power and move into the hyphen, the place where those being engaged with also have suspended their own agenda or agendas as well as power.

We often have video calls with two of our grandchildren living in New Zealand and Saipan, cousins Blaire and Ellie, sometimes for a couple of minutes and other times for an hour or so. These sessions are enjoyed by both of us as well as Blaire and Ellie, as there is absolutely no agenda, and we suspend any power as grandparents to the two girls. They mostly decide what we will talk about, what games we will play and how long we will be having Real Meeting. All of this time, with each video call with the children, we are in Real Meeting, we are in Kairos Time.

When spending time with Blaire, mostly on Saturday mornings, she would often pick up a book, pretend that she was reading a story, even though at that time, she was too young and unable to read. We would tell her stories, play Barbie dolls, have dress ups, and play kitchen-kitchen and much more. We all moved into the hyphen of I-Thou, no preconceived ideas, and thoughts of what to talk about, it was simply just having fun, building relationships, building trust and bonding.

On the other hand, when talking to Ellie, at the time, around three to four years of age, our Meetings were different to those with Blaire. Ellie having a strong sense of humour, and lots of energy, our discussions were not so much about her dolls, but about her three motocross bikes, her poster of me doing motocross which hangs on the wall in her bedroom, jumping on the bed, and anything that would make us all laugh and simply have fun. Her brother Raymond was later born, and the Real Meetings are now with both of them, although Raymond, at the time, of writing this book was too young to put many words together, however observing the gestures, body language and laughs was our way of building relationships with him as well.

As mentioned above, we treated our Meetings with each of the grandchildren differently as they are individuals, having their own interests, having their own stories, and most definitely having different ways and means of telling their stories and letting us experience their ideas of the world with them. These meeting are always about us suspending our own agenda, our own authority and giving our time to them and the three of them giving their time to us. All of this centred in the I-Thou.

As the grandchildren all lived in New Zealand at the time, and during the first couple of years, Aneta only met with them via FaceTime, or other means of video calls, however even these sessions were about getting to know the family and the family getting to know Aneta. It was all about Real Meeting. Some years later, we visited New Zealand and when the girls saw Aneta getting out of the car, they were excited, running up to her with open arms and jumping into her embracement.

There was no shyness, it was as if they had known her throughout their lives, this all because they had fun with her via technology, in Real Meeting. Aneta and the girls got to know each other, through experiencing a bond even though remotely. *Figure 47.* is Aneta having *Fun with Blaire. Figure 48.* shows *Ellie Having Fun* on the beach with Aneta during a photoshoot.

Figure 47. Fun with Blaire

Figure 48. Ellie Having Fun

Figure 49. Time with Ellie

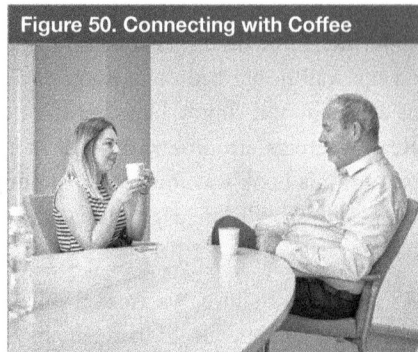
Figure 50. Connecting with Coffee

The above probably comes naturally for most parents and grandparents, and it works in building relationships of openness and based on trust, moving into the hyphen of the I-Thou. The question then is, why do we not practise the same principles in our professional lives, why do leaders often remain in the I-It and seldom move into the I-Thou mode? Why do leaders prefer holding meetings and steer away from Real Meetings with their colleagues and team members? Having specific biases as a leader (manager probably the better word) lends itself to people believing that they must take control of discussions, meetings, that they must direct the discussions with their sub-ordinates. This lends itself to more of a telling approach rather than a listening one. However, this should not be the case in many instances. By letting the discussions be open, letting the team contribute has positive benefits, not only as a team working together, but in decision making, developing, and implementing actions going forward. *Figure 49.* is Brian sharing *Time with Ellie* and *Figure 50.* reflects *Connecting with Coffee* in discussion with Paula, a colleague of mine.

By no means are we saying that leaders do not have to take control and direct discussions, for example chairing of meetings, making decisions, managing situations, considering, or deciding on certain actions, directing discussions, requesting information, instructing others, to name only a few. In leadership there is the need for all these elements of management, the need to be in the I-It mode, but good leaders do not stay in the I-It all the time. Once in discussion with Graham Long, I recall him saying that those people that remain for most of their time and efforts in the I-It become lonely and miserable. There is the need to challenge oneself as a leader or person in general to move out of the I-It and into the I-Thou. This is explained in more detail in Chapter 3, using the "I-It to I-Thou Model".

Building relationships, developing trust, showing interest, displaying a caring approach, practising active listening and simply engaging, to name only a few traits is key as a leader. This is not possible when leaders remain in the I-It mode and seldomly move out into the I-Thou. Good leaders spend time with their people which I call "boots on the ground". This does not necessarily mean inviting someone into one's office and having a discussion, as this might not be the best place for a person to feel comfortable and relaxed to have an open discussion. The semiotics of the leader's office could have the opposite effect on the employee. For example, the degrees on the walls reflect a level of intelligence and achievement, the high back chair and dark wooden desk depicting authority and control. Even more stressful is having the personal assistant ask the employee to take a seat outside of the leader's office, until called in to join the leader for a discussion. The waiting to enter the corner office, adding stress even before the discussion starts. All of these semiotics, continuously communicating with the conscious mind and even more importantly the unconscious mind as well as the collective unconscious.

To promote good engagement, consider inviting someone for a simple discussion, sharing a cup of coffee together and just engaging in an informal chat, in a neutral area, where the employee feels more relaxed. Even better, how about as a leader going into the company canteen and sitting with some of the employees for lunch and in an open chat, one would be surprised on where the discussions lead to and in doing so whilst practising active listening, suspending any agenda, building trust amongst the teams. If any leaders are keen on getting a feel of the culture on the shop floor, the best place to start is listening to discussions and spending time engaging with employees in the canteen area.

Some years ago, we were running a large rebuild project at one of the paper mills for the company that I work for. The project ran over a four-month period, rebuilding a large recovery boiler, and involving thousands of contractors from all over the world. It was a high-risk period, filled with lots of stress, long hours and taking a toll on many leaders, and employees. Once a month, we would gather our team of around twelve people, order pizzas, water and cool-drinks and sit under some trees on the site. During the lunch, we would have open engagement about what was going well, discussing the concerns, and sharing general feelings and comments. More importantly, we would ask the team to tell us how they felt, how were they holding up and whether they were getting enough rest and looking after their own mental wellbeing. We used the iCue listening model or better known as the Engagement Board to capture the discussions. There was no set agenda, no authority levels, just simply chatting and moving into the hyphen of the I-Thou, although at times also touching on the I-It. As the site is located in KwaZulu-Natal in South Africa, the team were also sitting close to some zebra and antelope grazing on the grass close by. At times, the odd wildebeest would walk by, and the loud hadada birds or Egyptian geese would fly in. The space and place contributing to the relaxed feeling all found themselves in, during these lunches.

Leadership is "Being with Others"

"Being with others" is a metaphor reflecting issues such as engaging with others, supporting them in times of need, times of uncertainty, times of difficulty and even when things are running smoothly and according to plan. When talking about being with others as a leader, what is meant, is that leaders should be aware of how they treat people, how they reflect a sense of caring and in turn how they serve others. I wonder how often leaders reflect on whether they, at times, enter the I-Thou and if they show a sincere level of caring, understanding and helping when engaging with persons working closely with them, as well as individuals or teams in the various departments and on the shop floor.

The following example is one that highlights, how a leader can ignore the fundamentals of showing care and all that is mentioned in the above paragraph.

"He Lost His Young Daughter Two Weeks Ago"

In the early days of my career, some thirty odd years ago, an acquaintance of mine (Hennie) worked for an organisation which conducted audits of companies at that time in South Africa, as well as other parts of Africa. The main areas of speciality were on risk, safety and health issues. Living and working close to Johannesburg, South Africa, an area having many underground gold mines, Hennie was given the task to conduct an audit at one of the gold mines. Auditing deep underground mines obviously includes spending most of the site visit below the surface, engaging and talking to the miners working in the hot, damp or dusty and often tough and labour-intensive conditions.

As Hennie knew that I was keen to visit an underground facility, he kindly obtained permission for me to join him on the audit and site visit. I had never been underground before, and therefore, on receiving the invitation, I immediately, without thinking twice, accepted the offer, and a week later, we pulled up to the security gate where we were met by a senior manager from the mine. After a cup of coffee, a welcoming and information presentation, we proceeded to the changerooms to fit the required overalls and collect our personal protective equipment. We then proceeded to the shaft where we entered a lift, or more like a cage and before long, jammed together with many miners, like sardines in a can, we were descending down the vertical mine shaft into the dark depths of the mine. I recall my heart racing with excitement at the opportunity that I had been given.

We arrived at one of the levels in the mine and started walking through the various man-made tunnels, carved into the earth, eventually coming across a rest area that was apparently below the desired standard of housekeeping and orderliness. The manager accompanying us approached an employee without any introductions of who we were, no shaking of hands or any type of icebreaking contact or comment. In contrast, he immediately showed his disappointment about the standard of the housekeeping of the workstation, and sternly raised his concern and then instructed the employee to without delay, address the issues identified, giving him a clear deadline of when it should be all sorted out.

On ending what was a short discussion or more like a blaming session, we proceeded towards another section of the mine at which the employees were conducting drilling activities in preparation for blasting activities at the rock face. Whilst walking, the manager informed Hennie and me that the person that he had just spoken to, at the rest area, had just returned from time off work, and therefore, that could have been the reason the area was not up to the desired standard. It then transpired that the employee had unexpectedly lost his young child due to illness during the previous week. I remember my thoughts at the time, shocked at what I had just heard, and I immediately lost respect for the manager with whom we were spending the day. I actually felt so saddened as well as embarrassed at the situation, as we were there with him during the discussion, but unbeknown to us that the employee was still grieving from the loss of his daughter. Shamefully, the manager in his discussion with the employee, at no time showed any signs of sympathy or sorrow at the employee's misfortune. Not once did he consider the emotions and the distress of the person, he never offered his condolences for the employee's loss. At no stage did the manager enter the I-Thou, he was only focused on the I-It, the physical standards, and conditions of the working area. Probably more concerned about his audit score, than the person in sorrow and still embodied in mourning.

One can only imagine how the employee must have felt, what he must have thought about us all as we walked away from the area. We will never know, but for sure, if I were in his shoes and was treated in such a bullying and unsympathetic way, I would have lost all trust in leadership, and the company as a whole. For days, I regretted not walking back to the employee and showing sympathy and in turn given him my sincere condolences, given him a bit of time, being with him in Real Meeting. This treatment was a significant contrast to the care and support that I would receive from my manager around thirty years later when my wife passed away; the two were so vastly different.

Sometimes, one does not have to say a word when a person is in a saddened moment or period in their lives. Just a simple hug or arm around the person's shoulder could be enough. It is not uncommon to hear the words when someone passes away like, "I do not know what to say to him or her with his or her loss". Maybe it is better not to fill the space with words. People say things like, "he was too young to die", or "she is in a better place", "come back to work, it will take your mind off your sadness", words like these could bring on more emotional pain for the grieving person. If one feels the need to say something, then one could use the words, "please accept my deepest condolences for your loss". This was all that was needed by the manager that day in the mine, sadly though, it had not crossed his mind.

"Being with Others" is Not a KPI, but Rather a Social Contract

Social Contracts an Ancient Idea

Social contracts are an ancient phenomenon, we have many stories and examples from centuries of writings that reflect social contracts with others, where there is no written agreement, no need to enforce engagement, no need to measure how many times people are given the time of their leaders, times to talk, times to engage and times in Real Meeting. Being social is related to being with others, interacting with the individual or the group and contributing to welfare of human beings as members of society. As one example, we read about such stories in the Holy Bible where it was normal for one to be with another in Real Meeting.

Being with others is about giving of one's own undivided attention, one's own time to another. And in doing so making them feel important and valued, making them feel significant and as an important part of the team. It is about making the other person, or persons feel that they have a voice and more importantly giving them the feeling that they are actually being heard. If leaders do this with genuine care for another, they are engulfed in Kairos Time, in the moment, in Real Meeting. Without any doubt when we are fully in the moment, Kairos Time and in Real Meeting, connection with others is at another level, one that builds trust, and as a result improves the outcomes of the discussions and engagement being held.

We as humans practise this in our daily lives with our spouses, children, grandchildren, friends, and partners. Be it, for example, at home on a weekend around the barbecue, on the beach, lying on the deck of a boat after scuba diving, playing a round of golf or enjoying a picnic in the park. However, when at work, leaders often fall into the routine of the I-It, and thereby returning into Chronos Time, and as a result spend little time in the social contract element.

When in the moment or in Real Meeting there is always the possibility of losing concentration, being distracted and shifting one's attention away from the discussions, away from listening with intent, away from being fully engaged. When this happens, our facial expressions or lack of expression, our eyes immediately tell the other person that we are no longer in the moment, that we have probably lost interest. Therefore, as leaders it is important that we concentrate on remaining focused during a discussion. I (Brian) have a condition that I have been informed is a type of synaesthesia which results in involuntary perceptions that cross over between senses. So, when I watch a movie or I am in discussion and I see or hear something that triggers my memories, I can smell whatever it is. For example, if I watch motocross on television, I can smell dust, or if someone mentions diesel in a discussion, I get the smell of diesel. This might sound great, however, it at times takes my concentration away from the movie, a book I might be reading or the discussion that I am having with another person. As a result, I really have to focus my attention on what is being said during the discussion or engagement.

"I Haven't Seen my Manager in Two Years"

As part of the enquiry into understanding an incident, I recall having a discussion in the mid-2000s with an employee, who was involved in an incident that resulted in him being injured, and as an outcome, he was off work for a couple of weeks. I still remember the look of the office that we were in, as well as his name, Peter, and some of the discussions that we had, as if it were yesterday. As part of an enquiry to understand the details of the incident I had a discussion with him and during which, I happened to ask him about the support provided by his leader. I was rather taken aback to hear that Peter had not seen his manager on the shop floor in almost two years. I asked him why he thought that was, and he said that his job was probably not that important in the context of things, and therefore, his impression was that he as a person and his job were of little significance to his manager. He used a metaphor that put it in a nutshell for me", "I am just a pair of hands to keep the process going, so the company can make money". Thinking back on the discussion, Peter was probably correct, he was just a number, he was being used, he was treated as an object to keep production going and contribute to the process and profits. Never mind there not being any Real Meeting in two years, there was not even any meeting at all in that period.

I shared this discussion with one of the middle managers and raised my concern, and then came the next shocking comment, he mentioned that this was not only the case for Peter, but for many others in the company, as the manager treats most persons with the same approach. He said something that put it into context for me, (although probably tongue in cheek) he explained that apart from his senior team, the only two people, who are likely to see the manager on a daily basis, is the security guard, who opens the boom gate when the manager arrives at the site each morning and when leaving in the afternoon, and the other is his secretary.

Having to Encourage and Measure Engagement

It is common for companies to have key performance indicators, or KPIs for their leaders, middle management and first line leaders. These are also often linked to bonus calculations and are a way of encouraging their respective leaders to achieve the requirements of each indicator. However, is it not sad that, at times, we have to use KPIs to encourage leaders, at all levels of organisations to switch off their computers, stand up from behind their desks, and get out of their offices to be with others, to engage, to partake in Real Meeting. Be it in the canteen, the engagement area, the coffee corner, the shop floor or just popping into someone's office for a chat.

Being with others should not necessarily be a KPI, however, I understand why companies do regard it as one, as by doing so forces leaders to engage with others. "Wow", if only some leaders would not have to be encouraged or forced to be in engagement with people. Being with others is a Social Contract and if the sub-culture of the various management teams is at a good level, the company would not have to depend on the KPI to encourage engagement.

Marriage Does not Necessarily Mean Love

As an example, let us consider a marriage between two people; a couple fall in love and over time get engaged and eventually married. As with many cultures the couple get married by either a legal ceremony, at a public venue or one inside a religious place, to name a few options. Prior to the wedding, a contract is often signed between the two parties, agreeing on certain conditions and what happens if things go wrong. On the day of the wedding, the matrimony and joining of the couple as they are blessed, and this is probably followed by the couple as well as witnesses signing the legal documentation.

The above is all good and needed, however mostly focused on the objects, the I-It and little on the I-Thou apart from various parts of the ceremony, including rituals and symbols, and where the couple connect, looking at each other and joining hands in sharing their vows and following the traditional instruction of, "you may kiss the bride", and where the mother in-law starts to cry. The vows are not recorded on any legal document, they are simply a social contract between the two, making various promises to each other. The contract, marriage certificate and ring do not necessarily prove that they love each other. They could be married on paper but not in reality, which could be the case, for example, in an arranged, forced marriage or a joining of two taken solely for legal reasons.

We have a friend who fell pregnant as a teenager and when together with her boyfriend nervously broke the news to her parents, her father made it clear to them both that they would not embarrass the family and that without any discussion, they would get married and that there would be no other option, even though, they both were not that keen to become husband and wife at such a young age. Some twenty-two years later, this has turned into a marriage only on paper, with a couple of signatures with an official stamp in the corner, but sadly not a marriage in reality. This couple were legally married, however, there is a total social disconnect between the two of them. When observing the couple at dinners or functions, over the years, there was nothing to see, but a total disconnect between the two of them, in most instances they did not sit next to each other, they made derogative comments about each other, and it was no longer a surprise when they threw insults at each other continuously. They openly said that they were only together for the sake of their daughter.

True marriage is when couples are connected in the I-Thou, where they are connected by mutual feelings, emotions, sharing, respect, understanding and love. In other words, true marriage is when the couple connect by their hearts, where there is clearly a devotion, loving, caring and trusting connection that cannot be calculated, measured, or be represented as a KPI that rates their marriage. True marriage is a social contract, and although legalities like contracts, paperwork, witnesses, legal stamps, and signatures are in place, they are of little true significance in their togetherness. Their love for one another, their understanding of marriage is a social contract through mutual connection and experience, it is totally in the I-Thou.

We use the metaphor; "nothing and no-thing". This relates to the situation where one person sees the partner as a thing, where there is no social contract, where one experiences or uses the other. This is the case where a partner sees the other as simply someone who will take care of them, keep the home tidy, clean up after them and sadly refer to them as the breadwinner. All of these are simply in the I-It, where people are treated as objects or as a thing, even worse as nothing, and for the benefit of another, and definitely nowhere near the same as being with someone, being in the I-Thou as described by Martin Buber.

The "Eight Seconds" Gifted to a Visually Impaired Young Girl

Anyone who has met Brian knows that he is a Manchester United supporter at heart, and because of this is not a fan of the arch-rivals, Manchester City; in fact, he does not like them at all. However, Brian was watching a football game in the lounge of our home in Greece, being played between Manchester City and Sevilla and as football is not my preferred sport (I much rather watch Rugby Union), I was busy with other things and would glance over at the television when entering the lounge, and every now and then have a chat with Brian. Well, at one stage, I entered the lounge and noticed Brian wiping a tear from his cheek. I glanced over at the television and happened to see the trophy about to be handed to the captain of the team from the blue side of Manchester. I knew that Brian dislikes Manchester City, however I thought it was rather amusing that he had tears, because he was sad that they had won another cup final.

I joked with Brian, putting my arm around his shoulders, and telling him that it was not that bad, with a smile on my face, and told him that one day his beloved Manchester United will once again get the opportunity to win a title and lift a cup. This is when Brian told me why he had felt a sense of emotion and explained what had just happened.

When the players of both teams walked up onto the stage to receive their silver and gold medals respectively, they were greeted and congratulated by a number of dignitaries, including a young girl who was visually impaired and dressed in a football outfit. Sadly, most of the players walked past the young girl, without acknowledging her, received their medals and then passed the trophy that was standing on a pedestal on the stage. Brian then explained that some of the Manchester City players had touched the trophy as they walked past it, totally focused on the medal around their necks and the coveted trophy, both being simple objects. My thoughts immediately went to what is better described by Martin Buber as being in the I-It.

This included Erling Haaland, who had received his medal and then as he slowly walked past the trophy, he touched it. Just behind him was Jack Grealish, the number ten player. The President of UEFA had his hand out to congratulate Jack on the win and hand him his winner's gold medal. This is when Jack held up the queue of players waiting to receive their medals, as he held the young girl's hands and started to talk to her. Jack had connected with her; he had entered the hyphen in the I-Thou. Yes, winning the trophy and being awarded a gold medal was probably as important for him as for any of the other players, but in his case, he placed the young girl at the centre of his focus, he had placed the person before the objects. In his eyes, the gold medal and the trophy could wait.

When rewatching the highlights of the ceremony, there is a moment where Erling Haaland, one of the Manchester City so-called "heroes", walks past the well-polished shining and newly engraved trophy, positioned in the middle of the stage and touches it whilst at the same moment, Jack is holding the hands of the young girl and giving her all of his undivided attention. What a contrast, one player connecting with an object and the second player connecting with a person, a good example of the difference between the I-It and the I-Thou. After all the players had received medals the manager of the team, Pep Guardiola, walked up to the young girl, placed his right hand on her cheek and either whispered something in her ear or gave her a kiss on the cheek. Both the deeds of Jack and Pep were heartwarming moments, something that the young girl will probably cherish for ever. Both of these men had given of their time to the young girl, they were not concerned about the Chronos Time, but were locked for a brief moment in Kairos Time. At one stage, the President of UEFA placed his hand on Jack's arm, which seemed like he was indicating that Jack should move on, but Jack ignored the gesture and then continued to give the young girl his time. It is as if the President was stuck in a Chronos Time mindset, wanting to proceed with the medal ceremony and then hand the coveted trophy to the captain of the team.

We watched the ceremony a couple of times, with our focus on the social elements, and have since used the video in training that I conduct in Social Psychology of Risk. There were many social influences taking place during the awards ceremony, however one of them that stood out, was how the players from both teams reacted when walking past the trophy. Some of the losing team players purposely refrained from looking at the trophy as they walked past it and then they were followed by the winning team players, who looked at and even touched the trophy as they walked past. In both instances, it seemed like they had regarded the trophy as being almost human, something that they could have a relationship with, something that impacted their emotions, head, heart, and gut. If only the players had treated the young girl in the same way, recognising her with even a soft touch on her shoulder or shaking of her hand. The true heroes of the day were not the winners, the goal scorers, or Player of the Match, but rather Jack Grealish and Pep Guardiola. Additionally, I can assure that the whole interaction did not take longer than around "eight seconds", but it was the eight seconds that others did not want to give to that young girl.

I must note here that Brian is still not a Manchester City fan, but has developed the greatest respect for both Jack Grealish and Pep Guardiola for the human approach that they showed.

Sadly, the same at times applies to leaders of organisations across the world who are often stuck in the I-It, where their focus is fixated on the objects, bar charts, the outputs, pushing the efficiencies, achieving the accolades and awards for production records, for innovation only to name a few. However, in doing so they fail to recognise the individuals, who make up the teams that make the difference, which achieve the results, which keep the machines running, that keep the company striving. Maybe by recognising the individuals, giving attention, showing respect and care, the results will be even better. Leaders should see their team members as the *"Blind Young Girl"* who has feelings, and who also needs recognition from the leader, their own *"Jack Grealish"*. Surprisingly enough, some of those interactions would not take more than eight seconds, a tap on the shoulder, a shake of a hand or even just acknowledging someone when passing in the passage or on the shop floor. The question worth asking ourselves is, how much is eight seconds worth to us, and even more, how much does eight seconds of connection mean to someone else?

At Times, the Things we Cannot Measure are as Important, if not More Important

Yes, many companies have some kind of key performance indicators (KPIs), which focus on lagging and leading indicators, which forms part of the I-It element of running a business. Peter Drucker has said, "you can't manage what you don't measure" and this term has since been used in leadership training and development courses across the world. I recall challenging this quote in a working group discussion at a leadership course in Switzerland some years ago with one of the participants. She made the comment that if you do not have a measurement then how do you know how you are performing, whether doing well or poorly. She cited numerous examples of how it is important to measure performance from early days at school, where students obtain a rating for their work and their exams, right through to the business world where companies measure all sorts of issues and include them in their key performance indicators, from machine efficiency, production rates, injury rates, EBIDTA, ROCE and many more. This is of course true, but what about those issues that cannot be measured but are as important in life, or at times even of more significance.

As with the story above with Jack Grealish, or the discussions with our children and grandchildren, whilst being in Kairos Time, living the moment, being with other, and in Real Meeting, there is no way of measuring the emotions, the inspirations, the feelings, the embodied feeling of one's thoughts, gut feel and heartfelt feelings.

Think back to the story at the beginning of this chapter, about Mandy, who was stressed and striving to pass her final exams to achieve her dreams and earn her "wings" as a fighter pilot. Yes, her performances were rated (measured) during each test flight and every exam, however what cannot be measured is the support that was provided to her, the emotions she felt when realising that the others were backing her and wanted her to succeed. We repeat, these are as important, if not more important as the things that we can measure.

Here is a nice example of how important the things are that cannot be measured in everyday life. Ask a married person what their wedding ring means to them, and the typical answers include relationship, loyalty, care, trust, love, partnership, togetherness, support, amongst others. Then ask them to rate these elements from 1 to 10, with 1 being bad and 10 being good. Some respond with 10, whilst others say 8, some 7, others 2 – because maybe on that specific morning they had an argument with their spouse; nevertheless, the majority of individuals would say that the question is strange, as it is difficult to measure love. This proves that one cannot measure these things, yet they are as important as things that can be measured in life.

Summarising it in the Measurement and Emotions Model

Clearly not all models are perfect, and many are open to interpretation and discussion, however in the following model (see *Figure 51. Measurement and Emotions Model*), we attempt to explain the various things that we measure in life.

This model reflects:

The lower circles represent the "lag indicators", "current indicators", and "lead indicators" that exist in companies around the world and are predominantly aligned with the I-It principle. Although lead indicators are mostly focused on measurement, some companies have developed lead indicators that require no measurement at all and that place people at the centre of the focus. The upper circle titled "other" represents the things that one cannot measure, but are as significant if not, at times, more significant than the lower circles, as mentioned in the paragraphs above. The upper circle is aligned to the I-Thou principle.

On the right side of the model, one sees that the lower three circles are predominantly in Chronos Time, whilst the upper circle is in Kairos Time.

The icon on the left with gears in the centre, reflects those indicators that are physical controls, things that can be measured. The middle icon with the head in the centre indicates the psychological influences and the upper icon with persons in the centre, indicates the culture influences, both of these being things that cannot be measured.

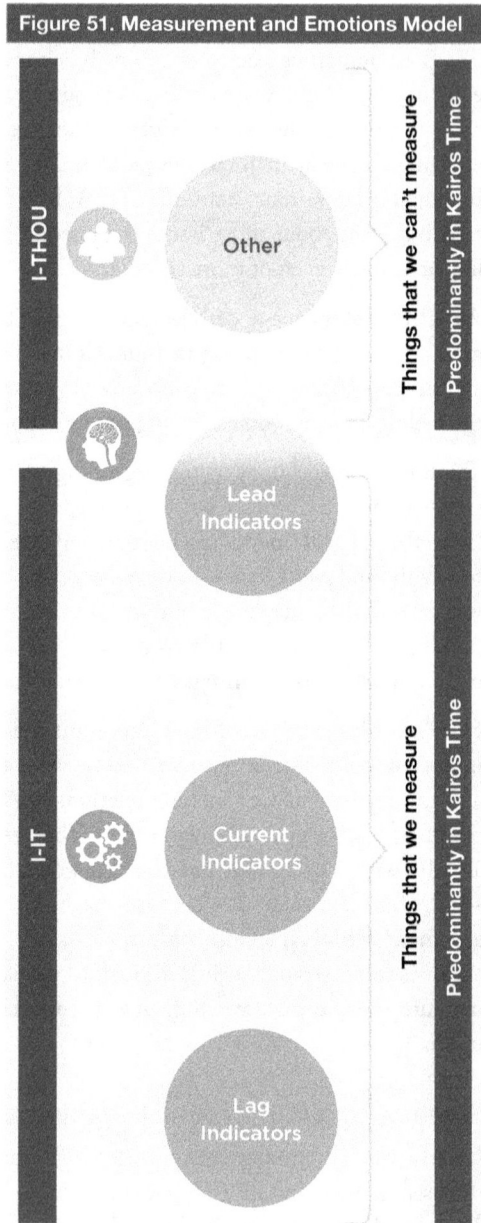

Figure 51. Measurement and Emotions Model

SELF-REFLECTION

Chapter 6 – Leadership in Being with Others

Our selection of elements for self-reflection from the chapter are as follows:

- Do I encourage teamwork and give credit where credit is due, or do I act in a way that is detrimental to others for my own personal gain?

- I see myself as being social with others, interacting with the individual and the group and thereby, contributing to the welfare of human beings as members of society.

- When engaging with others, do I often suspend my own agenda and power by letting others direct and control the discussion?

- At times, I treat things that cannot be measured as important, if not more important, than those that can be measured.

- Thinking about Jack Grealish and the visually impaired young girl at the football ceremony, do I give of myself in Kairos Time with others, thereby, focused on persons rather the objects? Am I seen as the *"Jack Grealish"* by my team?

- How much is time ("eight seconds") worth to me? Is it worth more than a good relationship in connection with another?

CHAPTER 7

Importance of Self-Reflection

"Your vision will become clear only when you can look into your own heart. Who looks outside, dreams, who looks inside, awakes".

Dr Carl Gustav Jung

Swiss Psychiatrist and Psychotherapist

When we were planning on writing this chapter on reflection, we asked several leaders from many walks of life whether they self-reflect on their actions, discussions, meetings, events and life in general, be it at work or in their private lives. We asked this question to amongst others, a chief executive officer, a hotel general manager, a university professor, two medical doctors, a nurse, several production plant managers, and a mechanical engineer. Only one of around fifteen persons, a teacher from Auckland, who we had asked mentioned that she often reflects on her day at work and the engagement with the children whom she teaches as well as the parents with whom she meets. Strangely enough the only other person who said, "yes, I often self-reflect" was a female taxi driver who was driving me to the airport in Canberra, Australia.

We also asked a family member of ours, Katia Guerreiro, a well-known Portuguese Fado singer, whether she practises self-reflection after her concerts. Without any hesitation, she said that she reflects after each performance as well as rehearsal. Katia mentioned that when returning to the dressing room after a concert, she reflects briefly on the performance, then when returning to her hotel room and at times at dinner on her own, she then spends more time in self-reflection. Her thoughts are focused on how she performed, the engagement she had with the audience, being in the moment and how she connected with her musicians. She said, she finds so much benefit in self-reflection, as it helps her ensure continuous improvement and in maintaining what works best in connecting with the audiences.

Many leaders, who we spoke to, were quick to answer that they are involved in reflection with their teams regularly. When asking what they reflect on, they mentioned things like considering the previous months, quarter, or year's performance in planning for the following period lying ahead. I know that in the company that I (Brian) work for, there are much needed meetings and working groups in various departments and disciplines, which is probably the same in most large organisations. As an example, our capital investment department, as well as safety and health teams will reflect on large construction and engineering projects to identify issues of concern, what went well, what could be improved, were there any surprises, both positive and negative, were the objectives met, the budget and timelines achieved and so on. This is all good as part of management, however, it is important for leaders to practise self-reflection.

Yes, we do understand that there are many who find relaxation in meditation or yoga, and a number of the leaders who we spoke to, mentioned that they find yoga and meditation useful in destressing, however these are not the same as self-reflection. We were wondering how many leaders actually practise self-reflection after a day's work or discussion with others. Caught up in the "rat race" and busyness at the office, the plant or wherever they find themselves, leaders tend to get stuck in the groove of managing the day, impacted by the swing of things and various duties and activities, often stuck in the I-It and at times moving to the I-Thou in discussion with others. However, these might not always be as "smooth sailing" as one wishes, or even believes. Therefore, self-reflection is an important element for any leader, and we hope this chapter gives some direction and understanding of how we see self-reflection.

Self-reflection allows one to reflect on what has happened during the day, after a discussion or any other event. It directs one in identifying and considering the positive experiences, what was not that good, and on ways of doing things differently in future.

During self-reflection, one can feel good about what has been done well, how dealing with others impacted or influenced them in a positive manner. This was definitely the case with the teacher in Auckland, who mentioned that she regularly practises self-reflection.

Self-reflection also allows one to think about those things that were not as positive or more challenging and then processing what was not the best and how to learn from them going forward. The additional advantage coming out of self-reflection is the ability to realise any positive or negative patterns in one's thinking, decision making and more importantly engagement with others. No leader is perfect, everyone has his or her own heuristics and biases and these impact one's focus, style of management, decision making, assumptions and worldview both in private and work life. As humans, we learn all the time and by learning we get better at what we do. Self-reflection is part of learning, part of becoming a better person, part of becoming a better leader in a social context. As humans, most actions and thoughts are of an unconscious manner, and when in the unconscious we do not recognise them. Practising self-reflection brings one out of oneself and brings the unconscious to the conscious.

Whilst conducting a proofread of this chapter, I (Brian) was sitting on a KLM plane flying between Amsterdam and Calgary and happened to have the flight map running on the monitor that was positioned right behind my laptop screen. As with most of my flights, I practise self-reflection of some sorts, however this time rather than reflecting on my day, I was reflecting on this chapter of the book. I happened to look at the monitor at the exact time that it reflected a compass showing the direction of our flight. This made me think that reflection is all about taking stock of our behaviours, the way we treat people, the difference we make to community, how we connect in Real Meeting; however, it is also about the metaphor "checking our compass", finding our bearings and realigning ourselves to our due north.

Our good friend Robert Long introduced us to the benefits of keeping a journal, thereby capturing thoughts, observations, discussions, events, and semiotics, amongst others. I found this a wonderful way of practising self-reflection, be it whilst writing or sketching my thoughts in the journal or when reading my notes at a later stage. When Rob suggested the use of a journal, I could not imagine the benefit it would have on me. It was not long before Aneta followed suit as part of her studies with Rob and during her research and work towards her PhD.

A colleague of mine working in South Africa often uses the analogy of the "Boiling Frog", meaning that when you place a frog into cold water and slowly turn up the heat, the frog does not realise that the water is getting hotter and hotter. The same applies to leaders: if there is no reflection on our actions, our behaviours, our inner self, we too become like the boiling frog, we do not realise that our ways, our biases and the way we connect with people might not be as effective and caring as we think.

Herewith some of our tips on practising self-reflection:

Keep a Personal Journal

As we did with Rob, we suggest that you start a journal and make it a living document, thereby updating it regularly as well as referring to what you have captured in words and sketches. Use the journal to, amongst other things, capture the positives, the mistakes, the failures, the ideas, your feelings about various circumstances, the way you treated others, the way others treated you, did you enter the hyphen in the I-Thou, did you find opportunities to be in Kairos Time or were you stuck in Chronos Time. Do this whilst being honest with yourself, capture the elements that matter and capture in text and sketches in a way and in detail, so that you can return to the reflection at a later stage and still have a good idea of what occurred, what your feelings and emotions were and what decisions came out of the initial reflection.

Note your embodied feelings, what you thought of at the time, what your gut feelings were and how it impacted your inner feelings and emotions. The embodied feeling encompasses all feelings, head, heart, and gut as well as the influences on your senses. Capture the emotions of the meeting, the decisions, the engagement that influenced your thoughts whilst writing or sketching in the journal.

Use the reflection to consider what you need to change, improve on, keep doing or stop doing. Through this, one ensures continuous improvement in his or her leadership style.

Find the Time and Suitable Space and Place

We both believe that there is no right or wrong place for reflection, it should however be in a space and place where one can relax, feel safe and be in the moment, a moment of thought, a moment of self-reflection. I (Brian) find the best place for me to self-reflect, is on a plane traveling between destinations for work or privately. I find that in most instances, especially on intercontinental flights, many passengers are quiet, in their own world, either watching a movie, reading, talking softly or sleeping. This gives me some quiet time to reflect on work related issues, discussions held with others, and inner feelings as well as life in general. Aneta finds her reflection time in walking through a park, or sitting next to a lake or sea, or even better sitting close to a waterfall and whilst reflecting, listening to the sound of the water falling and gushing over the rocks below.

Everyone is different, and therefore, leaders need to find that place where it makes it possible to break away, be alone for a while and practise the art of reflection. It could be in one's office (although not my preference due to interruptions), walking back from the production area to one's office, driving home at the end of the day, going for a run, sitting around a fireplace. Reflection for us is simply taking a couple of minutes after a meeting or discussion to reflect on what happened, how decisions were handled, were discussions open and transparent, were one's body language and gestures suitable, was there trust in the discussions, were people treated with respect and dignity and were they given the opportunity to tell their stories? Most importantly, was there a good balance between the I-It and the I-Thou during the meeting?

Make Reflection a Routine

Using the metaphors like amongst others, "time is running", "not enough hours in the day" or "I did not even have time to think", "I am running out of time" is so common in today's world, everything seems to be at full speed for many persons, including us as leaders. No wonder, we hear of cases of burnout, mental wellbeing challenges and stress related issues. Therefore, as mentioned above, leaders need to find the time for self-reflection on how they are dealing with circumstances, dialogue, engagement and building positive relationships with others.

For me, the best way is to make it a habit, and as mentioned, that is sitting on a plane gathering my thoughts, whilst not been interrupted by a telephone call, messages or someone popping in for a discussion. There is also no computer screen in front of me showing new emails arriving, and importantly no digital clock fixating me in realms of Chronos Time. Making it a routine in some degree and in whichever way suits the individual contributes to reflection becoming a regular event.

Structure Self-Reflection Time

When researching and reading on reflection some years ago, I (Brian) came across a couple of models that have assisted me in practising self-reflection, giving me a structured approach and guiding me in regular reflection. The models that I am referring to include the "Gibbs' Reflective Cycle" created by Graham Gibbs in 1988, and "The Integrated Reflective Cycle" created by Barbara Bassot in 2013, which I recommend to leaders to follow, especially when starting to practise self-reflection. In time it becomes a habit, with little or no need to think consciously about the elements of the model.

The reflection model below is slightly altered to fit our theme of Real Meeting, however, is mainly based on the "Gibbs' Reflection Cycle" as well as Bassot's "Integrated Reflective Cycle".

Step 1 – Find the Time and Place

How long is a piece of string? Reflection can at times be short or long, depending on the situation and the engagement outcomes, however, as it is important to find sufficient time and a suitable place to be able to have a value adding reflection and to ensure this, consider the following:

- Is the space and place suitable for reflection?

- Is there sufficient time for reflection?

- Do I have material to jot down or record my reflection?

As mentioned, I in most instances, practise my reflections when I am on a plane, whilst running through things in my mind without jotting anything down. Then, at times, I capture my reflections in a journal, so that I can refer to the thoughts at a later stage if needed. There is definitely no right or wrong way of conducting self-reflection, it is important that it suits and works for the individual. I know some people who carry a pocket booklet with them and capture their reflection after having a discussion with someone or a team of people, and after leaving their work area. Others like to practise reflection in silence with no need for keeping a journal or notes.

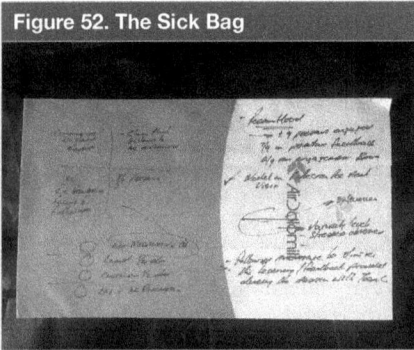

Figure 52. The Sick Bag

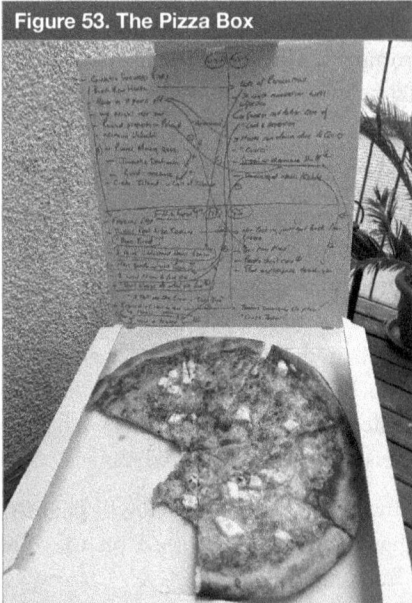

Figure 53. The Pizza Box

I recall once, being on a flight practising reflection and wanting to capture some of my thoughts immediately, as not to forget them, and as I wanted to transfer them to my journal once I returned home. I was sitting at the window seat, the person sitting in the middle seat was reading and the passenger in the aisle seat was fast asleep. My note pad was in my bag in the overhead storage and as I did not want to wake my fellow passengers, I pulled out the "sick bag" from the seat pocket in front of me on which I could capture my thoughts. The funny part was that the person sitting next to me seemed slightly nervous when seeing me take out the "sick bag". He seemed more relaxed when he noticed me pull out a pen from my jacket pocket and start making some notes on the bag.

One Saturday afternoon sitting on the patio in Crete, Aneta and I were debating and reflecting on an issue whilst enjoying our take-away pizzas. As we wanted to capture our thoughts using the iCue listening process, we grabbed a board marker and captured our thoughts on the pizza box. To record what we had discussed, we took a photo of the pizza box for future reference. *Figure 52.* shows my reflections on *The Sick Bag* and *Figure 53.* reflects our notes on *The Pizza Box.*

Step 2 – Reflection on Creating the Contact

In this element, one can reflect on how the engagement panned out and could include reflection on:

- How did I approach the person(s)?
- Who was present prior to my arrival and during the engagement?
- What was the reaction of those involved?
- How did I introduce the engagement?

It is important to make others feel comfortable when approaching them and wanting to have a talk. Simply walking up to someone or a team of employees and without introducing oneself, greeting with respect and introducing the reasons for the engagement, the chance of having an open discussion is lost. A positive "icebreaker" is always a good starting point and places people at ease.

During reflection after the session, there is benefit in improving one's own behaviour by considering how the contact went and focusing on the above four issues. Nobody is perfect and, at times, we forget some of the key aspects of good engagement. Through reflecting, we bring things from the unconscious to the conscious and that assists in improving our style and future opportunities when interacting with others and entering into discussions.

Reflecting on the body language observed when approaching others provides a good indication on how they experienced the interaction, be it positive, negative, relaxed, bothered, irritated or under stress. Consider who was present, did the discussion involve all participants, and were some excluded from the conversation, both voluntarily or only by chance. In reflection, consider who left when noticing you arrive, this is always a good indication of how one is perceived by the team.

Step 3 – Reflection Related to the I-Thou

As a lot of our focus is based on the writings of Martin Buber, we included the I-Thou in our steps of self-reflection, which includes consideration of the following:

- Was the connection found (I-Thou)?

- Did I suspend my power?

- Did I suspend my agenda?

- Did I allow the other person to tell their story?

- Did I listen for metaphors?

- Did I listen and react on confessions (gifts)?

To ensure understanding of what is meant by the last two bullet points above, regarding metaphors and confessions or also referred to as gifts, herewith explanations.

A metaphor is a figure of speech that describes an object or action in a way that is not literally true, but helps to explain an idea or makes a comparison. At their most basic, metaphors are used to make a direct comparison between two different things, in order to ascribe a particular quality to the first. We all speak in metaphors; however, leaders often miss the metaphor in discussions, engagements and whilst Meeting others. Metaphors are mostly spoken in the unconscious mind; we do not think of saying things in the form of a metaphor. By picking up on a metaphor shows that the leaders are listening and by following through on a metaphor, often changes the flow of the discussions bringing up or surfacing issues that were not known or come as a surprise.

In training we both often use the scenario of a leader leaving the factory on a Friday afternoon at 4:15 p.m., and on his way to the main gate, he notices a crane operator (Bill) lifting a large water tank to be fitted on the roof of the production building. The load is not secured properly, and the slings used are not of the correct design for such a heavy load. Now, let us imagine the two different scenarios of the discussions.

Discussion 1 – The Traditional Style

Leader – "Hey, Bill, your load is not secured correctly, and your lifting slings are the wrong ones as they are not suitable for the weight of the object being lifted".

Bill – "Hey boss, it is 4:15 p.m., and as you know it's Friday afternoon, I was planning to leave and go home in fifteen minutes, it's *'been a long week'* and *'I am dead tired'*, the load is fine, let me just finish the task quickly, all will be ok with the lift, I promise".

Leader – "No, first secure the load, use the correct slings, and then lift it into position. Once the task is complete then you can go home, I will make sure that we pay you overtime for staying longer".

Discussion 2 - Listening to the metaphors and confessions (gifts)

Leader – "Hi Bill, how are you, do you have a minute for a short chat"?

Leader – "I noticed that your load is not secured correctly, and your lifting slings are the wrong ones as they are not suitable for the weight of the load being lifted".

Bill – "Hey boss, it is 4:15 p.m., and as you know it's Friday afternoon, I was planning to leave and go home in fifteen minutes, it's *'been a long week'* and *'I am dead tired'*, the load is fine, let me just finish the task quickly, all will be ok with the lift, I promise".

Leader – "Can you tell me more about what you mean by it has *'been a long week'* and being *'dead tired'*"?

Bill – "I have been working for sixteen hours a day since Monday as we are short of enough crane operators (confession or gift) and as you know, we have a lot of maintenance work to complete, and I have been helping various teams with numerous tasks".

Leader – "Ok thanks, I understand, please stop the work and we will ask our crane supervisor, Warren, to arrange for a second crane operator (Joe) to secure and lift the load safely into place. I will also ask Warren to arrange additional crane operators to support you next week in the number of tasks being planned. Thanks for your dedication, however, in the meantime, you can go home, and I hope you have a great weekend and get some well-deserved rest. Many thanks for your efforts, and we will see you on Monday".

Let us now reflect briefly on the engagement between the leader and Bill.

In the first scenario, the leader missed the two metaphors, it has been a "long week" and "I am dead tired", and therefore, the discussion went straight back to the object and controls of lifting the load. There was no consideration for the operator's well-being or his mental and physical tiredness. In this scenario, yes, the load would be lifted and hopefully without any incident, however the operator would be frustrated and being aware that the leader did not care or consider what he had to say. In this instance trust and respect is often lost by the operator and negatively influences company culture as well as sub-cultures.

In the second scenario, the leader picked up on the two metaphors, "long week" and "I am dead tired" and asked the operator to tell him more about the two metaphors used. In this instance the operator mentioned the long hours that he had been working, resulting in him feeling tired and fatigued. The discussion then moved from focusing on the objects, being the load and the slings, to focusing on the personhood and well-being of the operator. Yes, the load would still be lifted into place, probably safer without incident, however, by another operator, who had just come onto shift and was well-rested. In this case, the leader showed that he was listening to the comments made by Bill, showed understanding and empathy and then allowed him to leave the site and return home for a much-needed rest. The leader also picked up on the issue that there were insufficient crane operators for the number of tasks to be conducted which obviously contributed to the long working hours of Bill. The Meeting here was totally different to that in the first scenario, and through engaging and showing care, probably building trust between the two persons.

Right now, you might think to yourself "who's got time for all that?" To some degree, you are right. The problem is that if as a leader, you will not "find the time" – you will face only a temporary solution. The "non-listening" approach is usually only a short-term fix. If you want to build something with a future, start incorporating attentive listening into your daily routine.

A couple of years ago, my boss asked me (Aneta) to write an academic article, because as I heard from the Dean, my other colleagues, "did not have the time to write something on their own and the university needed points for publications". Due to circumstances, I politely declined saying that I had already submitted my article months earlier, and I was at the time on vacation in New Zealand, and I informed her that I was getting married (mind you, it was the first time when I had ever said anything about my personal life to my boss). The response that I heard was, "yeah, but you are probably getting married on Saturday, so you still have the whole Sunday to write the article. I expect twenty pages by Monday, or else". At that time, it was two days prior to my wedding and finding out what "or else" meant was not at the top of my priority list. Therefore, when Sunday afternoon came along, a day after our wedding, as the promise on the day earlier went "for better or for worse" together with Brian, we sat down and wrote an academic article about Social Psychology of Risk. After a whole night of writing, my boss had the material on her desk by 8:00 a.m. on the Monday morning. So, my colleagues' lack of working ethic was covered, and the university got their points, The result, for the short term everything was "fixed". Long term…I resigned as soon as I could, even though I loved teaching there, I liked my students, and I enjoyed the learning that we shared. Today, almost two years later, even hearing the name of this university sends shivers down my spine. Amazing how the style of a leader can change the course of one's life.

Now, what is meant by confessions or gifts? These are comments made that were not asked for during the discussion or engagement. Similar to the scenarios of the discussion above where Bill mentioned that there were not enough crane operators on site. Confessions (gifts) are as important as listening for metaphors and it is critical to follow through or chase such comments during the discussions. By doing so, once again the leader is showing that he or she is listening with intent to the person(s) that he or she is engaging with. By listening to the confessions or gifts, and following through on them, often the discussion goes in a slightly different direction and as a result with different outcomes.

As an example, a leader is talking to one of the colleagues about a work-related topic and the discussion develops as follows:

Leader – "Hi Sandra, could you tell me what your thoughts are on the outcome of the price negotiations for the frame agreement with the potential suppliers of inks and chemicals for the printers at all our sites around the globe"?

Sandra – "Yes, all went well, we received offers from six companies. However, one of them is quoting fantastic prices. I compared them to other suppliers who submitted offers as well as our current supplier and their prices are much lower".

Leader – "Fantastic, we should set up a follow up meeting to negotiate the service agreement with the company having the lowest price offer".

Sandra – "No problem, I will do so, I know they will not be available for meetings in the next two weeks due to some court case, however, will push for a meeting thereafter".

Leader – "Can you tell me a bit more about the court case that you mentioned"?

Sandra – "I heard from a friend of mine that they have been investigated for child labour in one of the countries where they produce the chemicals".

Leader – "This changes the perspective, therefore let's look at the offers from the other suppliers and exclude this company from the list".

And now let us reflect on the engagement between the leader and Sandra.

The leader picked up on the confession (gift) where Sandra mentioned the court case. This was something he did not ask or expect to hear about. However, when following through on the comment, it surfaced that the company providing the best offer has been charged with employing underaged children to work in their chemical and ink processing plants.

By following through on the confession, the leader immediately excluded them from the negotiations or making use of the company. This would probably prevent any reputational issues going forward and ensured that the company adheres to the ethics and human rights issues aligned to legislation and best practise.

Step 4 – Reflection on the Engagement (Experience)

In this step, consider what your experience was during the engagement with the other person(s), as this will assist in self-coaching and improving future engagements. To do so, consider the following:

- How comfortable did I feel during the engagement?

- How comfortable do I think the other person(s) felt during the engagement?

- Was I respectful during the engagement?

- What is my impression on how others felt during the engagement?

- What is my impression on how people will feel after the engagement ended?

Talking to persons who leaders know and work with makes the starting of the conversation better, however, at times when approaching persons who are not well-known or total strangers, is at times, more difficult as there is the unknown of how the person(s) will react. Therefore, it is important to think of how you will approach others and how you will start the engagement. If one feels uncomfortable when making the contact, the rest of the discussion might be difficult or uneasy. Approaching whilst looking friendly and relaxed is already an icebreaker in itself without having to say a word. Making the other person feel comfortable is important, and showing respect throughout the discussions, be it positive or on a negative basis, is of utmost importance. Once respect is lost, everything thereafter is lost as well.

When reflecting on the discussion, consider what your impression is, of how the persons felt when ending the engagement and leaving the area or workplace. This is always only an impression as one cannot know exactly what they feel, however, gut feel can give some indication.

Step 5 – Action

During Step 5, one plans on how to learn from the experiences and to take things forward, to do things differently in the future, to become a better leader, to show interest in others and their stories and placing people at the centre of things that we do.

There is not always the need for additional actions, however reflection lends itself to ensuring continuous learning and getting better at moving oneself into the hyphen of the I and Thou. The more we consciously think of moving at times out of the I-It and into the I-Thou, the better leaders we become. By talking and engaging with people in a manner that gives them the opportunity to tell their story, giving others the platform to share their experience, ideas and even concerns, builds trust, and contributes to an improved company culture as well as sub-cultures.

Yes, there will be times that we forget some of the key aspects, and therefore, learning through reflection adds value in many ways. Reflection supports one, in considering how engagements were handled and what can be done in future to improve and become even better leaders.

As mentioned, it is not necessary to jot down the reflections, some people prefer to just think about things and learn from their thought process, some like to keep notes and others like me, prefer a balance between both options.

When thinking about the actions, consider what can be done differently, how can we remind ourselves of the fundamentals prior to making contact or engaging.

The Reflection Cycle Model

The Reflection Cycle Model depicts the steps needed to continuously work at getting better at engaging with others as a leader. Nobody is perfect, we can always improve, we make mistakes, we forget key issues at times that contribute to fruitful engagement sessions and in discussion with others. Finding the suitable space and place is important, and then creating the contact with the person(s), moving out of the I-It and into the I-Thou. Then later reflecting on the experience and taking action to improve, is a key element to becoming a caring and inspiring leader. *Figure 54.* reflects (excuse

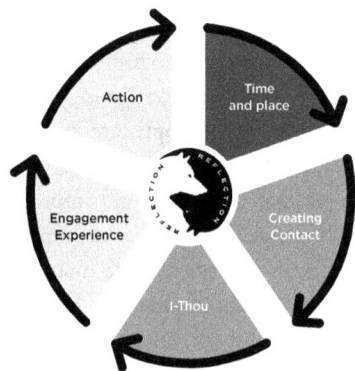

Figure 54. Reflection Cycle Model

the pun), the *Reflection Cycle Model*, highlighting the Five Key Points for reflection. Obviously, our model includes the two wolves in the centre, reminding us to look at the positives and the negatives during self-reflection.

Reflection in Understanding our Ontology

Whilst attending two modules on Social Psychology in Canberra, the participants were required to capture what their ontology is and what they stand for, as well as what their "world view" is. This too for us was a great session of reflection. Since Robert Long always says that learning happens when there is an e-motion, we were asked to draw our ontologies on a yoga mat. We must admit that capturing our thoughts on a yoga mat after having a session of meditation was a unique way of reflecting and capturing one's thoughts. *Figure 55.* shows *Our Reflections.* Two opposite ends of the spectrum, first, meditation and then reflection. Meditation being the practise in which an individual uses a technique – such as mindfulness, or focusing the mind on a particular object, thought, or activity – to train attention and awareness, and achieve a mentally clear, emotionally calm and stable state. Then followed by reflection, consciously thinking, and then putting your thoughts together.

It is useful for leaders to understand their own style as it reveals their actual nature of being a leader. It opens up and reveals the source of one's actions when exercising leadership.

Being a Reflective Leader

Figure 55. Our Reflections

Practising leadership through reflection is about "finding time" as a leader, finding the space and the time to look into the mirror and reflect on one's own actions, leadership style, language used (both spoken and unspoken) and the way people are treated and respected. It supports reflecting on one's own strengths and improvement opportunities. Good and honest self-reflection assists leaders in improving their leadership style and the way others perceive them as a leader. Reflection is focused on how engagements with others were conducted, to consider whether they were just meeting or were based on the concept of Real Meeting.

I like the analogy of reflection being the rhythm, movement, and steps of a dance, bringing all aspects together in an embodied experience. The dance requires flexibility, energy, passion, and to be successful the dancers have to move as one and feel the rhythm of the music. This is the same in business, on some days our style as leaders runs smoothly as practised, as imagined, however on other days all might not have gone as planned, we could have forgotten some key aspects of our approach to dealing and engaging with others, we might have used someone for our own benefit, not acknowledged someone walking past us in the hallway or passage of the office, we might not have listened with intent and we might have spent the majority of our day stuck in the I-It and failed to enter the I-Thou. Just like persons enjoying a dance together, be it the Tango, Foxtrot, the Austrian Waltz, or any other dance, we as leaders are in the rhythm, however not forgetting that we are fallible, we will make mistakes, but through reflection and practise we can improve, sharpen our skills as leaders, and in doing so, improve on our leadership dance.

As mentioned earlier in this book, self-reflection as a leader is a key aspect in leadership. No matter in which industry one finds oneself in, self-reflection is key to identifying where one is in conflict with certain principles, ethics and morals.

SELF-REFLECTION

Chapter 7 – Importance of Self-Reflection

Our selection of elements for self-reflection from the chapter are as follows:

- Do I find the time for reflection on the way I have handled a situation?

- I find the right place to reflect on my leadership style without interruptions or disturbances.

- As a leader, do I reflect regularly on how I have treated others?

- When reflecting on a contact, do I practise the following:

  - Did I find the connection (I-Thou)?

  - Did I suspend my authority?

  - Did I suspend my agenda?

  - Did I allow the other person to tell their story?

  - Did I listen for metaphors?

  - Did I listen and react on confessions (gifts)?

- How does my "dance" look like, am I in rhythm and in step with accepted morals, ethics and principles whilst engaging and in relationship with others?

CHAPTER 8

Shock and Trauma, the Total Opposite of Meeting, a Dehumanising Approach

"If there is a God, he will have to beg me for my forgiveness".

Unknown
Etched into the prison walls of the Mauthausen Concentration Camp

Mauthausen Concentration Camp

Never a nice place to visit, however since moving to Austria in 2005, I have visited the camp around six times taking family and friends to see the camp and experience the sadness, coldness and understand the brutality of the guards of the time that the place existed as a concentration camp. Mauthausen was built in 1938, and is located on the top of a hill in the town of Mauthausen in Upper Austria. It was one of the main Nazi camps and housed around 85 000 prisoners from 8 August 1938, after Austria was annexed by Germany, until it was liberated by the American soldiers on 5 May 1945.

History shows that the Mauthausen concentration camp was one of the most brutal and severe of the Nazi concentration camps, with prisoners suffering from malnutrition, constant abuse and beatings and forced to perform exceptionally difficult tasks like carrying stone blocks up the "stairs of death" (Todesstiege) from the quarry to the camp. Bear in mind that the average weight of the prisoners was less than fifty kilograms. The SS recruited female prisoners from the Ravensbrück concentration camp, who were sent to the Mauthausen camp and forced to be sex workers. This is a typical example of being in the I-It by experiencing another of one's own benefit.

When visiting the camp for the first time, I found walking up the stairs requiring effort and energy sapping, and this without any load on my back. I recall my thoughts moving to the prisoners being whipped and beaten by the guards whilst ascending those difficult stairs.

Every action taken by the Nazi officers and guards was designed to dehumanise the prisoners and with the aim of destroying any social contract between people. The SS Captain Albert Sauer was in charge of the camp and remained in that role until middle February 1939. He was succeeded by Franz Ziereis from 1939, until the camp's liberation in 1945. Franz Ziereis was shot and interrogated after the liberation of the camp, and he said around 65 000 prisoners were murdered in the camp.

On arrival to the camp, prisoners were forced to stand naked outside in the freezing cold conditions, sprayed with water and then some left to die of the cold. Others were sent to the gas chambers, many shot, many beaten to death and some even thrown against the electrical fencing and dying due to electrocution. The prisoners were forced to carry out physical work under horrific conditions that sadly caused many deaths.

I recall during my first trip to the camp shortly after moving to Austria, we were walking through the prison cell block within the camp and on one of the walls, one of the prisoners had expressed his or her feelings by scratching words into the plaster of a wall in the cell. The words engraved into the walls were, "if there is a God, he will have to beg me for my forgiveness". Already feeling depressed and saddened when walking through the camp and prior to entering this specific cell, these words sent shivers down my spine, brought tears to my eyes as I tried to fathom how this person must have felt, and how desperate he or she must have been at the time.

I recently visited the camp as a semiotic walk with Aneta and Rob Long, and with other colleagues from various companies. Halfway through the visit, I remembered the feeling I had when reading the words eighteen years before, I decided to go sit at the prison cell, alone, in my own thoughts, and reflect on what the Mauthausen camp symbolised, not only to me, but more importantly to all those prisoners who entered through the large wooden gates of the camp, (which I call "the gates of despair") and surely noticing the Nazi Eagle holding the swastika symbol, on the arch above their heads as they passed through and into the dreaded courtyard. I recall seeing a photograph of the prisoners pulling the eagle down after the camp was liberated, therefore, a clear indication how they despised the artifact and its meaning.

During my reflection whilst sitting in the camp prison, I composed a poem depicting my emotions, feelings, my embodied feelings and the sadness in my heart, and later sitting outside of the camp, I sketches the "gates of despair" on a page in my journal. The poem goes as follows:

The Gates of Despair

Walking through the rooms of the Mauthausen Camp,
An eery feeling, so dark and so damp.
So much pain and suffering, is fact and for sure,
Many emotional scars, for which there is no cure.
From Race to religion, ethnic group, and all,
They left this Earth, but not at God's call.
Love, hope and faith, etched on the walls, we see,
A reminder for all, also you and me.
This should never happen, ever again,
Such brutality and hate, is just so insane.
Entering the camp gates, not knowing what's ahead,
Your fears must have been strong, it surely must be said.
Being separated from your family for so many years,
Brought sadness and sorrow, and so many tears.
Not knowing where they were or if even alive,
Your emotions a mess and bringing on much strife.
All those who entered this horrible place,
For many their lives taken, without any trace.
The others that left, it was for sure a different life,
Losing sons, daughters, also husband and wife.
Those that were able to leave these places of shame,
We understand your suffering, is difficult to explain.
For those who passed, may you rest in peace, we say,
For your souls and your loved ones, we can only pray.

The prisoners of the camp were stripped of their dignity, labelled by tattooed numbers and symbols, stripped of their personal belongings. Every attempt was made by the guards and the officers, their so called "leaders", to ensure prisoners would be deprived of their socialisation and to dehumanise each and every person sent to the camp. This started by stripping them down of their clothing on arrival at the camp, shaving their hair and shouting abuse and screaming at them. One cannot even imagine what these prisoners must have been thinking, being separated from their loved ones, the uncertainty and fear of what was happening to them.

On arrival the prisoners were issued with blue and white striped prison pants, jacket and cap, no matter if they fitted well, whether used, or having the incorrect symbols sewn onto them. These actions were all part of dehumanising the prisoners. On the other hand, the prison officers and guards wore smart German uniforms, well ironed, and fitted with all kinds of symbols and insignia. See *Figure 56. A Prisoner's Cap.*

The so called "leadership" of the camp would have regular meetings on how to destroy the social contract between people, how they could be more brutal with the prisoners, agreeing on techniques to do so and agreeing on actions that could increase the number of persons killed and at a faster pace.

All this fixed in the I-It, treating people with disrespect, not seeing them in a human context, using them for experiments, which included removing of internal organs to see how long the patients would survive. They also experimented with chemicals, and injecting phenol directly into their hearts.

For us what is so difficult to understand is that the same SS officers and guards that brutalised prisoners during the day, would return to their families in the evening and be the total opposite, to how they were behaving when inside the camp, carrying out their duties and the atrocities that they imposed. They definitely moved out of the I-It, where they treated humans as objects, and into the I-Thou, spending time with their families, having dinner and wine and simply engaging. Probably spending time in Real Meeting, focused on people, their emotions and listening to their stories. A total contradiction between their two lives that they were living. I sometimes wonder, if any of those camp guards as well as officers reflected on their dehumanising behaviour, the treatment of other human beings, and the brutality of the camps. I am sure, if they did years later, their reflections as well as dreams and nightmares, must have haunted them. I wonder what the words of their own poems would have looked like, if they had reflected on their behaviours, the way they dehumanised persons during their times in the camp.

All their actions contradicted all the elements of being social; creating group think with the guards being the in-group and prisoners the out-group, treating others as objects, using others for their own benefit, labelling people with symbols and tattoos, stripping them of their dignity, forcing them to be naked amongst others, enforcing solitary confinement, anti-caring and the list goes on and on, with all of it denying the humanity of the prisoners.

Figure 57. Memorial Wall shows one of the many memorial walls filled with plaques around the camp. In *Figure 58.* one sees a section of the *"Stairs of Death"* and in *Figure 59. The Passage* in the prison cells leading to the cell where I once read those profound words deeply engraved into one of the walls; "if there is a God, he will have to beg me for my forgiveness".

Figure 56. A Prisoner's Cap

Figure 57. Memorial Wall

Figure 58. "Stairs of Death"

Figure 59. The Passage

SELF-REFLECTION

Chapter 8 – Shock and Trauma, the Total Opposite of Meeting, a Dehumanising Approach

We considered and debated on what self-reflections we should include into this chapter. Having visited the Mauthausen concentration camp on several occasions as well as other concentration, labour, and death camps over the years, including Auschwitz, we both felt that words cannot explain the emotions felt during each of these visits, and self -reflection is so personal on these atrocities.

My self-reflection of the Mauthausen concentration camp was sitting in the prison cell in the camp writing the poem in reflection of my feelings and later on in the day, sitting on the grass outside the camp making some sketches, including the one of the gates to the camp, what I thought of as the "Gates of Despair".

Finally, we decided that we could not find the words to prompt any type of self-reflection of this chapter and of what sadly happened in the Mauthausen concentration camp between 1938 and 1945. We, therefore, decided to leave it up to you, the Reader, to decide on any reflection that comes to mind.

We have left the open space below for your self-reflection:

CHAPTER 9

Leaders who Understand Real Meeting

"What counts in life is not the mere fact that we have lived. It is what difference we have made to the lives of others that will determine the significance of the life we lead".

Nelson Rolihlahla Mandela
Former President of South Africa

Nelson Rolihlahla Mandela (Prisoner 46664)

When finalising my second book titled, "Humanising Leadership in Risk", I was sitting on a plane flying between Vienna and Lisbon, deep in my thoughts, and I challenged myself to name someone, who I believed was an inspiring leader, one who met many of the qualities mentioned throughout the chapters of this book, a leader who helped others, cared for humanity and truly understood the meaning of Real Meeting. I thought of a number of people, who I had been privileged of knowing in my life, personally or through the media.

My immediate thoughts went to my parents Raymond and Margaret, my good friend and mentor Bob Hunt, with whom I worked for many years in various roles in South Africa, and others who had inspired me over the years. However, one person stood out amongst them all and that is the late Nelson Mandela. He was a man who inspired many, brought a nation together, treated everyone as equal and with respect, had time for everyone, helped and cared for humanity. Whilst writing my previous book, I often related to words of Mandela. His writings and various quotes kept inspiring me. So when writing this book, Aneta and I had many discussions about Mandela as a leader and as we were writing about Leadership it would be a no-brainer not to have a chapter on this wonderful man, this inspiring former President who played such an active and important role in South Africa, and in the world, a Leader that had time stolen from him, twenty-seven years in prison, time that could have been used in shaping a better South Africa, a better world.

In August 1962, Mandela was arrested and imprisoned in Johannesburg and then at the maximum-security prison in Pretoria, South Africa. In 1964, Mandela was transferred from Pretoria to Robben Island prison, just off the shores of Cape Town, overlooking the well-known Table Mountain. He would spend the next eighteen years on the island in his damp prison cell of a mere five square metres. During his time, he was verbally and physically harassed by some of the prison wardens. Many of these wardens were stuck in the I-It and probably never moving into the I-Thou, and definitely not putting much emphasis into creating any Real Meeting. However, Mandela did create a unique bond with one of his prison wardens and apparently as a result they shared stories, spent many hours together and partook in Real Meeting, much of it in the I-Thou.

Mandela was released from Victor Verster Prison on 11th of February 1990, and later elected as President of South Africa on 10th of May 1994. The apartheid regime had come to an end and South Africa had entered a new era. It was just over a year prior to the Rugby World Cup which was due to be held in South Africa, an event that would once again reflect the leadership style of Mandela. A style of a Leader who understood the dynamics of persons, cultures, sub-cultures and even the significance of signs and symbols, as well as the importance of them, in uniting a nation.

The Rugby World Cup

In 1995, the South African National Rugby Team, known as the Springboks, were allowed, for the first time due to political reasons, after being expelled for years, to take part in the Rugby World Cup and compete for the coveted William Webb-Ellis Trophy. They were never expected to reach the final, never mind beating one of their arch-rivals Australia in the opening game in Cape Town. It was during the lead up to and during the tournament that many of Mandela's strengths as a Leader surfaced and became known. These are well-documented in the famous film titled "Invictus", directed by the well-known Clint Eastwood. The film tells the story of how President Mandela and the Springbok Captain, Francois Pienaar joined forces to help unite South Africa, erase the scars of the past and overcome racial division as well as preventing possible civil war.

As former President Mandela stands out for us as a true Leader, probably one of the best in modern history, we used the film "Invictus" as our inspiration in writing what follows, which is based on Mandela's Leadership.

Mandela attended a test match at the Ellis Park stadium in Johannesburg in 1994, which was played between the Springboks and England. Unfortunately, England beat South Africa. Whilst attending this match against England leading up to the World Cup, Mandela walked out onto the pitch and there was a mixture of cheers and jeers, people booing from all around the stadium, old South African National Flags were being waved in the crowd. Despite the commotion, Mandela stepped off the pitch, into the crowd and addressed people in the stand. He thanked one of the supporters who was flying the new South African national flag. Although he had focused on the object, he had entered the I-Thou with the supporters.

It was during this match that Mandela was informed by one of his ministers that if the Springboks lost, it could be a good opportunity to get rid of the beloved Springbok emblem and that the game could be the last time they would see the South African team, playing in the famous green and gold colours. It seems like these words brought "food to thought" and Mandela came to realise the importance of using the game of rugby to build and unite the nation, a nation that was so divided, a nation that needed healing, a nation that under his leadership, his Presidency would become known worldwide as the Rainbow Nation.

During the game, Mandela turned to his assistant and mentioned that, amazingly, in the stands on the day, all the white supporters were cheering for the Springboks and all the black supporters were cheering for England. He also said that it was exactly what they did on Robben Island, the prisoners would cheer for any other team, but never the Springboks. Apparently, this would make the prison wardens very angry. We guess that was the prisoners' way of using the I-Thou in a manner of protesting against being imprisoned, a protest against white domination, a protest against oppression of others.

Sometime after the game, members of the African National Congress (ANC) met and as part of the agenda of the day was to take a vote to eliminate the colours (green and gold), the Springbok emblem and the name "Springboks" immediately. The rugby team would be known in future as the Proteas. The majority of the votes by show of hand was to eliminate the three elements related to the National Rugby Team.

Mandela came to hear about the decision taken, and immediately had his driver and escorts take him to the venue where the members had met. He walked in on the meeting whilst they were singing the National Anthem, "Nkosi Sikelel' iAfrika", which was duly stopped by the chairperson of the committee when noticing Mandela walking into the room. Mandela, in his ever calm and distinctive voice, addressed the participants.

He said that he had heard of the decision made by the members with insufficient information and insights, and he then called for the colours, the Springbok emblem, and the name "Springboks" to be reinstated immediately. He told them how he had come to know the Afrikaners during his twenty-seven years in prison, as he had to get to know his enemy at the time. He then said that the Afrikaners were no longer the enemy, they were now their partners, and that they treasure Springbok Rugby. Mandela then made it clear that if the committee went ahead and took the colours, emblem, and name away, the partnership would be lost, and that the whites would fear the worst. The fear of what they thought would happen when releasing Mandela from prison and relinquishing power. Mandela made it clear that they had to be better than the oppressors, they had to show compassion and generosity. He added that there was no time for revenge, and that it was time to build the nation using every single brick available, even if that brick comes wrapped in green and gold (fantastic metaphor). Whilst driving back to the office, Mandela's assistant asked him if rugby was being used as a political calculation, to which Mandela responded, "it is a human calculation".

The human element is something that leaders often forget about, when they are mostly stuck in the I-It and not moving into the I-Thou, focusing on the human element as mentioned by Mandela.

Mandela invited Pienaar to his office at the Union Buildings in Pretoria, and one of the first questions after welcoming him, asked Pienaar how his ankle was feeling; this showed care and interest in his injury, his recovery and how he was feeling, and the film depicts the surprise on Pienaar's face when being asked the question. (A huge difference to the lack of care reflected by the Mine Manager in Chapter 6.) Mandela had once again suspended his power, authority, moved into the I-Thou, showing humbleness and during the discussion even poured a cup of tea for Pienaar. Not mentioning the humbleness of Pienaar in meeting the President, another great South African Leader, a leader who together with Mandela would later have a huge, positive impact on the moulding of the new South Africa. This was what we call a Real Meeting, showing support, listening to the other, providing inspiration to Pienaar as the Captain who would take the Springboks to glory, who would, some months later, take the country to overwhelming joy, who would unite a nation through sport, through the wonderful game of rugby, even if in the past it was the game of the oppressors in South Africa. Mandela focused on inspiration and a quote in the film that was really inspirational was, "that we achieve success through the work of others". Other key words coming out of the discussion in the movie were, "lead by example", "getting others to be better than they think they can be", and "inspiring others to greatness".

In the movie, the two men are shown sitting comfortably opposite each other on some lounge chairs, engaging and listening to each other's words with intent. At one stage Mandela stood up, took his cup of tea and moved to the chair closer to Pienaar, entering his space and again entering the I-Thou mode. The film shows Pienaar getting back into his car, after the meeting, sitting quietly, not saying a word, and staring into the distance, he was reflecting on the discussions that had just taken place. As mentioned in Chapter 7, good leaders reflect on conversations held, decisions taken and how they handled various circumstances. Pienaar's reflection, at the time, was more than likely no different.

Mandela started getting advice on the rules of rugby, started watching games, taking a keen interest in what was happening and followed all the games very closely. During the week leading up to the opening game of the World Cup between the Springboks and Australia, Mandela landed in a helicopter on the training ground (where the Springboks were going through their moves and polishing their skills) to engage with the players and wish them all the best for the game. He apologised for taking their time before starting the conversation, so humble in his approach. Something that leaders often lack, and unfortunately, they often believe that they do not have to ask someone for their time to have a discussion, they tend to own the space and immediately go directly to the issue that they want to raise.

On his way to the airport earlier that day, Mandela had rehearsed the names of each and every member of the Springbok squad, and duly addressed them by name. Knowing their names reflected interest and support for each of them, showing encouragement, once again entering the hyphen between the I and the Thou, he had suspended his power, authority, his agenda and gave time to the team. After talking to the players, he was given a Springbok Cap by one of the players, Hennie Le-Roux, for which he showed total appreciation. When walking back to the helicopter, Mandela asked Pienaar to join him. This is when he handed Pienaar a folded piece of paper, containing his favourite poem "Invictus" that he had with him while in prison, from which he often found inspiration.

In today's tumultuous world, poetry has a valuable place, a place for recording sentiments and feelings, events and reactions. For centuries, leaders throughout the world have turned to poetry for solace and for a call to action. Mandela, the anti-apartheid leader who was imprisoned for twenty-seven years for his activism and in 1994, became President of South Africa, regularly recited the poem "Invictus" during his imprisonment. Invictus, meaning unconquerable or undefeated in Latin, was written in 1875, by the influential British poet William Ernest Henley.

Invictus

Out of the night that covers me,

Black as the pit from pole to pole,

I thank whatever Gods may be

For my unconquerable soul.

In the fell clutch of circumstance

I have not winced nor cried aloud.

Under the bludgeoning's of chance

My head is bloody, but unbowed.

Beyond this place of wrath and tears

Looms but the Horror of the shade,

And yet the menace of the years

Finds and shall find me unafraid.

It matters not how strait the gate,

How charged with punishments the scroll,

I am the master of my fate,

I am the captain of my soul.

We guess that Henley probably had no idea that his words would inspire one of the world's greatest leaders 120 years later.

I recall watching the final with friends on the day, all of us proud to be South African, but obviously nervous and excited at the same time. After the two teams had run out and stood in formation in preparation for singing their respective National Anthems, Mandela walked out of the tunnel and onto the field, he was wearing a Springbok jersey, with the number six on his back, the same number as the Captain Pienaar.

In an interview with the BBC some eighteen years after winning the match, Pienaar explained how Mandela walked into the dressing room prior to the match wearing the Springbok Jersey, and after wishing them the best of luck for the game, he turned around to leave the dressing room and that was the moment that Pienaar noticed there was a number six on the back of the jersey. In the interview Pienaar said that he was tearing up and emotional, he had to bite his lip, trying not to show his emotions. Mandela probably knew that if he wore the jersey with pride, he would inspire the team in beating the mighty New Zealand Rugby Union team, better known as the All Blacks and would also be an inspiration to those in the stadium and those watching on television. In the interview Pienaar also remembered that he could not even sing the National Anthem whilst lined up on the field with his team prior to the game, because he was so emotional.

Mandela was also wearing a Springbok cap, I guess it was the one that Hennie Le Roux had given him on the day that he had visited them on the training ground, once again showing appreciation for a simple gift given to him.

As Mandela exited the tunnel and entered the field, most of the crowd in the stadium started chanting, "Nelson, Nelson, Nelson, Nelson", a true hair-raising moment for all South Africans present in the stadium and watching on television. I am sure that many people sitting in the stands as well as watching around the world, enjoying the spectacle experienced goosebumps, as the chanting got louder. Seeing Mandela waving in appreciation at the crowds in the fully packed stadium, with that wonderful smile on his face said it all. Even the All Blacks supporters sitting in the stands must have known this was a unique moment.

The game went as planned and the Springboks beat their old arch-rivals by fifteen points to twelve, and the dreams of the team, the dreams of Mandela and the dreams of the nation had come true. With the final whistle blown, there were emphatic celebrations around the stadium and across all corners of South Africa, the Rainbow Nation was ecstatic, in unity with one another. However, the highlight was still to come and that was when Pienaar stepped onto the podium and was handed the William Webb-Ellis trophy by his President, Mandela, both of them having huge smiles on their faces in total celebration of the moment. Pienaar lifted the trophy as high as he could above his head; the Springbok team were for the first time and at the first attempt, Champions of the World! They had won the most important game ever played between the two teams since the inaugural game in 1921. A game played by two teams, which is arguably known as the biggest rivalry in World Rugby history.

In the interview before being handed the trophy, a journalist approached Pienaar and said, "great game, but you couldn't have done it without the amazing support of sixty-three thousand South Africans here today", to which without any hesitation, Pienaar responded, "we didn't have the support of sixty-thousand South Africans, we had the support of forty-three million South Africans", to which his response once again raised the roof of the cheering crowd in the stadium.

Before handing over the trophy, both Mandela and Pienaar thanked each other for what they had done for South Africa. True Leaders with both giving the credit to the other and not taking the credit for themselves. This is the skill of a true Leader, in all walks of life, privately and professionally. Sometimes leaders should reflect on whether they give credit where credit is due, by recognising others for their efforts, ideas, and initiatives, both to teams and individuals.

The Springboks' victory over the mighty All Blacks on the day and winning the title of World Champions for the first time is probably one of the greatest moments in South African sport and truly a watershed moment in bringing the citizens of the country together.

Away From the Rugby – Two Great Leaders

Mandela was a true inspiration, a global icon, however like all humans a fallible person. He never projected himself as a hero; he just entered into reality and infused that reality with his vision for persons, ethics, political will, and his community (South Africa). Such real leadership is not beyond anyone. We do not need language of the "ultimate" leader or the "heroic" leader, such language becomes a distraction from the everyday realities of vision, when helping and engaging with people. Isn't it amazing how a fallible leader can inspire, achieve, and envision? A Leader who as a fallible man changed a whole country, and to some degree, a Leader who inspired the world. A well-deserved recipient of the 1993 Nobel Peace Prize, which was jointly awarded to Mandela and former President Frederik Willem de Klerk for their work for the peaceful termination of the apartheid regime, and for laying the foundations for a new democratic South Africa.

Mandela was a person who fully understood the meaning and importance of the I-Thou as written by Martin Buber. He always knew what the hyphen was between two persons engaging in the I-Thou. Mandela had a destiny, he was released after spending eighteen years as a political prisoner on Robben Island, just off Cape Town in South Africa, followed by an additional eight years in Pollsmoor and Victor Verster Prisons. He walked out of prison knowing what was needed to unite a country previously torn apart.

Watching the film "Invictus" of which I have watched around six times, it is evident that Mandela understood the physical aspects, however and more importantly the psychological controls needed. Through his understanding of the fundamentals of I-Thou, Mandela transformed South Africa. Unfortunately, most of the presidents who have followed him have all focused on themselves and not on the I-Thou fundamentals.

The language of the leader is of great significance, be it in sport or at the workplace or even as a parent, words matter, be they spoken or unspoken. Support and inspiration of the leader moves people to striving to be better and show appreciation. Signs and symbols communicate with the conscious and the unconscious minds, words posted on the walls, company icons, and all have significance. Mandela understood all of this as a leader and so too did Pienaar through inspiration by Mandela. Two great leaders coming from opposite spectrums of South Africa's society, joining together in inspiring each other, inspiring the Springbok Team and in turn inspiring and uniting a nation.

When writing, "Humanising Leadership in Risk", Mandela received my vote of most inspiring Leader and two years later still remains my favourite. Aneta through her readings of Mandela's life as well as watching various documentaries came to a similar conclusion, that Mandela was one of the most inspiring Leaders she has read or heard about, and therefore, we decided that he would be a fitting example to this book.

As for Pienaar, he too, gets my nod as someone who is an inspiring Leader, whom I was fortunate to meet in the early 1990's at his home in South Africa, and as he knew I was an avid collector of original players rugby jerseys and other memorabilia, he gifted me with a tie that he had worn during a Test Series between the Springboks and Wales. *Figure 60.* shows *Francois' Tie* framed with a photo of him after leading the Springboks to a nineteen points to twelve win over the Australian Wallabies in Sydney in 1993.

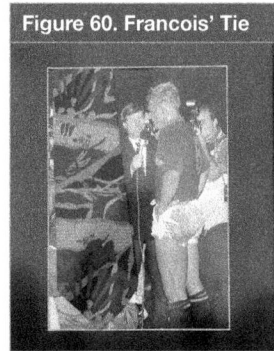

Figure 60. Francois' Tie

Whilst writing this chapter we were on planes between Vienna, Austria and Auckland, New Zealand and during one of the stops we had a layover in Dubai. Aneta and I sat down in a sports bar at the airport to watch the All Blacks play Namibia which was live on television in a pool match of the 2023, World Cup finals. I turned around to grab the attention of the waiter, when I noticed a large, framed photograph hanging on the wall, it was the renowned photograph of Mandela handing the World Cup Trophy over to Pienaar in 1995. This coincidence, once again, gave me goosebumps and reminded me of two great Leaders

Figure 61. Aneta in Dubai

coming out of South Africa. What a great ending to writing this chapter. *Figure 61.* shows *Aneta in Dubai* in front of the iconic photograph during our layover.

SELF-REFLECTION

Chapter 9 – Leaders who Understand Real Meeting

Our selection of elements for self-reflection from the chapter are as follows:

- Similar to Mandela, do I have a quote, poem or song that is foundational to the way I conduct myself as a leader?

- As a leader, I understand what is of significance to others within their cultures, beliefs and ethics.

- Do I understand the power of Real Meeting in bringing others together?

- Do I understand the significance of symbols used in the workplace as well as personal spheres?

- I refrain from taking the credits, but rather co-share our successes as a team.

- Do I regard myself as the "ultimate or heroic leader", rather than a humble one, showing care, engaging and helping others?

- I often reflect on what difference I, as a leader, have made to the lives of others on a professional and personal level.

CHAPTER 10

The Need for Leaders to Tell Their Story

"Telling a story is one of the best ways we have of coming up with new ideas, and also of learning about each other and our world. It's been happening since humans first inhabited the earth".

Sir Richard Branson

Entrepreneur and Author

The Art of Storytelling

For some leaders, storytelling is not serious business, although when telling stories, we reflect on what has happened, a reminder of lessons learnt, and many stories attain the status of being truthful. Leaders in the true sense of the word know how to listen, and sadly managers know how to tell or instruct. Many Indigenous tribes around the world like in Australia and Canada believe that the elder telling a story is feeding them and it is up to those listening to discover what they are being fed. Some of these stories explain the history, the various worldviews, teach who we are, where we come from and why we have developed certain heuristics and biases. Other stories enlighten those listening and often appease the inquiring and inquisitive minds of people, no matter what age. All of these types of stories are part of our development and continuous learning process.

Storytelling is an art and is one of the oldest methods of transferring knowledge and understanding to others. For Indigenous People, storytelling by the elders is key in transferring the stories of their ancestors, culture, and knowledge from generation to generation. However, in their storytelling there is lots of semiotics, dance, songs, rituals, gestures, myths, sound effects, beating of drums and entertainment. These all support the art of storytelling and in the e-motion, the stories are well understood and remembered. When storytelling brings in a touch of humour, it too makes storytelling easier when the humour is acknowledged by those listening with laughter. In the Indigenous culture it is believed that laughter is the greatest healer. For the Indigenous tribes in Canada, storytelling forms a big part of ceremonies. For this reason, we have included stories in Chapter 5, that have been told to us by Indigenous People, in the Australian Capital Territory (ACT), Australia and in Alberta, Canada.

Every story has four basic elements which are listening, understanding, memorising, and sharing. This is no different to stories told at the workplace. There is probably less emphasis on traditions, sound effects, dancing and the beating of drums, however when leaders share their stories, there is a much better chance that those with whom they are engaging with will remember the stories that are connected to the topic and the discussion. In most instances stories take the listeners on a journey of discovering new things or in remembering things that they have forgotten about or relating to the issue being addressed.

I came across this quotation; however, I could not find the author of it, but I feel it is so fitting to this chapter and is as follows, "A story is a description of someone's ethics which can become one's ethos of behaviours that bring people together through a centralised narrative".

Listening to Sid Tell His Story of the God - Lord Murugan

Whilst writing this book, Brian and I had conducted some training in Kuala Lumpur and decided to stay a few days to do some scuba diving in the Malacca Strait or the Andaman Sea. However, when contacting the diving centre, we were informed that because of the monsoon season, diving was not recommended. Although a little disappointed, we decided not to chance anything and enjoy the week relaxing and seeing a bit of the country.

On one of the days, we visited the Batu Caves Temple located in Gombak, Malaysia. The caves are believed to be over four-hundred million years old and eventually became a popular Hindi shrine in the late 1800s, which even now is one of the most significant sites of pilgrimage for those in the Hindi faith. The caves were often a place for shelter for the Temuan people, an Indigenous group of people belonging to the Orang Asli tribe and have since become one of the most popular Hindi shrines outside of India. The caves are dedicated to Lord Murugan, the God of War. Being a Hindu religious site, one can only imagine the semiotics of the place, filled with temples, shrines, statues of the Gods, Goddesses, colours and of course one the tallest statues in the world, that of Lord Murugan. Towards the end of the nineteenth century an Indian trader installed a statue of Lord Murugan and dedicated the cave as a place of worship. The cave has since become the venue for the Thaipusam festival, which takes place every year. Before starting the climb of the two hundred and seventy-two rainbow-coloured stairs to the temple, one passes the almost 43 m tall golden statue of Lord Murugan. We climbed the colourful stairs, stopping at times to get our breath back, constantly surrounded by an abundance of long-tailed macaques monkeys, and taking photographs of the view below looking over the shoulder of Lord Murugan. See *Figure 62. Statue of Lord Murugan* and *Figure 63. Rainbow Coloured Stairs.*

Figure 62. Statue of Lord Murugan

Figure 63. Rainbow Coloured Stairs

Eventually, we entered the cave, and when walking through the various levels, we found the shrine for Lord Murugan. We took in, all the semiotics in and around the shrine, however with little understanding what each of the artifacts meant. When turning around, we noticed a young lady and her son sitting on the floor against a pillar in front of the shrine. I approached her, we introduced ourselves and I asked if she would mind giving us a few minutes of her time to explain the shrine and all its meanings. With a huge smile on her face, she used the words "of course, I would love to", however we were pleasantly surprised when her young son, named Sid, asked his mother, Madhu, if he could tell the story of the Lord Murugan, let us rephrase that, "his God Murugan". Thinking about it now, actually with a sparkle in his eyes, he begged his mother to be allowed to tell the story.

We then both got comfortable, sitting down on the bare floor with them, as Sid started telling his story, with every now and then his mother chipping in and adding some information, filling the gaps. However, each time she did this, Sid made it clear that his intent was to share the story all by himself. When Sid had finished telling his story, with the proud look on her face, Madhu then asked him if he would like to sing a song about his Gods, to which he immediately agreed and without hesitation started singing, at times being joined in song by his mother Madhu. When finished, Madhu informed us what the words of the song meant. I continued talking to Madhu and listening to her inspiring story, as Sid took Brian by the hand taking him closer to the Lord Murugan's shrine and commenced telling Brian what each of the symbols meant, how the spear in the right hand symbolises the defeat of the asura (titan) Surapadma, all supported by some explanation and story. Sid made it clear that the spear is not for attacking persons, but rather for giving them power. See *Figure 64. Sitting on the Floor* with Madhu and Sid and *Figure 65. Sid and Brian* at Lord Murugan's shrine.

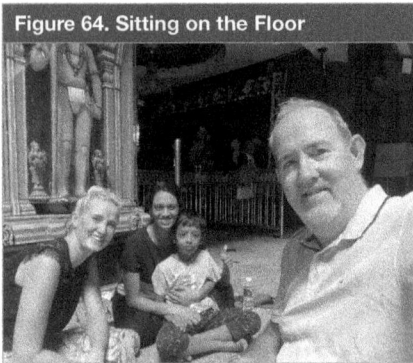
Figure 64. Sitting on the Floor

Figure 65. Sid and Brian

Without asking, Madhu started telling us how her husband had gone to a wedding, but she wanted to spend some time in the cave and the temple, sitting with Sid in front of the shrine, reflecting and thanking Lord Murugan for helping her and answering her prayers through a difficult time earlier in the year, related to her family back home in the south of India. In understanding the importance of letting others tell their stories, suspending our own agenda and just listening with intent, we both sat on the floor giving them our time of listening, after all, we had asked for their time to answer a question that we had. We must have sat with them for at least forty minutes. We had both suspended our agenda, refrained from asking our questions, and in turn gifted them the time to tell their story. We were in the moment, inspired and in awe listening to them, we were in Kairos Time, not needing to go anywhere, no rush and no deadlines.

What touched both of us the most was when we were leaving, Brian asked Sid if he liked ice-cream and after Sid sheepishly confirmed that he did, Brian gave him some money to buy himself one when they left the cave. Immediately after placing the money in his hand, Sid stood up and walked over to the shrine to give the money up as an offering to his Lord Murugan in appreciation for protecting his mother and him.

Both Brian and I had learnt so much about the Hindu faith, and Lord Murugan, together with all the meanings of the myths, signs, symbols and all the artifacts related to the God that both Madhu and Sid have so much faith in, and the God that has instilled so much trust in not only Madhu, but our little friend Sid. We had entered the hyphen in the I-Thou with both Madhu and Sid, connecting with them through their interest, their world, their religion and their God. We had connected in something that was important to them, something with so much meaning and so much significance.

On leaving the cave and descending the stairs, we arrived at the entrance to another temple located at the foot of the Lord Murugan statue. After taking our sandals off, we entered the temple, once again in awe with all the semiotics, including a sleeping, Goddess. Whilst inside the temple, I immediately noticed a lady placing different powder-like substances of two colours on her forehead. When she was finished praying, we approached her and asked if she could tell us what the powders meant, to which she gladly agreed. We introduced ourselves to her and she to us. She mentioned that it is called Tilaka Tilaka which is applied when praying to the Gods and consists of a red paste which apparently is a symbol of Hinduism and part of prayer and worship. After explaining it to us, she offered to make the markings on our foreheads as well, to which we both agreed. After she had done so, she eagerly explained other symbols in the temple and their meanings to us. We could see that she was keen to tell the story of her religion, the story of the temple and how much significance all of it has to her and her husband's life. See *Figure 66.* lady *Marking my Forehead* and *Figure 67. The Sleeping Goddess.*

Two days later, we had arranged to go on a boat trip on the Klang River to experience the glowing plankton and fireflies at night. On the way to the meeting point, the driver offered to stop at the Sri Shakti Devasthanam Temple. Once again, like all the other temples that we had visited, there was an abundance of semiotics to take in, hundreds of carefully sculptured statues and inside, many Gods and

Figure 66. Marking my Forehead

Figure 67. The Sleeping Goddess

Goddesses of significance to the Hindus as well as the smell of burning incense. When entering the temple, we met the Hindu Priest, or better known as Pujari. He also marked our foreheads with a paste, similar to what the lady had done to us in the temple two days before. Yes, you probably guessed it, after he had marked our foreheads and blessed us, I asked him if he could tell us his story of the temple. He gladly did so and explained that the centre of the temple housed the well-meaning, kind and widely encountered Goddess, the Goddess Sri Shakti Mari Amman, beautifully carved out of granite rock in a sitting position. He explained that she is the embodiment of divine energy, and she welcomes all who visit the temple. The Pujari mentioned other Gods and Goddesses in the temple, including the statue of Lord Murugan which was positioned in the rear right-hand corner of the temple. We walked over to the shrine of Lord Murugan, it was so nice to have some degree of pre-knowledge and understanding of the artifacts, signs and symbols around the shrine, all because we had two days prior allowed our little friend Sid to tell his story to us at the Batu Caves. See *Figure 68. Standing with the Pujari* inside the temple next to the Shrine of Goddess Sri Shakti Mari Amman and *Figure 69. The* Sri Shakti Devasthanam *Temple.*

Figure 68. Standing with the Pujari

Figure 69. The Temple

What is common in the stories we heard from Sid, Madhu, the lady in the temple and the Pujari is that Brian and I, in all three situations, suspended our agenda, we asked them if they were willing to share their stories, to which we listened with intent, not interrupting and thereby showing interest and entering into the hyphen of the I-Thou. The hyphen for Sid being his God Lord Murugan, the Sleeping Goddess for the lady in the temple and for the Pujari, it was Goddess Sri Shakti Mari Amman. This should be no different at the workplace, giving others the opportunity to tell their stories and in entering the hyphen of the I-Thou, leads to a totally different discussion, builds trust, reflects interest and shows caring by listening with intent.

Inspiring Leaders Tell Their Stories

Over time, some of the best leaders have told their stories, be it at seminars, university lecture rooms, college halls, TED talks, videos, documentaries, in meetings and in written form, be it in the tabloids, the Times Magazine, and other means. This includes leaders from all walks of life, including politicians, industry CEOs, clergymen, medical professionals, pilots, engineers, university and college lecturers, and philosophers, to name a few.

Most leaders rely on various kinds of methods and tools to encourage and inspire their audience, their teams, their business partners in the drive for team building, improved performance, intuitive thinking, however, one of the most powerful methods that leaders tend to refrain from, is the telling of personal stories. Storytelling is a method of expressing feelings, sharing details with others for preserving culture, training and learning purposes. Storytelling encourages and inspires the listener or audiences, both individually or in groups through imagination by focusing on words and actions and in turn impacts the collective unconscious.

Yes, it is understandable that when speaking or presenting to an audience, leaders tend to refer to numbers, past performance, data, graphs, tables, and at times throwing in the odd picture or two. No matter how interesting the data is, powerful presentations or speeches include the personal stories, and what I find is that the inclusion of photographs taken by the speaker adds additional interest and inspiration to the presentation or speech. Leaders should embrace storytelling as one of their key methods of inspiring others. Storytelling supports the listener in remembering, and therefore, is key to education and learning.

So, why do leaders tend to refrain from telling their personal stories? There are a couple of reasons for this, including feeling vulnerable, showing weakness, fault or even failure, losing face or credibility, fear of becoming emotional, to name a few. In 2012, I was encouraged by a good friend of mine to consider telling a very personal story as part of my presentation to an International Conference. At first, I hesitated, as I too felt vulnerable and was unsure, if I would be able to handle my emotions when presenting and telling the story. Eventually my gut feel was that I would be all right and I decided to jump in the deep end and tell my story. It was about my late wife, Bela, who ended up in a coma with twenty-one fractures to her face after falling down three stairs of our home in Austria. Due to the nature of the presentation, I decided to name the presentation "Safety from the Heart". Yes, it was emotionally draining for me to present my story, but the feedback I received from many of the persons attending was overwhelming. This convinced me to make use of personal stories related to private issues as well as examples from my professional life, site visits, travels and much more. I had exposed myself, as I used a tough story to share with the audience, but it worked, although sad, it touched others and inspired my approach going forward.

Dr Robert Long, who co-wrote my first book "It Works!", encouraged me once again to start the book off with the emotional story of the passing of Bela in 2019. At first, I was not too keen to do so, however after some reflection and in remembering the effect a personal story had during my presentation in 2012, I decided to go along with the recommendation. I repeated the same approach of telling stories in my second book "Humanising Leadership in Risk". Many persons who have commented on the "Safety from the Heart" sessions or later provided feedback on my two books, mentioning the impact the personal stories, at the beginning of the books as well as throughout the two books, have had on them.

When leaders, just like I had done in 2012, tell their personal stories, they too enter the hyphen of the I-Thou. In telling their stories, they have an impact on others, and without a doubt the stories they tell are most often remembered by those who had heard them. This is evident as I still receive comments from people on how my stories touched them when hearing them and still remembered years later. This included touching stories related to my personal life, but also to other events that I have experienced, both positive and negative at the workplace.

When people hear a good story they consciously or unconsciously create images, with their embodied mind feel emotions either happy or sad ones, they imagine the environment, the colours and even the sounds. These stories help them to remember the topic or the discussion far better than a presentation of numbers and what I call "Death by PowerPoint". In many instances, the stories that are told will be remembered for a long time to come. We, as adults, all still remember stories told to us by our parents and even grandparents.

I belonged to the Boy Scouts as a young boy and I can still remember some of the stories told to us by our Scout Master, Robert; stories about hiking, pathfinding, a close call with a venomous snake, the stars and much more, with many of these stories told to us around a campfire of two Scouts Jamborees that I had attended. Almost half a century later (tells my age), I still remember many stories and retold them whilst sitting around campfires in a nature reserve in South Africa. In doing so, engaging with Aneta as well as some British and German tourists, who had shared a game viewing vehicle with us over two days. It is amazing what the biosemiotics of a crackling fireplace, nature's sounds in the background and a good bottle of South African Pinotage red wine can do in creating connection. Sharing stories, be it from the bush experience, other adventure holiday destinations and even being stranded on a remote island can do this. Although this was about us enjoying socialising with others around the crackling fire, reminiscing about holiday destinations, it is very similar to Sir Richard Branson's approach where he refers to the storytelling around a campfire. More about Sir Richard Branson later in the chapter.

Leaders Who Inspire Others Through Storytelling

Through research and reading, we have over time, come across many quotes by persons from different backgrounds and professions on the importance of storytelling, of which some of our favourite ones include:

"Sometimes reality is too complex. Stories give it form".

Jean-Luc Godard

Screenwriter, Critic and Director

"Stories constitute the single most powerful weapon in a leader's arsenal".

Dr Howard Gardner

Professor, Harvard University

"Storytelling is our obligation to the next generation. If all we are doing is marketing, we are doing a disservice, and not only to our profession, but to our children and their children. Give something of meaning to your audience by inspiring, engaging, and educating them with story. Stop marketing. Start storytelling".

Laura Holloway

Founder and Chief of the Storyteller Agency

"Stories are memory aids, instruction manuals and moral compasses".

Aleks Krotoski

Author, Journalist, Broadcaster and Psychologist

"The fact of storytelling hints at a fundamental human unease, hints at human imperfection. Where there is perfection, there is no story to tell".

Ben Okri

Poet and Novelist

Sir Richard Branson – a Believer in Storytelling

In an interview titled "The Power of Storytelling to Drive Change", Sir Richard Branson mentioned that when illustrating a point through storytelling, the storyteller brings the specific point alive. He also said that his dad was a good storyteller and his generation and the generations before that, did not have television and would sit around the campfire telling wonderful stories that got passed down from generation to generation. Watching the interview and hearing this comment took my thoughts back to sitting around the fire at the "Tent Embassy" in Canberra listening to the stories of "Uncle Kev" about his culture, the culture of the Aboriginal persons in Australia.

When writing the book "Humanising Leadership in Risk", I developed the quote, "Leadership is time and a simple cup of coffee", which in my view to some degree, aligns to Sir Richard Branson's idea of sitting around a fire, and in aligning with my quote then in this case, "Leadership is time and a simple chat around the fireplace".

Sadly, through television and social media these days, we tend to agree that storytelling has lost a bit of its importance to many. Sir Richard Branson also mentioned that the reason he tells his stories in his books that he has written is so that hopefully people get some ideas from the stories.

Reading any of his books, or listening to his interviews is always inspiring, however, what I liked in his book titled "Finding my Virginity" was that he made a comment on the first page of the book, "If your life is one long success story, it won't make for a good read". He not only tells stories about his successes, but also his difficulties and failures. This aligns with the quote by the poet and novelist, Ben Okri, "The fact of storytelling hints at a fundamental human unease, hints at human imperfection. Where there is perfection, there is no story to tell".

Apparently, Sir Richard Branson's day ends with a group dinner where stories are shared, and ideas are born. He also said that he prefers to have meetings in different places and to lighten the mood, including events like a shared meal and at times walking meetings when he is pressed for time.

I recall a couple of Leadership forums held by the company that I work for, where we were encouraged to take an hour and walk around a lake, in the park, networking with people in the company, who we do not usually meet. I have always found these moving to Real Meeting and connecting with others.

A colleague and friend of ours was having a difficult time and was at crossroads in both her private as well as professional life and was at the edge of suffering burnout. She called me and needed to have a chat and a shoulder to lean on during her challenging times. Having in mind the words of Sir Richard Branson, I decided not to as usual meet with her in the office, but rather invite her to a coffee and a friendly chat in the park, close to the office. It was one of the best things I could have done for her, the biosemiotics of the park was serene, with only the sound of the ducks splashing in the water. She was able to open up and speak her heart out, and even shed some tears. When we parted around forty-five minutes later, she seemed more relaxed and had a smile on her face. The emotions and discussions would never have been the same, if we had met in the office environment. I had learnt and practised something new, thanks to Sir Richard Branson; I guess, contrary to common beliefs, an old dog can learn new tricks.

Benefits of Telling Stories

As mentioned, there are numerous reasons why it is important that leaders tell their personal stories, even though at times it could expose them somewhat. Telling one's story is a significant element of leaders connecting with their teams. In doing so, storytelling builds trust, and we all know that trust is a fundamental quality when building community and in influencing the culture and sub-cultures of an organisation.

Storytelling does, at times, expose the leaders, however in return, depending on the story told, reflects the human side, the caring and emotional elements which in turn resonate and inspire others and hopefully encourage them to tell their stories with their respective teams.

It is without any doubt that by telling stories, be it in meetings, presentations, writing articles, explaining scenarios or in training sessions, the impact of the message is stronger and will be remembered long beyond the details of the material, the numbers and the images used. Telling the stories is often persuasive and in turn makes a difference in understanding and learning.

After all, storytelling often brings up the emotions in others, as well as shows the feelings of the person telling the story.

Challenging Ourselves as Leaders

So, to summarise, if a leader strives to become an effective leader who inspires others, be it a company chief executive officer, person of the cloth, engineer, teacher, lecturer, or someone in any other walk of life, one should hone their skills in the art of storytelling. Many companies have team events, team builds, seminars, leadership forums and other types of get-togethers, but a good suggestion taken out of Sir Richard Branson's book is that sometimes maybe all you need is a campfire or (like in my case) that simple walk in the park.

Some questions for leaders to ask themselves whether they truly have Real Meeting with others:

- When meeting someone in our office, whether a formal meeting or an informal chat, and the phone rings, do I stand up and take the call, or do I ignore the ringing telephone and continue with giving the other person or persons my undivided attention?

- When at a function, be it a conference or standing lunch between sessions, talking to someone, when I see a person passing by who I know, do I interrupt the discussion and greet the person passing?

- How often do I invite someone for a cup of coffee for an informal chat, suspend the agenda and authority and have Real Meeting?

- Do I recognise those at all levels who conduct the work and recognise them, giving credit where credit is due, be it a simple handshake or friendly tap on the shoulder, some honest and kind words and, of course, saying thank you?

- Am I patient with others, suspending my agenda and even authority at times, making the other person feel heard and in turn significant?

- Do I practise curiosity, understanding that others could know more than me, knowing that by listening with interest I learn from others?

- Do I have the ability to be humble and be open to Real Meeting with any person in the organisation, be it at an executive level or a person cleaning the restrooms?

- Do I create an atmosphere where others feel that I am true to the idea of Real Meeting, which is key to open communication, and allowing others to tell their story, their point of view, their issues of concern, their suggestions or simply needing someone to talk to?

- Do I have Real Meeting which enables others and where I develop significant relationships showing trust, authenticity and appreciation of others?

- Do I promote shoulder to shoulder, friendly and respective face to face relationships, rather than one at an arm's length away with little reflection of Real Meeting?

- Do I have a balance between listening and understanding, and telling and controlling?

- Do I invite someone for a walk along the river, at a nearby park for a walking meeting, just to network or discuss a certain topic, without the traditional PowerPoint presentation?

- Do I create PowerPoint slides filled with words and lines of text, or do I make use of photographs or pictures and then support them with a story?

- Do I give time in Real Meeting to address issues that need Real Meeting, and do I encourage others to do the same?

- Do I listen with the intent to learn from others, and do I understand that power of remaining silent and not directing the conversations?

In summary, when walking down the passage of an office block, the company parking lot, the reception or entrance area, the production floor, do we as leaders greet people, shake hands, recognise them and if time permits stop for a talk? In other words, are we as leaders visible to the employees or are we too good to leave our offices and engage in Real Meeting with others, entering the hyphen between the I-Thou?

The Poem "The Storyteller"

Taffy Thomas MBE, a writer and professional storyteller, has over years inspired us with his stories and especially his words, "storytelling preserves the past, reveals the present and creates the future". "The Storyteller" originally a song by folk singer Mike Jones was reproduced as a poem by Taffy Thomas and is about the art and practise of storytelling. The poem goes as follows:

Storyteller

I'm a teller of tales, a spinner of yarns,
A weaver of dreams and a liar.
I'll teach you some stories to tell to your friends,
While sitting at home by the fire.
You may not believe everything that I say
But there's one thing I'll tell you that's true
For my stories were given as presents to me
And now they are my gifts to you.
My stories are as old as the mountains and rivers
That flow through the land they were born in
They were told in the homes of peasants in rags
And kings with fine clothes adorning.
There's no need for silver or gold in great store
For a tale becomes richer with telling
And as long as each listener has a pair of good ears
It matters not where they are dwelling.
A story well told can lift up your hearts
And help you forget all your sorrows
It can give you the strength and the courage to stand
And face all your troubles tomorrow.
For there's wisdom and wit, beauty and charm
There's laughter and sometimes there's tears
But when the story is over and the spell it is broken
You'll find that there's nothing to fear
My stories were learned in my grandparent's home
Where their grandparents also had heard them
They were given as payment by travelling folk
For a warm place to lay down their burdens
My stories are ageless, they never grow old
With each telling they are born anew
And when my story is ended, I'll still be alive
In the tales that I've given to you.

SELF-REFLECTION

Chapter 10 – The Need for Leaders to Tell Their Story

Our selection of elements for self-reflection from the chapter are as follows:

- Like the story of a colleague and friend, who needed someone to talk to in the park, do I as a leader give him or her the time and space when they simply need someone to talk to?

- I regularly tell my story to members of my team and, at the same time, encourage them to tell their stories.

- When last have I had that "simple cup of coffee" whilst in discussion with someone in my private or professional life?

- I try to ensure that my presentations are not "Death by PowerPoint", but have minimal text (where possible) and include photographs and stories.

- Do I have a "Sid" in my team or my life, who simply needs the time to tell his or her story and would appreciate my time listening with intent?

CHAPTER 11

Various Practical Examples and Tools

"We change our tools and then our tools change us".

Jeff Bezos

Executive Chairman of Amazon

This chapter is not designed to provide all the details of initiatives, models, training programmes and tools used, but rather to provide some insight in what methods are available in supporting understanding of what is required to have Real Meeting.

iCue Listening

Over our years in various leadership positions, we have both been exposed to many leaders who are unable to engage with their teams proactively and effectively. This has always struck us as strange, as we are sure that as family members, they are most of their time engaging with their families, listing to their partners, having discussions and letting the others tell their stories. The question is, why then they find it challenging to engage with their fellow employees at the workplace?

This is a problem identified at so many levels in management, I have done site visits with senior managers, with middle management and first line managers (better known as supervisors or foremen), and at all these levels, I have observed many of them focusing on physical aspects and controls (I-It) with little engagement with the persons on the shopfloor, in the offices and other parts of the company, thereby seldom entering the hyphen of the I-Thou. This is no fault of their own, it is more the issue that they are not given the tools and learning opportunities in how to engage and actively listen to the people, who work for them or those working in other departments of an organisation.

I was once talking to the managing director of a large beverage company over a dinner at a conference that I was attending in the Netherlands. He had told me that an incident had recently occurred at his operation, where an employee was seriously

---

injured as a result of being crushed between two forklifts in the warehouse. After the investigation had been completed, he met with his operations leadership team consisting, of around fifteen people and informed them that for the next four weeks, he would like them to be present on the shopfloor for 10% of their time, talking to the employees. The aim of the initiative was to engage and find out what works well, what initiatives do not add any value, what are the risks faced by the employees and to get a feeling of what the sub-culture of the various department on the site is. He then mentioned that after informing them of the plan, the discussions started and with the exception of three of the leaders, they started making comments that they do not feel comfortable talking to the employees in their own departments, and even less in the other departments on the site. One even made the comment that she felt that the request was a punishment to the leaders for the incident and mentioned that the plan should not go ahead. The managing director told me that he was annoyed as well as disappointed by the response by most of his leadership team, he had reiterated to the team that he would not budge and that the request that time be spent on the shopfloor would proceed as requested. For the managing director it was clear that the leadership team were not taking the safety issues seriously and considering that a fellow colleague had been critically injured, it was disappointing that they were not willing to make changes and sacrifice their time. I believe that the issue was slightly different: the leadership team had over the years probably been stuck in the I-It elements of managing their respective departments, and seldom moved into the I-Thou leadership elements, engaging with team members.

I suggested to the managing director that they probably needed some coaching in how to engage with other persons, how to approach them, break the ice in the discussion, listen with intent, give them time to tell their stories and suspend their own agenda and power, to which he agreed. Had they had this type of training and coaching, there is a good probability that the request from the managing director would have been accepted by the team. At the end of the dinner, he said that he would suspend the initiative, provide the coaching and support to his leadership team, and then revisit the idea six months later. I often, in reflection, wondered if the managing director took the advice, of actually suspending the initiative and employed a person to provide the training and coaching of his team, but we never exchanged our contact details, so there is no way of following up on it, but I truly hope he did.

As part of our studies in Social Psychology of Risk, we were both introduced, at different times, to the iCue listening tool. This is a tool developed by Dr Robert

Long to support engagement, one that provides the employees with a platform to share their feelings, their ideas, their concerns and to participate actively in discussions, and therefore, being part of the team, feeling significant and getting the sense that they are being listened to and appreciated. The tool also supports teams in finding the balance in discussions between workplace controls, the psychological and cultural elements. The tool is a semiotic representation of these three elements and endeavours to assist individuals and teams to think visually and spatially about these three layers of risk and learning.

From the outset, I found the tool very interesting, it appealed to me as I knew this would bring a new dimension to the discussions with employees at the company that I have been working at for more than thirty-seven years. When returning to Europe, after one of the many sessions together with Rob Long in Australia, I was keen to introduce this tool to my senior team and then later, roll it out in the company across all our sites around the world. The tool is now called the Engagement Board and has without any doubt changed the language of the company through engagement with the employees and contractors working on our sites across the globe.

When understanding the tool, one realises that, in today's world, leaders need to do a lot less telling and a lot more listening, if they want their efforts to add value. There is a strong need for engagement amongst all levels in an organisation, where leaders move from solely a telling approach, to running of engagement sessions, during which there is two-way communication and engagement on the topic being discussed. Obtaining commitment and buy-in will follow, and the time spent will add value to those attending, as well as to the company as a whole.

When attending the session in Canberra, it was clear that the four quadrants related to Workspace (positive and negative), Headspace (psychological) and Groupspace (cultural) supported the discussions and in doing so found the balance and placed people at the centre of what leaders do in all departments and all professions. The key was to ensure that the tool was well understood, to prevent it from being used incorrectly and finally just becoming a tickbox approach, one that adds little value and as a result eventually disappears into the background.

Over time in the company that I am employed, and at companies for which Aneta through her company Embodied Leadership has trained and coached, this tool has evolved and is being used by many leaders. Training sessions have been conducted in many countries, thereby coaching leaders across the globe in the correct use of the Engagement Board process (iCue Listening). As true learning comes from e-motion, coaching in doing was key in ensuring the correct understanding and knowledge of the tool. This coaching included gamification, group activities, solving puzzles, using the Engagement Board for addressing selected topics, including critiquing sessions to support the learning process. *Figure 70. Roadshow Session* reflects one of the training and coaching sessions conducted in Malaysia and *Figure 71. Aneta Using the Tool.*

Figure 70. Roadshow Session

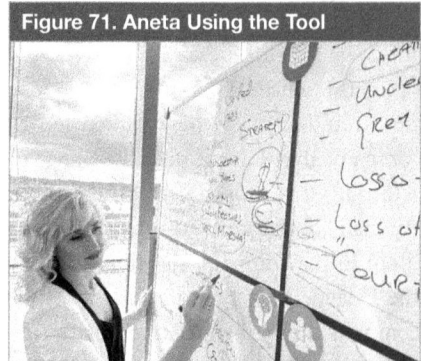

Figure 71. Aneta Using the Tool

When initially introducing the Engagement Board to one of our sites, attendees of a training session were split into five working groups, consisting of senior leaders in the organisation. In turn, each group was given a specific topic to use in developing a typical pre-shift talk or better known as a toolbox talk in industry. Each group was then required to present their respective talk to the wider group.

Each person in all five groups, were given a rating score sheet and were asked to rate each of the talks conducted by the other groups. Rating would vary between 1 and 5 points, with 1 being poor and 5 being good. The four categories included the following:

- The toolbox talk covered the critical elements of the specific topic.

- The toolbox talk made a difference in understanding of the topic.

- The toolbox talk added value to the audience, and supported learning.

- The toolbox talk promoted engagement between the presenter and the audience.

Not surprisingly, the scores of the wider group were low for three of the four items above, with the exception being critical elements discussed. It is not uncommon in industry, for leaders to conduct safety talks by reading the document and telling their teams what is required. They then believe that the contents have been understood and that the time spent has ensured buy-in and will make a difference.

Often toolbox talks are treated as a tickbox exercise and are conducted only because it is a requirement by the company, or even local legislation. The approach is, therefore, "let's get this done, so that we can start the work". This approach is absurd. It adds no value and is a waste of time, effort, and money. Obviously, toolbox talks are an important part of the puzzle in providing a safe working environment and in the drive to send everyone home safely at the end of the day. However, doing it properly and steering away from a telling approach to a two-way communication and engagement approach would bring much benefit. When running the same exercise using the Engagement Board process, the scores for the four categories were between 4 and 5, thereby reflecting the benefit of the process.

Addressing Illiteracy

Having run training and used the Engagement Board process and tool across many sites around the world, we came to realise that it can be used in numerous settings, be it training venues, meeting rooms, operational control rooms, coffee corners, to name only a few. Some sessions took place in the African bush during team discussions a couple of years ago. This is all good, however, we have since realised that there can be a challenge in industries with low levels of literacy and an overburden of paper-based systems, forms, and assessments. This is even more of a challenge when having discussion with persons with little or no schooling, who are unable to read and write, and therefore, we believed that we should expand the tool to suit. The question however was, how could we do this, to ensure effectiveness and learning?

Brian and I had completed a boat dive in the Maldives and were sitting on the sun deck of the boat, catching up on some vitamin D, simply relaxing and snacking on pieces of a coconut. Whilst reminiscing and sharing our experiences and observations of the dive, the "penny dropped" and we came up with the idea that using scuba diving as an example on how to explain the Engagement Board would be a perfect opportunity. As there is so much workspace, and especially headspace and groupspace elements connected to scuba diving, this would be a perfect example to use. We then agreed to develop a video showing the various stages of a dive, from preparing one's kit to fitting the equipment, conducting the so called "buddy check", taking care of each other prior to stepping off the boat, checking on each other once in the water, to watching out for each other whilst submerged and then continuously during the dive, finally supporting each other after completion of the dive and returning to the boat or the shore.

In addition to the video, we developed a set of Engagement Board Coaching Cards, containing eighty cards with photographs and twenty-word cards, all connected to various diving equipment, risks, activities and covering the three elements of workspace, headspace and groupspace. These cards are now used in training to promote experiential learning by teams through placing the photocards and word cards in the various quadrants of the Engagement Board, followed by group discussion. The cards that have an impact on the social or cultural elements are then connected to highlight how controls and people impact others.

This process has been extended by the teams working in the forest environment in South Africa With many of the employees being illiterate, the cards related to their working environment have been instrumental in ensuring understanding of the risks, supported through the use of the Engagement Boards. The forests related Coaching Cards also promote good discussion and engagement amongst the teams on the ground. *Figure 72.* shows the *Cards Being Used* in a training session and *Figure 73.* reflects *Connecting the Cards* on the Engagement Board.

Figure 72. Cards Being Used

Figure 73. Connecting the Cards

Understanding the Language of the Team

Many of the social influences that impact the perception and perspective of people are through language as well as what is embedded in discourse in what is said, understood, and believed. It is not uncommon for leaders to have no understanding of the language of their respective teams, what is understood by the team, how issues are regarded and what comments are made. This is because in many instances, leaders do not engage with their teams on specific items. Understanding the "language" used by the teams can be done in a number of ways. One method is running the Engagement Board sessions with various shifts and then capturing the key words that are constantly mentioned during the discussions. Often this will give an insight to the leader of the language and even sub-cultures of the various departments and teams on the site.

For example, a site is battling with a certain aspect, let us say they do not feel comfortable in speaking up, if there is any malpractice taking place. With the use of the Engagement Board, the facilitator meets with members of a certain shift and engages with them on the topic, whilst capturing the discussion on the Engagement Board. Let us say, for example, words or metaphors such as: mistrust, bullying, the management style causes fear and blaming keep coming up, and more than once these are captured and highlighted on the board; then the same facilitator meets with other shifts, runs the Engagement Board sessions and then for each shift captures the common words and metaphors used. Once completing the sessions with various shifts the common words and metaphors are consolidated, giving the facilitator a clearer understanding of the language used. Language audits are useful in determining focus actions to influence and improve the company culture and sub-cultures.

Another method is to conduct an audit of the language used. We will not go into this in detail, however what it entails is giving each participant in the training, or engagement session ten pieces of paper and asking them within sixty seconds to capture the first ten words that come to their mind, when the facilitator mentions a topic. The group is then divided into several teams, depending on the size of the audience. They are then required to discuss their words and as a team agree on ten of the words selected. These are then further discussed amongst the bigger group. By going through the selected words, the facilitator has the opportunity to understand the language of the teams and the group. This then provides insight into how to address the issues, how to conduct the session and how to pitch the training, be it at a high level or at a basic level of training. This is important as the trainer does not want to lose the audience by being too basic or too detailed during the training. *Figure 74. Aneta Facilitating* a Language Audit, and in *Figure 75.* conducting a *Language Audit.*

Figure 74. Aneta Facilitating

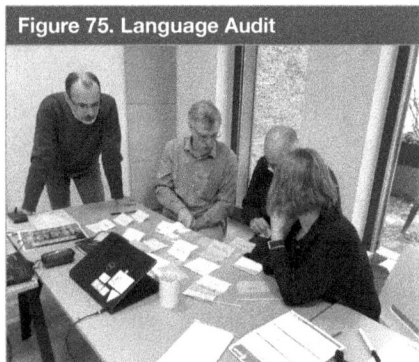
Figure 75. Language Audit

Dos and Don'ts Dialogue Cards

Good leaders understand that having a telling approach in their leadership style has its limits and is by no means a sustainable one. This approach is evidence of an existence of a superiority and inferiority culture within the team. Anyone growing up in the 1960s through 1980s would most likely have experienced this whilst at school. This approach is in direct contrast to having a culture where leaders promote open dialogue, where people are not afraid to voice their opinions or even raise their concerns and in addition, feel comfortable in speaking up. A leader, who understands the importance of listening to others through dialogue and engagement, is a leader who promotes learning amongst all and in turn creates a sense of ownership. Without having ownership there is little learning.

In conducting training sessions with persons in leadership roles in various companies and with persons in different levels from senior management, middle management, and those in first line leadership roles, it is clear that many leaders do not have the skills or means of ensuring good engagement with others. Many leaders find it challenging to have good dialogue with their team members and even less with persons outside of their respective teams. Some of the leaders, who we have engaged with, have openly said that they dislike engaging with the employees as they feel uncomfortable in doing so. If one cannot openly engage with another, then there is little or no chance of Real Meeting or entering the hyphen in the I-Thou.

In addition to the Engagement Board process, one of the tools that have been developed is called the Dos and Don'ts Dialogue Cards that are used to train others in good dialogue techniques. *Figure 76.* shows *The Dialogue Cards* and *Figure 77. Various Cards Used* in a training and coaching session.

Figure 76. The Dialogue Cards

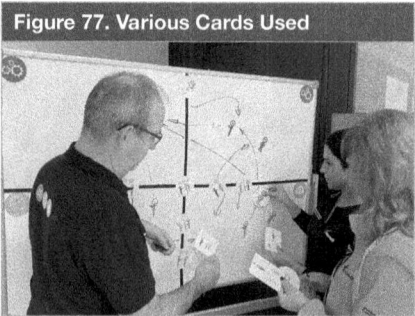

Figure 77. Various Cards Used

These cards are aimed at supporting dialogue by focusing on various issues, including the following four elements:

The Basics of Dialogue

It is, at times, rather worrying how we miss so much in dialogue with others. A set of Dialogue Cards has been developed and is used in training to focus on the basics of good dialogue and teaching people to be aware of various issues such as body language (good and bad), directing discussions, not missing the metaphors or gifts, refraining from interrupting others, and losing focus. The idea is to have two persons engaged in dialogue, whilst others use the cards to identify positives and negatives in the discussions held.

The Power of Silence

"The power of silence", these words were mentioned frequently during our training sessions some years ago. At first, they were not making much sense, however after further discussion, the meaning was understood. Leaders should know that they do not have to fill the conversation with their own comments, questions, or remarks, or even interrupting, as at times, it is better just to stay quiet and wait for others to continue talking.

Try this skill when in discussion with others and experience the benefit of the power of silence. When allowing the other person to tell their story, there often comes a time when the person stops talking, believing that they have said enough to answer a question or in giving their impression or comments on a certain topic. However, if the leader does not immediately start talking, but instead remains mute, the other person involved in the discussion will more than likely continue talking.

By doing the above, allows the leader to have an even better understanding of the topic than they would have had, if they had filled the space with words. As leaders, we should understand that there is no need to fill the space or the pauses in a conversation, just remain silent and there is a chance of the discussion continuing. Like all elements of good dialogue, this needs practise and conscious thought process when engaging with others. The silence, at times, is more powerful than the words spoken.

Listening to Metaphors

For most persons, a metaphor is regarded as an extraordinary way of explaining something, and most of us cannot speak without the use of metaphors. Some people believe that metaphors are of no significance in our language or the way that we communicate with others. When reading the book, "Metaphors We Live By" written by George Lakoff and Mark Johnson, one realises that the use of metaphors is key to everyday language as well as in our thoughts and actions. The use of metaphors in our language is often from the unconscious mind, with us not even realising that we are speaking metaphorically. When engaging with others, leaders should switch on to listening consciously to metaphors used and in doing so having a better understanding of what is being discussed. There are so many common metaphors used continuously in our daily lives at work, with some of them including the following:

- Time is money.
- Time has flown past.
- She will never win the argument.
- Mind over matter.
- Let us unpack this idea.
- Jumping with joy.
- He ran out of luck.
- Sitting in the hot seat.
- He has no leg to stand on.
- I immediately fell into a deep sleep.
- What does the future hold for them.
- We took the wind out of their sails.
- Put your money where your mouth is.
- The results hit the ceiling last year.
- He has no backbone or stomach to handle the situation.
- She is a back seat driver.
- It is going to be an uphill battle.
- Up a creek without a paddle.

We believe that it is not possible to be switched on to listening to metaphors all the time, and therefore, one needs to train oneself in listening to metaphors when in discussion with others. Doing so, not only, improves the understanding of what is meant, but also could support in, "driving the discussion into a different direction". When training leaders, and in gauging their understanding of metaphors, it is surprising how people struggle to think of some metaphors, even though, they are used continuously in their daily language. However, when giving some examples, one sees the "aha moment" kicking in as they realise how many of the metaphors, they have either heard or used themselves.

This chapter is not designed to be an in-depth lesson on metaphors, but rather simply to raise the awareness of how, when switching on to metaphors, one can facilitate or "chase" the discussions into different directions, issues of significance that will have a totally different outcome from engagement with others than what was expected.

In the Chapter 7 on self-reflection, we gave an example of how listening to metaphors in a discussion with someone else had a totally different outcome to addressing the problem related to a lifting task. Looking at the paragraph above we used a number of metaphors without even realising it, at the time of writing. When reading the paragraph, we identified the metaphors used. This is an example of how, even in our written communication, we make use of metaphors. To explain this further, the metaphors used in the above paragraphs include:

- "Key to everyday language".
- "Not possible to be switched on to listening to metaphors".
- "Driving the discussion into a different direction".
- "In gauging their understanding of metaphors".
- "Surprising how many struggle to think".
- "Aha moment' kicking in".
- "This chapter is not aimed at an in-depth writing".
- "Raise the awareness on how when switching on".
- "Chase the discussion into different directions".
- "On self-reflection, we gave an example".
- "Addressing the problem".
- "Make use of metaphors".

As mentioned, one is not automatically and consciously switched on to listening to metaphors, however, when focusing on improving dialogue with others there is huge benefit in switching oneself on to listening to the metaphors used. Having dialogue cards in training supports the notion of listening to metaphors.

If one strives to understanding metaphors clearly, then the book titled "Metaphors We Live By" is an excellent read – one of the important books for good leaders to read, if they want to improve their skills of listening and in turn having Real Meeting. Without a doubt, a book that is amongst both our lists of favourite books that we have read and referred to when developing training material.

Listening to the "Gifts"

Listening to the gifts (sometimes referred to as confessions) that others give during discussion is as important as switching on to the metaphors used. A "gift" is defined as comments made that are not necessarily related to the topic of a discussion. An example of listening to a gift was provided in Chapter 7 on self-reflection. These Dialogue Cards are used to coach leaders to listen for these gifts, and as with metaphors chase the discussion based on any relevant gifts provided by the words of others. Often these gifts are from the unconscious mind and take discussions into a different direction. We have experienced, at times, surprisingly where a discussion ends up, only because the metaphors and gifts were chased and followed through on. In many instances resulting in significant issues being surfaced and addressed accordingly.

Engagement Walkabouts (Boots on the Ground)

In practising Real Meeting, one of the key aspects of leadership is getting out of one's office, away from the boardrooms, out of the comfort zone of sitting behind one's desk and getting out onto the floor where the rubber hits the tar, where the action takes place, where the employees are adding value, where some are at the coalface. Be it in the office block, the production areas, maintenance workshops, warehouses, energy plants, hospital wards, canteens, lecture rooms, plantations, to name only a few.

These walkabouts must be aimed at engaging with the employees, entering the hyphen in the I-Thou and in Real Meeting with others. However, for many, this does not come naturally, therefore, training and coaching is needed to provide leaders at all levels of the organisation with the skills and fundamentals of talking and engaging with their respective teams. Even with the correct training and instruction, regular coaching is required to further hone the skills of leaders.

The key aspect of engagement walkabouts is focusing on the person or persons and not solely of the work activity, for example, the controls, procedures, and deadlines. Yes, there is a time and place for focusing on the objects and controls, after all, leaders are in the role to focus also on things like profits, production numbers, efficiencies, product development, logistics and more. However, the focus of engagement walkabouts has an emphasis on the people issues, finding the balance between objects and people is key in leadership.

Engagement walkabouts, as mentioned above, and in the various chapters of this book, build open discussions, trust, promote engagement and more importantly contribute to developing the desired culture in an organisation. Many discussions with teams are about the things that can be measured. As previously mentioned in Chapter 6, there is the well-known quote by Peter Drucker, "you can't manage what you don't measure", yes, this is true to many aspects of management, however there are many facets of leadership that cannot be measured. These include the engagement that leaders have with employees, in discussion, building relationship, listening with intent, allowing others to tell their story and what happens in Real Meeting. However sadly, at times, leaders regard this as non-value adding and not important be it consciously or unconsciously.

The aspects that are not measurable are often more important than the aspects of business that organisations measure. Often the aspects of life that cannot be measured have a stronger impact and contribution of the overall culture of an organisation. One can have the best tools, computer programs, systems, office space, production machines, canteen facilities and more, but if there is no true sense of care for others, giving people time as a leader, showing interest, engaging, with others and having Real Meeting, then there is a good possibility that building the desired culture will not be achieved. As a simple bit of encouragement, as a leader, get out from behind the desk at times, and engage with others.

There are many ways of ensuring Real Meetings with others when out on site talking to employees, the "icebreaker" usually sets the tone for good engagement with others. When visiting work areas, and noticing that someone has a tattoo, I find this as a good start to a discussion. By informing the person that you noticed their tattoo and asking, if they would like to share its meaning, often is a good start, as most tattoos have significance, and you will find that the majority of those with tattoos are pleased that they are asked and share the details with pleasure. I also find that asking someone to share what object they have on their keyring, starts off a good discussion. There are many ways in addition to these two examples that one can show interest and engage with others, for example asking what they have as a screen saver on their phone, or who are the persons in a photograph on their desk. All of these have significance to the persons and by asking, you show your interest in the person. Once the connection is made, the leader can move into the discussion regarding the work-related topic. I have only experienced one occasion, when the person with whom I was engaging did not want to share the details of their specific tattoo. Seeing the person's facial expression (sadness) it was clear there was some significant emotion attached, and therefore, I refrained from continuing the discussion. I then immediately diverted to the work-related discussion with the person. See *Figure 78. Tattoo Discussion* and in *Figure 79. Keyring Discussion*.

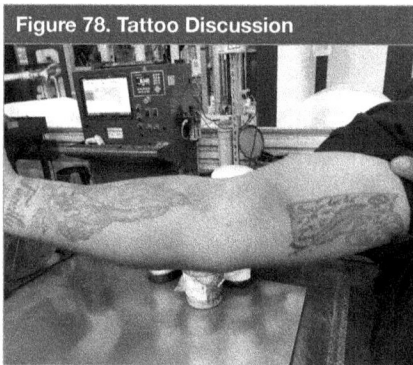
Figure 78. Tattoo Discussion

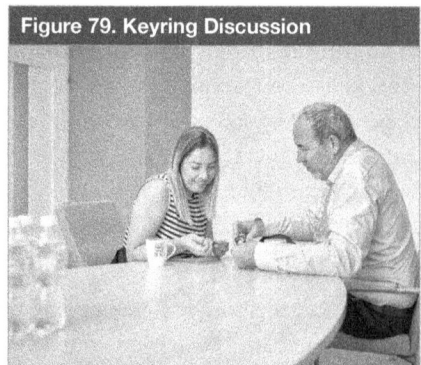
Figure 79. Keyring Discussion

Tying the Key Elements Together

We often take a walk prior to calling it a day as part of our reflection, and whilst out for one of our regular evening walks, through the streets of Malta and day one into the new year, we were talking about the final chapters of this book and deciding what should be covered. We agreed on the epilogue of the book, however felt that it was key to pull everything together into a model to reflect the link between the writings of Martin Buber and Social Psychology of Risk as developed by Robert Long and written about in our book titled "It Works!". Yes, we do understand that no model is perfect, that all models are interpreted differently; however, with that in mind we came up with our own interpretation, and therefore, we hope that our interpretation to you, as the reader, makes sense.

Workspace, Headspace and Groupspace

So much of what we do as leaders is focused on what is called Workspace elements, things that are physical, can be controlled and managed, things like profits, metrics, cash flow, incidents, meetings, emails, strategy setting, due dates, action plans, to name a few. All these are necessary and of importance in daily management of any successful company, however there is also the need to move towards the two other elements, being Headspace and Groupspace. Moving out of the boardroom or one's own office and meeting with people, in discussion, understanding their needs, their concerns and listening to their stories, be it individuals or in groups.

Although the idea of Workspace (Physical), Headspace (Psychological) and Groupspace (Cultural) was developed to capture the fundamentals of Social Psychology of Risk, we have no doubt that they are applicable to other aspects of leadership in general. If leaders place their focus solely on the physical dimension, there will be little understanding of the psychological issues and even less knowledge or influence on the cultural elements.

One Brain – Three Minds and Three Ways of Knowing or Deciding

We know that when we get stressed and anxious, our heart races, when we feel overwhelmed, we get "butterflies in our gut" and the same with some sensations such as excessive guilt and fear, we get physically sick, we get an ache in the gut. These sensations may come partly from the brain, yet they are triggered and communicated independently by the endocrine, nervous, and immune systems. Under acute stress the body shuts down, and most importantly the sensations are felt in the heart and gut. This is referred to as the "Three Ways of Knowing".

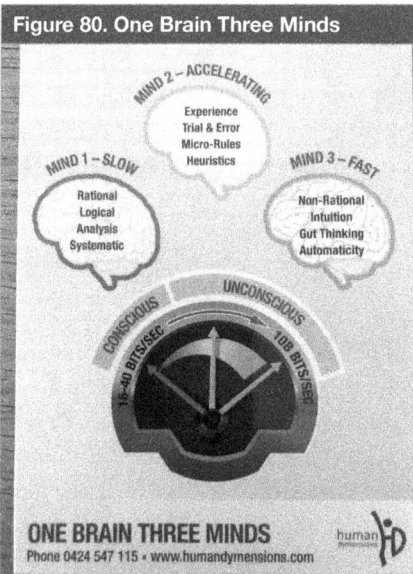

Figure 80. One Brain Three Minds

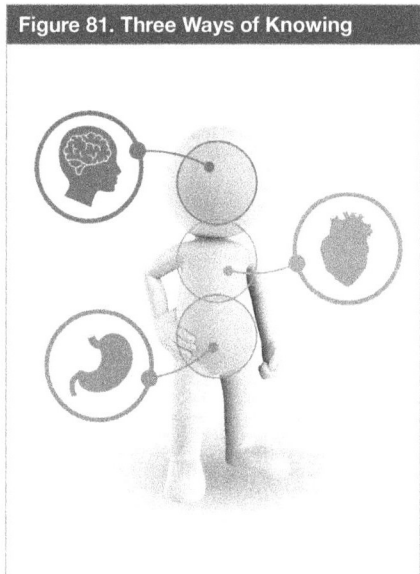

Figure 81. Three Ways of Knowing

In order to convey the embodied nature of decision-making Robert Long, uses three brain images as Minds across the semiotic of a speedometer. As much as every model has flaws and weaknesses, this model allows an understanding of how the human embodied Mind "thinks". This triarchic model seeks to explain both the automaticity of human decision making and also the slow rational mode of decision making and thinking. This model is expressed semiotically in *Figure 80. One Brain Three Minds*. Another model used and which is of significance in understanding how people think and act, is the One Person Three Ways of Knowing or Deciding. This is reflected in *Figure 81*. One Person *Three Ways of Knowing* or Deciding.

Mind 1- Slow Mind

In Mind 1, humans make slow rational decisions like completing a paper-based checklist or form. In Mind 1, the process of thinking requires methodical, systematic and rational thinking. A good example here is, the pilots together conducting the pre-flight checks, where they verbally run through and confirm the various checks conducted.

Mind 2 – Intermediate Mind

In Mind 2, it is all about thinking heuristically, for example thinking that relies on practical habits and developed shortcuts as humans. This kind of decision making is essential to be fast and efficient in what we do as a species and is based on trial and error, as well as infused into thinking through gaining of experience and often triggered by perception or memory. Much of this type of decision making is quick and efficient with little or no decision making, rational choice or analytical thinking. An example here is, when learning to drive a car, after a couple of weeks of trial and error, the learner driver starts getting the hang of things and therefore, does not consciously focus on all the aspects of driving, but rather only some of them.

Mind 3 – Fast Mind

In Mind 3, it is all about doing things automatically, there is no rational thinking, no deciding on what to do, no conscious thoughts or rational processing of things. This is often referred to as intuitional or gut thinking. Let us once again, use the example of driving a car. After years of driving, we tend to slip into the automatic mode, often focused on other things than the driving itself. How often do we as drivers drive to a destination and when arriving, we cannot remember elements of the drive?

When in dialogue with others, and when in the I-Thou, we are communicating in Mind 1, showing care and interest in another person or persons, and are also influencing the embodied thoughts and feelings in head, heart, and gut. Depending in the nature of the discussion, we as leaders, influence the other person or persons, be it stuck in the I-It mode or moving into the I-Thou. As mentioned, there is a need to have dialogue in anyone of the two, depending on the circumstances. However, having dialogue, no matter what kind, brings a person or persons from Minds 3 and 2 to Mind 1. The dialogue moves persons from the unconscious to the conscious.

We have tried to place all of the above into one model, bringing the I-Thou, I-It, Workspace, Headspace, Groupspace as well as One Brain-Three Minds together, thereby reflecting how they all intertwine with each other, almost as if in a dance. We have named our model, "The Mission and Movement Model". As mentioned earlier in the book, as with all models, this one is not perfect, however it is aimed at reflecting our thoughts and our interpretation of Martin Buber's writings and some elements of Social Psychology of Risk. See *Figure 82. The Mission and Movement Model.*

As the model is in black and white in the book and not as normally in colour, the explanation is as follows, to allow you the Reader to imagine what it looks like in its original form:

A = Red Colour (Workspace)

B = Yellow Colour (Headspace)

C = Green Colour (Groupspace)

On the lower section of the model (section A) is the management component and the wording reflects examples of elements of management that fall into the I-It mode. The upper section of the model (section C) is the leadership component, and the wording depicts examples of leadership qualities that are imbedded in the I-Thou mode. The middle section (section B) is the neutral part of the model, which is the period when the leader makes the decision to move out from the I-It and into the I-Thou.

The three round icons on the right-hand side of the model are reflecting the three elements of social psychology of risk: workspace (gears icon), headspace (head icon) and groupspace (people icon). The symbol of the person located (upper right) in the leadership component (section C), represents the three ways of knowing, being head, heart and gut. The figure on the bottom left (section A), indicates the manager focusing on management controls, the figure in section B, signifies the leader considering to move out of the I-It and towards the I-Thou mode, and the figure on top left ((section C), reflects the leader in the I-Thou mode. The symbol of the three figures (with communication bubbles) located slightly off centre in section C, reflects the leader in the I-Thou, and in engagement with others.

The model has two curving lines running from left to right, at different heights and shapes. These depict the importance of moving out of the I-It and into the I-Thou. The two lines also indicate that, at times, a leader would spend either longer or less time engaging with the teams, and sometimes engaging with many people and other times with less persons, even on a one-to-one basis.

Finaly, when in the management component, one finds oneself spending the majority of the time in Chronos time and when in the I-Thou one spends the majority of the time in Kairos time, time in Real Meeting. Once again, as mentioned in various chapters of this book, all of these elements depicted in this model are like a dance, moving between the I-It and the I-Thou, spending time in Chronos Time and Kairos Time, in meeting or in Real Meeting, being alone in one's office to engaging with employees on the shop floor. In actual fact, life itself is a continuous dance, it is up to us in which part of the dance, we want to spend our time in and for how long. One thing is for sure, we will spend time in all the various components, as they all are of significance in one way or another.

It is important to understand that nobody is permanently in the I-Thou, as we, as leaders, and in our personal lives need to spend time in managing things, and therefore, spending large periods of our lives in the I-It. This is why the curve of the lines in the model move up, however always come back down to the I-It component. Some people can be embedded in the I-It and seldom or never move into the I-Thou, however in doing so, is a contradiction to us as social beings. Being stuck in the I-It can only result in one becoming extremely lonely.

We like the quote from Martin Buber, "I knew nothing of books when I came forth from the womb of my mother, and I shall die without books, with another human hand in my own. I do, indeed, close my door at times and surrender myself to a book, but only because I can open the door again and see a human being looking at me". This quote fits so well with our model, where we reflect that, as leaders, we need to be in the I-It in our daily lives, to manage the business, however at times, we need to get up from behind the computer screen, open the office door and go engage with people on the shopfloor, in the canteens, coffee corners or in their offices, or wherever they might be.

Figure 82. The Mission and Movement Model

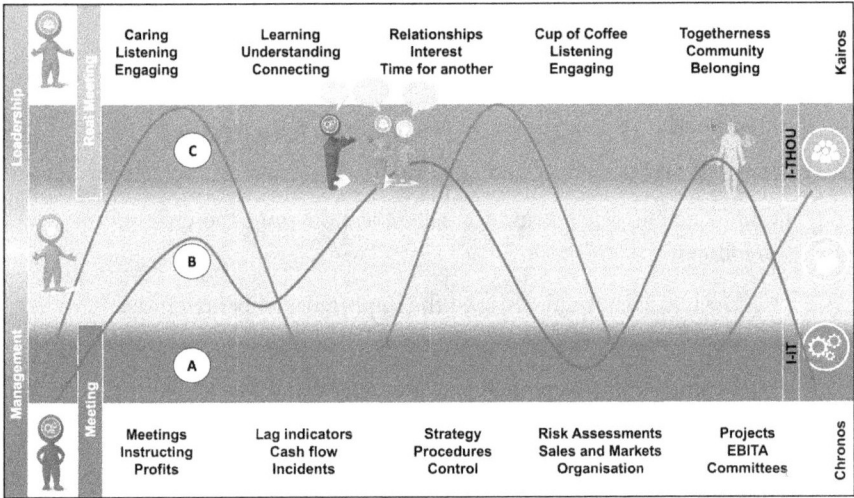

SELF-REFLECTION

Chapter 11 – Various Practical Examples and Tools

Our selection of elements for self-reflection from the chapter are as follows:

- Do I, as a leader, understand the importance of being on the shop floor, engaging with my teams?

- I ensure all my team members are trained and coached in the fundamentals of engaging with others.

- Do I understand the importance of switching on to metaphors and "gifts" when in discussion with others?

- I try to focus on the "power of silence" when engaging with others.

- What percentage of my time is spent with "boots on the ground"?

- I am aware that people think with their head, heart and gut, and therefore, deal with situations accordingly.

- How often do I move out of the red zone, section A (management) and into the green zone, section C (leadership) of the Mission and Movement Model?

CHAPTER 12

The Epilogue

"But how could you live and have no story to tell?"

Fyodor Dostoevsky

Novellist (Aneta's Favourite Writer)

Moving to Real Meeting as Leaders

Without doubt, many of us have fallen into the "rat race", the business of things, life as we know it today has speeded up, we have drifted from a predominantly caring approach to one that is about getting things done, as quickly and efficiently as possible, and at times not even acknowledging people whom we pass or interact with on a daily basis. We both know it from our own experiences and for both of us this is definitely the case, both in our private lives as well as in business. We are certainly not saying this is the wrong approach, however, it is evident that as leaders we tend to rush so much, stick to fixed agendas, do everything at extra fast pace, dictated by our watches or the clock in the bottom right-hand corner of our laptops and in doing so have lost the importance of having Real Meetings with others. Real Meeting where we listen to others with intent, where our teams see us as leaders with a leadership style that shows a sense of caring, guidance, support, promoting open discussion, and, of course, entering the hyphen of the I-Thou.

Life as we know it today, has become so busy, and the busier we become, the days and months as well as years tend to fly past in a "blink of an eye". How often do we hear people use metaphors like; "this year has flown past", or "I don't have enough hours in the day", "time flies" and "where has this month gone to!" It is not as if the year has fewer months, or a month has fewer days and days fewer hours, it is because we as a human race in today's world are continuously living at maximum speed, seldom switching off from work, responsibilities, or addicted to and reliant on technology. In doing so, we become less social and thereby dehumanise our approach on how we deal with others, we slip into the I-It and seldom enter the I-Thou.

Some decades back, when we were introduced to mobile phones, laptops became the norm, followed by items like the "Blackberry" and then smart phone technology arrived. Not surprisingly, most of these items have to some degree taken over and controlled our lives in many aspects – sadly though, affecting our heuristics of being social beings and also neglecting meeting in Real Meeting.

Just observe people sitting at restaurants with their families or friends, so often one or more of them are looking at the screens of their phones or typing a message, email or surfing the Internet. There is little engagement taking place, as those on their phones are locked in their own world. Sometimes it seems like the "influencers" on their social media are of more importance than the persons sitting face to face with them.

As children, living with our parents, we recall being friends with, or at least knowing, the neighbours who resided in the same street, the owners of the local shop, the local postal worker, the bank teller, milkman, and even the police officer. Fast forward thirty years, living in the centre of Vienna, one of the most beautiful cities in the world, we do only know two out of around fifteen people living in our block of apartments, never mind others living in the same street and even less the postal worker or local bank teller. Life has just become far too hectic – or is it just an excuse to avoid being social. Or perhaps every day, we make a conscious choice of being social, but only on social media.

Technology has improved, having a laptop and a smart phone often results in people taking work home to complete whatever was not finished at the office or addressed during the day. Sadly, as a result, families lose that valuable time together sharing experiences and entering the I-Thou or the opportunity of having Real Meetings with their partners, children as well as friends and family. Time that could have been spent in engagement, conversations, truly being with others, sports and having some fun, is at times, exchanged for "valuable" online "likes" and "subscriptions". A friend of ours who lost his wife in an accident, once said, "if only I had found the balance, if only I had given more time to my wife", and the "if onlys" went on and on. He had lost time of Real Meeting with his wife, time that can never be brought back.

This is no different to the working environment, leaders are so busy in their offices and meeting rooms, and because of technology often bogged down behind their desks and with closed doors, dealing with important issues. The emergence of emails complicated things even more, as it is easy to be added to distribution lists or copied in on emails for all types of issues, some core business, and others not. The downside of this is that leaders have less time to have "boots on the ground", engaging with their respective teams and the employees on the shop floor. Leaders tend to focus mainly on objects and have often, to some degree, lost that humanising approach to life at work and possibly a balanced life at home. It is also not uncommon for them to be conscious of time pressures and therefore, when on the shop floor engaging with people, they tend to limit the duration of discussions, making it a tickbox approach, and as a result do not listen with intent, fail to suspend their own agendas and miss so much in getting the potential benefit from the engagement session. All of this similar to the "if onlys" mentioned by our friend after losing his dear wife.

Being a True Leader or Losing Touch

The challenge for all leaders is to understand that their teams are made up of individual members of the society in which they live and work. Leaders can by no means rely on the idea that people can all be treated in the same way. All persons are made up of their own set of biases as well as heuristics; everyone is unique, and the overwhelming majority of their actions are influenced by their unconscious Minds as well as the impact of their social environments. No person is identical to another, and therefore, each one of us interprets things around us differently, be it signs, symbols, mantras, language, gestures, body language or our social environment, to name a few elements. Therefore, to ensure common understanding, leaders need to engage with their employees, understand the sub-cultures of their various teams and be aware of the dynamics thereof. Leaders also need to understand the heuristics and biases that contribute to the decision-making process. Leaders should through engagement bring to the surface issues and drive discussion from Workspace to Headspace and Groupspace and by doing so move unconscious thoughts to conscious.

Leaders who lose touch with the "shop floor" run the risk of shifting from being "Caring Leaders" to becoming "managers". The key elements of being a leader are often lost when we dehumanise the approach to leadership. Some key elements of a good Leader include:

- understanding that human beings are fallible, and therefore, will fail and make mistakes at times;

- understanding that the social environment impacts the way people behave and make decisions;

- being ethical and having a genuine caring-helping approach towards others;

- guiding, coaching and supporting others to achieve their best;
- having "boots on the ground" and being accessible to others;
- developing individuals as social beings;
- building trust and honesty;
- showing empathy;
- having a listening rather than telling approach (with the use of open questions);
- reliance on engagement and good dialogue techniques;
- use of methods, tools, models, techniques that are humanising and not brutalising or bullying;
- refraining from managing by fear or threats;
- showing respect;
- being aware and alert of the use of gestures, metaphors, and body language;
- remaining calm during challenging situations;
- ensuring a balanced focus between objects and subjects;
- acknowledging others as human beings, with needs, feelings and emotions;
- considering the trade-offs or discourse of language used;
- being consciously aware of the language used, their own behaviours as well as the examples that they set to their teams;
- and most importantly remembering to move out of the I-It, at times, and entering the hyphen of the I-Thou.

How can it ever be possible to regard oneself as being a Leader in the true sense of the word, if there is a disregard for the characteristics listed above? Certainly, no leader will be good at all of them (as well as other key characteristics) all of the time. So, too, no leader can be constantly "switched on" and be conscious of their behaviour, body language or gestures used. And yes, no leader can be constantly in the I-Thou as there is a need to focus on the I-It elements in managing business, navigating through life in general; however, reminding oneself to move to the I-Thou is of utmost importance in being an inspiring and caring leader. Taking all of this into account, it is key for any leader to take time out for self-reflection, to take stock of what we do, how we behave, how much we reflect care, and in doing so challenge oneself and continuously strive not only to be an inspiring leader, but also an inspiring person in everyday life.

From Switching off Life Support – to Swiss Chocolates

When thinking about a closing chapter to this book, I recalled a story once told to me by Brian, how he was faced with a seriously injured person, asking him to switch off the life support machines as she laid in the intensive care unit of a hospital, and how he felt the sadness in the ward on the day and had to think carefully about what words he would use to face the challenging request that he had to face. I am glad that Brian agreed to close this book off with the story, as it is a true reflection how a leader can change the perception about life, just by showing a caring approach, visiting someone in distress, lying in hospital, and whilst there for ten minutes entered the hyphen in the I-Thou. This story is a sad one, however frames the I-Thou principle and the aspect of Real Meeting.

The Ten Minutes of Care with Anne that Made a Difference

Many years ago, I (Brian) was sitting in the Lufthansa Senator Lounge at Frankfurt airport enjoying my breakfast and connecting my laptop to the lounge's Internet service. I had an hour earlier arrived back from a week-long trip and was waiting for my flight home to Vienna to repack my bags and some three hours later board a flight to the Philippines. I had been asked by a multi-national mining company to support them with an investigation into a fatality that they had experienced, due to someone being struck by a falling coconut tree on an exploration site on one of the islands. As I was tucking into my breakfast, enjoying a German frankfurter and warmly baked pretzel, whilst preparing to send some of the emails that I had written on the flight the night before, I received a call from the managing director of one of our operations, informing me of a serious incident that had occurred at the site during the night. He informed me that the employee (for the purpose of this book, I refer to her as Anne) who had been seriously injured had been transported to a local hospital and was admitted to the intensive care unit; and although stable, her injuries were concerning and probably life threatening.

After ending the conversation, obviously both shocked and saddened by the news, I was processing it all in my mind and reflecting on the distressing discussion I had just experienced with the managing director of the site, I could clearly hear the emotion in his voice. I immediately knew that under no circumstance would I be comfortable flying to the Philippines to support the team with the investigation, whilst knowing that our own company, our site in South Africa, had experienced a serious and life-threatening incident, and that our team members would have been in distress. I knew that my support would be appreciated by our senior team at the site during the difficult days that lay ahead, emotionally as well as during the incident investigation.

Even though still early on that Saturday morning, I decided to call my manager and the representative of the mining company. I explained the situation to them and mentioned that as a result, I would no longer be flying to the Philippines to participate in the fatality incident investigation, but instead, I would be boarding the long flight back to South Africa, on probably the same plane that I had just disembarked from that same morning. The representative of the mining company, who had initially asked me to investigate the incident and had made all the arrangements, fully understood the circumstances, and wholeheartedly supported my decision to change the plans. I did, however, feel that in my decision, I had let the incident investigation team down, however I knew that cancelling the planned trip to the Philippines was the right thing to do, for Anne as she laid in hospital, our team as well as my own conscience and peace of mind.

I caught the plane back to Austria, drove hundred and seventy kilometres home, washed up, repacked my travel bag, had a quick lunch and then drove back to Vienna to catch the flight to Frankfurt. Then after a short layover boarded the flight to travel from Frankfurt to my destination, enduring another more than ten hours of flying. At that stage, everything I had done and was still doing was based on the I-It as well as in Chronos Time; managing changes, booking flights, hotel reservations, preparing the documentation for the investigation, talking to the team at the site, and arranging the logistics for the week that lay ahead. This all would change so much when stepping into the hospital the next day, as I would move out of the I-It and into the world of I-Thou as described by Martin Buber, and for a short period move out of Chronos Time into Kairos Time by being present in the moment. Shifting me from focusing mainly on all the arrangements and logistics to connecting with another, showing genuine care for, and engaging with Anne, someone who I had never met, as well as to some degree connecting with her mother, who was preoccupied with fear of losing her daughter.

After landing the following morning, and catching one more connecting flight, I rented a car and drove directly to the hospital where I requested permission to see Anne. Not being a family member, it was always going to be difficult to enter the ward, however after some discussion with the health nurse, explaining who I was and why I would like to be permitted into the intensive care unit, she kindly obliged, in turn asking me not to be longer than ten to fifteen minutes due to Anne's condition. The nurse then escorted me to the section where Anne was lying in her bed behind a slightly opened curtain where she was being cared for. When entering through the opening in the curtain, I immediately noticed Anne being connected to all types of medical equipment, oxygen and what I believe were feeding tubes. I will never forget the look on her mother's face as she sat next to Anne holding her hand, the blank look on her face, with tears running down her cheeks. I introduced myself to Anne and her mother, explaining that I worked for the company and that I was from Vienna, and had come to see how she was doing.

With a slow-moving hand gesture, Anne called me closer to her and with an exhausted breath she asked me, if I would do her a favour. I immediately obliged, however was taken aback when Anne asked me to switch off the life support machines, and then explained that her mother had continuously refused to switch them off. Anne was crying, as she explained to me that she was in too much pain, that it was unbearable and that she no longer wanted to live, she wanted to give up the fight. Not sure how to respond, I looked over to her mother sitting on the opposite side of the bed, noticed the sadness on her face and fear in her eyes, before dropping her head into her hands, and starting to sob, as she had heard the request from Anne to me. I turned my attention back to Anne, battling to control my own emotions, instant sadness, and tears, as I had definitely not expected her request. I informed her that firstly, it was not legal for her mother or me to do such a thing (I was in the I-It, focused on the controls). I then asked her if she had any children, to which she responded, "yes, I have a two-year-old daughter". I then said to Anne that for the sake of her young daughter there was another reason why I could not grant her wish to switch off the life support machines (I had moved from the I-It to the I-Thou, focused on the relationship). I could see that she was emotional and was breathing with difficulty. I then mentioned to her that when (not if) she leaves the hospital, recovers fully, and returns to work, I would have lunch with her at the company canteen. I then decided to leave, as I noticed that she was breathing with difficulty and her slowly closing eyes showing signs of tiredness.

As I was about to leave the intensive care unit, Anne's mother approached me at the door and mentioned that her daughter had asked that I go back to her, as she wanted to talk to me. I returned to her bedside, and up to this day, I will never forget her words. In a belated breath, she said "when you return the next time, could you bring me Swiss chocolates". I looked at her and smiled, agreeing, and making a deal with her that I would bring her the chocolates with my next visit. Anne looked at me, wearing a smile on her face as I gave a brief wave as I said bye and left the ward.

After I had exited the hospital, I sat in the hired car in the hospital's car park for around ten minutes, reflecting on what had just happened, Anne's initial request, the fear in her eyes, and the tears on her face and that of her mother and the silence, my emotions were all over the place, I felt so much sadness within myself for Anne, and her mother, two people that I had never met before. I recalled witnessing her mother looking so sad and so terrified that she would lose her daughter. Although I did not realise it at that stage of my life, but I was so much in the I-Thou, I had connected with Anne, by showing care, holding her hand and bringing her young daughter from her unconscious to her conscious mind, and even though only with her for a short time, we were in Kairos Time. Within ten minutes standing next to Anne's bed, she had moved from wanting to die to wanting Swiss chocolates, "wow" such a turn-around, so unexpected, truly astonishing.

Some months later, Anne eventually left the hospital and as part of her rehabilitation was visiting our on-site clinic for a medical checkup and coincidentally, I happened to be on site on the specific day. I was so pleased to hear that she would be visiting and as promised, together with some of the occupational nurses, we had lunch together in the clinic with her and gave her the Swiss chocolates that she had requested so many months before, whilst fighting for her life. During lunch, Anne thanked me for the short time that we had spent together months before, the day after the incident, and this was when she mentioned that the care and support that was shown as well as the reference to her daughter pulled her through the pain and suffering. Her view had changed, her wish to die had changed, and her will to survive conquered all. Initially, when referring to the legalities of not switching the life support off, meant nothing to Anne, I was talking to her in the I-It. As soon as I referred to her daughter, I had (even not knowing) moved into the I-Thou, that is what made the difference to Anne.

Beatles Song – Help

Whenever reflecting on the time standing in the intensive care unit, comforting and talking to Anne, I think of the song by the Beatles "Help". Most humans at some stages of their lives feel down, want that shoulder to lean on, that ear to listen to them, that caring hug to comfort them. Be it in our private lives, at home, or at work. And sadly, at times this is not regarded as important by leaders, or sometimes even overlooked. Leaders who show care and support, listen to those in need, make a difference, they are true Leaders who inspire others and often their leadership style cascades down to other leaders within their teams.

The following lyrics from the song "Help", are so key in understanding that there are people out there, in our private lives, at work who need some support, some kind of care. Whenever I hear this song, it brings my memories to the surface, moving them from my unconscious to my conscious all the way back to the intensive care unit and ultimately to my friend and colleague, Anne.

Help

I need somebody

(Help) not just anybody

(Help) you know I need someone, help

So much younger than today

(I never need) I never needed anybody's help in any way

(Now) but now these days are gone (these days are gone)

I'm not so self-assured

(And now I find) now I find I've changed my mind

And opened up the doors

Help me if you can, I'm feeling down

And I do appreciate you being 'round

Help me get my feet back on the ground

Won't you please, please help me

In oh so many ways

(My independ-) my independence seems to vanish in the haze

(But) but every now and then (now and then)

I feel so insecure

(I know that I) I know that I just need you like

I've never done before

Help me if you can, I'm feeling down

And I do appreciate you being 'round

Help me get my feet back on the ground

Won't you please, please help me

When I was younger, so much younger than today
I never needed anybody's help in any way
(Now) but now these days are gone (these days are gone)
I'm not so self-assured
(And now I find) now I find I've changed my mind
And opened up the doors
Help me if you can, I'm feeling down
And I do appreciate you being 'round
Help me get my feet back on the ground
Won't you please, please help me, help me, help me, ooh

Reflection

Reading this book reflects that you, as a leader, are keen to sharpen your skills, to humanise your leadership style and to make personhood the centre of your focus. We trust that the contents of the chapters, as well as various stories told, did exactly that and prompted reflection on your leadership style, positive and negative; but at the end, that they have provided some guidance in being a Leader, which reflects the caring and helping approach and, importantly, the need for Real Meeting. Move from focusing solely on the I-It into the hyphen of the I-Thou. Shift from focusing on objects towards focusing on the person. See *Figure 83. The Traffic Cone*, Aneta having a discussion with a traffic cone, depicting the notion of the focus on the I-It and in *Figure 84. Talking to a Person*, Aneta speaking to our daughter, Jolene, talking about her tattoo and having entered the hyphen of the I-Thou.

Figure 83. The Traffic Cone

Figure 84. Talking to a Person

Our journey with numerous leaders, coaches and mentors over the years, has "opened our eyes" in many aspects of life and assisted in our own reflection regarding our styles of leadership. We came to realise that, although we both cared in general for others, some of the tools and methods used in leadership are in contradiction to the principles of caring and helping.

Meeting Graham Long on several Zoom sessions as well as in person, focusing on the writings of the "I and Thou" by Martin Buber, as well as our interests (especially Aneta's) in the writings of various philosophers of the twentieth century, provided us with much guidance about the importance of relationships, community, care, support and importantly the coming together in the I-Thou, and entering into the hyphen.

We hope that this book does the same for you, Dear Reader, and in your journey as a leader, no matter whether in a personal capacity or what industry, profession, or level of leadership you find yourself at the time of reading this book or in years to come.

One day, as work on this book was nearing completion, Brian was looking over a printed version that was lying on the kitchen table. It was a Friday afternoon, and I was preparing dinner and enjoying listening to some smooth jazz in the background when suddenly I heard a question, "Love ... if you had to name a special person in your life, who gave you his or her time and undivided attention to listen to your stories, who would that be?"

My immediate response was, "Besides you (when the Springbok Rugby team isn't playing) and my mom?"

He nodded, smiling. One would think that after writing a book titled "Real Meetings", I would have had several names in mind, but I did not... Actually, it took me a while to reply and that was when I realised that this innocent-sounding, apparently simple question had a very complex answer, which required much thought. In today's hectic world, with things evolving at such a fast pace, not many people have the time to give their undivided attention to others.

After some deliberation, one person came to mind. For me that special person was Mrs Maria Wlodarczyk, a family friend with whom I spent many fascinating hours during my early years (unfortunately she passed away in her late seventies, when I was sixteen years old). This special lady would always pay attention to people she met. She would give of her time, eager to listen, often with a cup of tea in her hand, and always willing to share her thoughts.

One day I asked her, how did she do it? Typically, as a teenager, I did not think that everything anyone said was worth listening to. She answered, "My child, everyone deserves to be heard. I learnt that, when I was a prisoner in the Auschwitz concentration camp in the Second World War. That place was filled with stories that no one wanted to listen to. Sometimes listening is all you can offer, and you might be surprised how often that is more than enough".

I then directed the question back to Brian, and he immediately named his late mother. However, he also had to take time to reflect on who such a person would be in his business encounters. Eventually, he mentioned two people, his good friend, mentor and leader for many years, Bob Hunt, who was always ready to spend time listening to him, mentoring and offering advice. The second was leadership coach Marie O'Hara, who supported Brian during some tough times.

As a last consideration, would your name be mentioned by your family members, friends, colleagues and team members, if they were asked the same question?

If through self-reflection, the answer is "no", then maybe as a start, it is time for that "simple cup of coffee", and to make it a regular occurrence, during which in Real Meeting, we give our time and undivided attention to listen to others.

We close this book with one final reflection, that we both believe in, and something, that we as human beings should continuously reflect on, and which comes from the quote of Mandela:

"What counts in life is not the mere fact that we have lived. It is what difference we have made to the lives of others".

SELF-REFLECTION

Chapter 12 – The Epilogue

Our selection of elements for self-reflection from the chapter are as follows:

- Am I stuck in the busyness of the "rat race" day in and day out, or do I take time out for myself and for others in Real Meeting?

- When with others, I refrain from having my mobile phone on the table, or in my hand, thereby, preventing any distraction from conversations.

- As a leader, have I lost touch with those on the "shop floor" and am I seen as their "manager" rather than a "Caring Leader"?

- In my personal life, I show care to others, be it someone I know or a total stranger. In other words, I turn their problems into that request for "Swiss Chocolates".

- Am I a leader who practises the mantra, "Leadership is time and a simple cup of coffee"?

- I give others my time, knowing that it will make a difference to them.

- Do I know the difference between a meeting and a Real Meeting, and do I switch myself on to giving of myself to others in Real Meeting and when doing so, do I enter the hyphen of the I-Thou?

CHAPTER 13

References

Reference List:

Books:

Allen, K. (2020). The Psychology of Belonging. The Psychology of Everything. (1st ed.). Routledge.

Buber Agassi J. (1999). Martin Buber on psychology and psychotherapy: essays, letters, and dialogue. New York: Syracuse University Press.

Buber, M. (1957). Pointing the way: collected essays M. Friedman. New York: Harper & Brothers.

Buber, M. (2002). The way of man: According to the teaching of Hasidism. London: Routledge.

Buber, M. (2004). Between man and man. Milton Park: Taylor & Francis.

Buber, M. (2016). Eclipse of God: Studies in the relation between religion and philosophy (1st ed.). New Jersey: Princeton University Press.

Buber, M. (1923) I and Thou (1st ed.). T. & T. Clark.

Buber, M. (1967). Meetings: Autobiographical Fragments. Vol. XII. Routledge.

Byars-Winston, A. (2014). Toward a framework for multicultural STEM-focused career interventions. The Career Development Quarterly, 62(4), 340–357. doi:10.1002/j.2161-0045.2014. 00087.x PMID:25750480

Callon, M. (1998). An essay on framing and overflowing: economic externalities revisited by sociology. In M. Callon. The laws of markets. Oxford: Blackwell.

Chandler, D. (2020). Semiotics: The Basics. Taylor & Francis Distribution.

Claxton, G. (2005). The Wayward Mind, An Intimate History of the Unconscious. Abacus.

Darlington, B. (2022). Humanising Leadership in Risk. Scotoma Press, Canberra.

Darlington, B., with Long, R. (2021). It Works! A New Approach to Risk and Safety. Scotoma Press, Canberra.

Egan, G. (2022). The Skilled Helper. (9th ed.). Brooks Cole.

Greenleaf, R. K. (2002). Servant Leadership: A Journey into the Nature of Legitimate Power and Greatness 25th Anniversary Edition (3rd ed.). Paulist Press.

Hanh, T. N., Ellsberg, R., & Laity, A. (2001). Thich Nhat Hanh: Essential Writings.

Hickson, M. (2020). An Officer, Not a Gentleman. The Inspirational Journey of a Pioneering Female Fighter Pilot. (1st ed.). Routledge.

Kohlrieser, G., & J. (2006). Hostage at the Table: How Leaders Can Overcome Conflict, Influence Others, and Raise Performance (1st ed.). Jossey-Bass.

Kohlrieser, G., Goldsworthy, S., & Coombe, D. (2012). Care to Dare: Unleashing Astonishing Potential Through Secure Base Leadership (1st ed.). Jossey-Bass.

Kruger, M. (2016). It Takes Two to Tango, Reflections on Safe Behaviour. Michael Kruger.

Lakoff, G., & Johnson, M. (1980). Metaphors we live by. (1st ed.). University of Chicago Press.

Long, G. (2013) Love Over Hate: Finding Life by the Wayside. The Slattery Media Group.

Long, R. (2012) Risk Makes Sense, Human Judgement and Risk. Scotoma Press, Canberra.

Long, R. (2013) For the Love of Zero, Human Fallibility and Risk. Scotoma Press, Canberra.

Long, R. (2013) Real Risk, Human Discerning and Risk. Scotoma Press, Canberra.

Long, R. (2014) Following-Leading in Risk, A Humanising Dynamic. Scotoma Press, Canberra.

Long, R. (2018) Fallibility and Risk, Living with Uncertainty. Scotoma Press. Canberra.

Long, R. (2019) The Social Psychology of Risk handbook: I-thou. Scotoma Press. Canberra.

Long, R. (2020) Envisioning Risk, Seeing, Vision and Meaning in Risk. Scotoma Press. Canberra.

Long, R., and Fitzgerald, R. (2017) Tackling Risk, A Field Guide to Risk and Learning. Scotoma Press, Canberra.

Long, R., Smith, G., and Ashhurst, C. (2016) Risky Conversations, The Law, Social Psychology and Risk. Scotoma Press. Canberra.

Machin, D., & Abousnnouga, G. (2013). The Language of War Monuments (Bloomsbury Advances in Semiotics). Bloomsbury Academic.

Mandela, N. (1995). by Mandela Long Walk to Freedom, The Autobiography of Mandela Abridged edition. Abacus.

Manzoni, J., & Barsoux, J. (2007). Set-up-to-Fail Syndrome: Overcoming the Undertow of Expectations (1st ed.). Harvard Business Review Press.

Mlodinow, L. (2013). Subliminal: How Your Unconscious Mind Rules Your Behavior (1st ed.). Vintage.

Murphy, K. (2020). You're Not Listening: What You're Missing and Why It Matters. Harvill Secker.

Pease, A., & Pease, B. (2017). Definitive Book of Body Language. Orion Paperbacks.

Thich Nhat, H. (2013). Silence. The Power of Quiet in a World Full of Noise. Ridler.

Van Der Kolk, B. (2015). Body Keeps the Score. (1st ed.). Penguin.

Websites:

Aboriginal and Torres Strait Islander culture and history - VPSC. (2024, May 28). VPSC. Retrieved from https://vpsc.vic.gov.au/workforce-programs/aboriginal-cultural-capability-toolkit/aboriginal-culture-and-history/

Buber, M., (2020). Stanford Encyclopedia of Philosophy. Retrieved from https://plato.stanford.edu/entries/buber/

Buber, M., Internet Encyclopedia of Philosophy. (n.d.). Retrieved from https://iep.utm.edu/martin-buber/

Buber, M., Internet Encyclopedia of Philosophy. (n.d.-c). Retrieved from https://iep.utm.edu/martin-buber/#:~:text=After%20I%20and%20Thou%2C%20Buber,30%20years%20after%20Rosenzweig%27s%20death

Burton, N. (2012). Jung: The Man and His Symbols. Psychology Today. Retrieved from https://www.psychologytoday.com/intl/blog/hide-and-seek/201204/jung-the-man-and-his-symbols

Carl Jung's Archetypes. (n.d.). Structural Learning. Retrieved from https://www.structural-learning.com/post/carl-jungs-archetypes

Carter, R. G. (2006). Of things said and unsaid: power, archival silences, and power in silence. Archivaria, 61(61), 215–233. Retrieved from https://archivaria.ca/index.php/archivaria/article/viewFile/12541/13687

Cherry, K. (2026, November 1). Kurt Lewin and Field Theory. Very well Mind. Retrieved from https://www.verywellmind.com/kurt-lewin-biography-1890-1947-2795540#:~:text=Lewin's%20field%20theory%20emphasized%20the,understanding%20of%20your%20own%20life.

Covert Learning for behavior change - Studies, products, and examples. (n.d.). Retrieved from https://www.besci.org/tactics/covert-learning#:~:text=Covert%20 learning%20refers%20to%20imparting,least%20generally%20what%20they%20are)

Darlington, A. (2024, July 5). Uncommon Sense. SHEQ Management. Retrieved from https://sheqmanagement.com/ commonality-between-speedway-and-work-identity/

Darlington, A. (2024, September 16). Commonality between speedway and work identity. SHEQ Management. Retrieved from https://sheqmanagement.com/ commonality-between-speedway-and-work-identity/

Darlington, B. (2018, July 16). A tough job. SHEQ Management. Retrieved from https://sheqmanagement.com/a-tough-job/

Darlington, B. (2018, July 16). Can we control culture. SHEQ Management. Retrieved from https://sheqmanagement.com/a-tough-job/https:// sheqmanagement.com/can-we-control-culture/

Darlington, B. (2019, October 18). Is our approach to safety crazy or committed? SHEQ Management. Retrieved from https://sheqmanagement.com/ is-our-approach-to-safety-crazy-or-committed/

Darlington, B. (2019a, August 21). Engagement is key to success. SHEQ Management. Retrieved from https://sheqmanagement.com/ engagement-is-key-to-success/

Darlington, B. (2020, October 8). Food for thought. SHEQ Management. Retrieved from https://sheqmanagement.com/food-for-thought-2/

Darlington, B. (2020a, April 24). Do we listen with intent? SHEQ Management. Retrieved from https://sheqmanagement.com/do-we-listen-with-intent/

Darlington, B. (2020a, August 12). Our world is not your ashtray! SHEQ Management. Retrieved from https://sheqmanagement.com/ our-world-is-not-your-ashtray/

Darlington, B. (2020a, August 17). Lessons from a semiotic walk on the Danube Island. SHEQ Management. Retrieved from https://sheqmanagement.com/lessons-from-a-semiotic-walk-on-the-danube-island/

Darlington, B. (2021, October 26). Mantras and trade-offs. SHEQ Management. Retrieved from https://sheqmanagement.com/mantras-and-trade-offs/

Darlington, B. (2021a, August 26). Envisioning through semiotics. SHEQ Management. Retrieved from https://sheqmanagement.com/envisioning-through-semiotics/

Darlington, B. (2021a, February 24). Learning from the Hudson River landing. SHEQ Management. Retrieved from https://sheqmanagement.com/learning-from-the-hudson-river-landing/

Darlington, B. (2021a, January 11). Do we care enough? SHEQ Management. Retrieved from https://sheqmanagement.com/do-we-care-enough/

Darlington, B. (2021a, June 23). Envisioning through semiotics – a flight between Vienna and Casablanca. SHEQ Management. Retrieved from https://sheqmanagement.com/envisioning-through-semiotics-a-flight-between-vienna-and-casablanca/

Darlington, B. (2021a, May 6). Signs and symbols: are we overdoing it? SHEQ Management. Retrieved from https://sheqmanagement.com/signs-and-symbols-are-we-overdoing-it/

Darlington, B. (2022, March 17). Wait, I've got this one! SHEQ Management. Retrieved from https://sheqmanagement.com/wait-ive-got-this-one/

Darlington, B. (2022a, January 26). Addressing the elephant in the room. SHEQ Management. Retrieved from https://sheqmanagement.com/addressing-the-elephant-in-the-room/

Gallo, C. (n.d.). Why Richard Branson Loves the Early Tradition of Campfire and Story. Carminegallo. Retrieved from https://www.carminegallo.com/richard-branson-loves-early-tradition-campfire-story/

Gilliam, W. C. (2017, September 9). Meeting and Mismeeting: Facilitating Transformational Communities/Conversations — Gilliam & Associates. Gilliam & Associates. Retrieved from https://gilliamandassociates.com/ittakesdeepgrace/2017/9/8/meeting-and-mismeeting-facilitating-transformational-communitiesconversations

Glover, S. (2016, April 1). How Trump Sees himself. cnn.com. Retrieved from https://edition.cnn.com/2016/04/01/politics/how-donald-trump-sees-himself/index.html

Glover, S. (2016, April 1). How Trump Sees himself. cnn.com. Retrieved from https://edition.cnn.com/2016/04/01/politics/how-donald-trump-sees-himself/index.html

Hegi, M. E., Diserens, A., Gorlia, T., Hamou, M., De Tribolet, N., Weller, M., Kros, J. M., Hainfellner, J. A., Mason, W., Mariani, L., Bromberg, J. E., Hau, P., Mirimanoff, R. O., Cairncross, J. G., Janzer, R. C., & Stupp, R. (2005). MGMTGene Silencing and Benefit from Temozolomide in Glioblastoma. New England Journal of Medicine, 352(10), 997–1003. Retrieved from https://doi.org/10.1056/nejmoa043331

Hilcenko, C., & Taubman-Bassirian, T. (2023). Artificial Intelligence and Ethics. Journal of Education Technology and Computer Science, 4(34), 119–136. Retrieved from https://doi.org/10.15584/jetacomps.2023.4.12

Huszár, O. (2016). The role of silence at the retreats of a Buddhist community. KOME, 4(2). Retrieved from https://doi.org/10.17646/kome.2016.25

I-Thou – New World Encyclopedia. (n.d.). Retrieved from https://www.newworldencyclopedia.org/entry/I-Thou

James Humes Quotes. (n.d.). BrainyQuote. Retrieved from https://www.brainyquote.com/quotes/james_humes_154730

Long, R. (n.d.). Podcast – What Jung Can Contribute to Safety – Part One. Safety risk - Humanising Safety and Embracing Real Risk. Retrieved from https://safetyrisk.net/podcast-what-jung-can-contribute-to-safety-part-one/

Marques, D (n.d.) The Importance of Community: 7 Key Benefits, Happiness. com Retrieved from https://www.happiness.com/magazine/relationships/the-importance-of-community/

Martel, Y. (2014). Buber: All real living is meeting. Retrieved from https://peoplethinkingaction.blogspot.com/2014/05/i-also-love-this-quote-from-buber-i.html

Mastering Common Research Methodologies. (n.d.). Voxco.com. Retrieved from https://www.voxco.com/blog/common-research-methodologies/

Mateo. (2024, September 21). The Two Wolves Story (Here's its Deeper Meaning). Loner Wolf. Retrieved from https://lonerwolf.com/two-wolves-story/#h-the-meaning-of-the-two-wolves-story-nbsp

Mba, M. W. (2024, March 6). Community for the Win — How collective solutions help individual problems. Better Up. Retrieved from https://www.betterup.com/blog/importance-of-community

McLeod, S. (2023, October 5). Social Facilitation Theory in Psychology. Simply Psychology. Retrieved from https://www.simplypsychology.org/social-facilitation.html

Menekse, M., Stump, G., Krause, S., & Chi, M. (n.d.). Differentiated Overt Learning Activities for Effective Instruction in Engineering Classrooms. Retrieved from https://education.asu.edu/sites/default/files/lcl/menekse_stump_et_al.pdf

Monique. (2023, April 21). What is Overt Teaching, and how does it help language students? - EC Partners | EC English Language Centres. EC Partners | EC English Language Centres. Retrieved from https://partners.ecenglish.com/news/what-is-overt-teaching-and-how-does-it-help-language-students/

Oprah Interviews Mandela. (2013, December 5). Oprah.Com. Retrieved from https://www.oprah.com/world/oprah-interviews-nelson-mandela

The Nobel Peace Prize 1993. (n.d.). NobelPrize.org. Retrieved from https://www.nobelprize.org/prizes/peace/1993/press-release/

Webmaster, C. (2019). Remembering Martin Buber and the I–Thou in counseling - Counseling Today. Counseling Today. Retrieved from https://ct.counseling.org/2019/05/remembering-martin-buber-and-the-i-thou-in-counseling/

Wikipedia contributors. (2022b, March 12). List of cognitive biases. Wikipedia. Retrieved from https://en.wikipedia.org/wiki/List_of_cognitive_biases

Woodside, A. G., Megehee, C. M., & Sood, S. (2012). Conversations with(in) the collective unconscious by consumers, brands, and relevant others. Journal of Business Research, 65(5), 594–602. Retrieved from https://doi.org/10.1016/j.jbusres.2011.02.016

Ying, Y., Lee, P. A., & Tsai, J. L. (2000). Cultural orientation and racial discrimination: Predictors of coherence in Chinese American young adults. Journal of Community Psychology, 28(4), 427–441. Retrieved from https://doi.org/10.1002/1520-6629(200007)

About the Authors

Aneta Darlington

Master's Economics Degree, Bachelor's in Communications, Master's in Social Psychology of Risk.

Aneta was born in the north of Poland and grew up in Swiecie. After completing school, she moved to the United States to conduct her university studies. She graduated with a Bachelor's Degree in communications from the Richard Stockton University of New Jersey and a Master's Degree in economics from the Lazarski University in Warsaw, Poland.

After working as a journalist for a couple of years in various countries, Aneta embarked on a new adventure, she became a safety ambassador, trainer and a brand representative for one of the biggest airlines in the world, located in the Middle East. During this period, Aneta took an interest in the various cultures of countries that she visited and with the different nationalities with whom she worked.

Aneta completed her Post Graduate Master's study in Social Psychology of Risk (SPoR) in 2024, in Australia and is the Director of SPoR in Europe, managing her own consulting and leadership training company called "Embodied Leadership" located in Vienna, Austria.

Among numerous interests, Aneta is: conducting her PhD studies focusing on Social Psychology of Risk, a published author of the book titled "50 Shades of Red" and is a proof-reader for two authors of books related to SPoR. Aneta is currently a columnist for a safety, health, environment and quality magazine "SHEQ Management" with her column titled" Finding the Balance".

Aneta is an avid scuba diver and is currently studying and training to become a Dive Master. Together with Brian, she has grandchildren living in Saipan and New Zealand.

Brian Darlington

Dipl. Safety and Health, Master's in Social Psychology of Risk, GradSaiosh.

Brian was born in South Africa and grew up in Pretoria. After completing two years of Military National service in 1982, he returned from South West Africa (now Namibia) to South Africa.

He continued his studies in an engineering trade while employed by a large iron and steel manufacturing company. Brian has worked for a multi-national company for almost forty years and has conducted training for leaders in Social Psychology of Risk and in the fundamentals of leadership around the globe. Brian completed his Post Graduate Master's study in Social Psychology of Risk in 2020, with the Centre for Leadership and Learning in Risk.

Brian co-authored the book "It Works!" with Dr Robert Long, based on some of the fundamentals of Social Psychology of Risk and the practical implementation thereof. Brian has authored a book titled "Humanising Leadership in Risk" and is currently co-writing two books, with one related to the Chernobyl Nuclear Disaster and the personal stories of persons involved.

Over the years, Brian has written articles for a number of magazines and is currently a columnist for a safety, health, environment and quality magazine "SHEQ Management". He started his regular column, titled "Embodied Safety", after presenting a paper titled "Safety from the Heart" at numerous international conferences. The column is focused on the caring and people-oriented approach and more recently has included elements of social psychology.

Brian has a son and two daughters, three granddaughters, and a grandson living in New Zealand, Saipan and Austria, and is an avid scuba diver, golfer and reader of military history and social psychology-related books.

Dear Reader,

now, our question to you, do you perhaps know of someone in your personal or professional life, who could use "your time and that simple cup of coffee"?

Kind Regards

Aneta and Brian

Sharing a good wine with Rob and Graham